SUSTAINABLE LEADERSHIP

SUSTAINABLE LEADERSHIP

SOURCING AND MULTIPLYING HAPPINESS

JACOB THOMAS, PhD

PARTRIDGE

To order additional copies of this book, contact
Partridge India
000 800 10062 62
orders.india@partridgepublishing.com

www.partridgepublishing.com/india

List of Figures

List of Tables

Jacob Thomas earned his doctoral degree in Agronomy from the Indian Agricultural Research Institute, New Delhi, and was a doctoral fellow in Human Resource Development with Research Guide from the Indian Institute of Management, Ahmedabad. Thomas is a strategist, environmentalist, and practitioner of yoga and meditation. He held CEO positions in several organizations in different sectors since the year 1991. He also coaches and mentors young leaders on their paths toward excellence. He is voted as the "Manorama Newsmaker of the year 2015" and is currently working for the cause of Good Governance.

Dedicated to all the young leaders in all nature and cultures.

Preface

It was in 1999 that I first moved from practicing leadership to teaching *leadership* in an MBA classroom, and it was full of theories of leadership with examples from the business world and the business leaders who were in search of excellence or moving their firms from good to great or reengineering their firms. Ten years later, in 2009, I taught *strategic leadership* from a practitioner's perspective as part of a strategic management course in another MBA classroom. This time, it was about the business leaders who craft the vision, clarify the mission, design the business models, and find blue oceans to maintain sustainable competitive advantages for their firms. Two years later, in 2011, I taught leadership again in another MBA classroom as part of a course in environmental management and the *environmental leaders* who love plants, animals, and nature and who write, act, campaign, and live for the preservation of nature in its original state. The leadership that was taught in 1999 has changed not only in MBA classrooms but also outside, in the practitioners world as well.

Most of us have practiced leadership at various levels during our growth stages—at school, college, university, workplaces, communities, religious institutions, clubs, and friendship groups.

This book is for leaders, for the managers and executives who would like to cross over to the realm of leadership, for the CEOs and leaders who would like to sustain their leadership positions, and for the leaders who would like to leave a legacy. Sustainable leadership is a perspective and skill set that can be acquired by understanding the process and practicing it by anyone who is currently planning, organizing, transforming, changing, influenzing, controlling, and monitoring. Transforming oneself from the planning and controlling functions to influencing the resource use, impacts of leadership actions, and well-being of followers is the aim of this book.

Many companies evolve into sustainable leadership when they see tangible economic benefits and/or as a response to pressures from civil society, investors, government, and other stakeholders.

Whatever the initial cause or stimulus, once initiated, many leaders pursue improvements in their leadership strategies, redefine the mission and vision, and move forward.

Sustainable leadership is presented as a process with inputs to leadership and outputs to leadership, with several mediating factors. The book is packaged with several novel frameworks to enable a leader to become a sustainable leader. Some of the frameworks illustrated in this book are:

- ❖ seven-*I* framework of influencing
- ❖ five-action framework of leading with insight
- ❖ bases of influence
- ❖ shaping the ideal self from expectations
- ❖ three-way connection for communication authenticity
- ❖ sustainable leadership's arena
- ❖ stability–instability–adaptation cycle
- ❖ analysis of the three-way sustainable leadership arena
- ❖ three-way stakeholder classification for the sustainable leader
- ❖ belief-to-purpose game plan for success
- ❖ enlightening the follower culture as a resource
- ❖ process map for the implementation of culturally rooted leadership strategy
- ❖ sustainable leadership model
- ❖ ingredients of sustainable leadership effectiveness
- ❖ seven-action sustainable leadership framework
- ❖ four-way leadership strategy framework
- ❖ four-way sustainable leadership strategy fit
- ❖ influence chain
- ❖ people strategy synergy matrix
- ❖ sustainable leadership process map.

From the first chapter, which gives the conceptual model of the sustainable leadership process, the reader is taken on a journey through leading with insights by looking forward, backward and sideways with a leadership strategy. The chapters are enriched with pieces of useful and interesting information in boxes to enlighten readers on other types and styles of leadership theories and practices. Self-assessment questions are given at the end of the chapters as a self-reflection guide.

Jacob Thomas, PhD

The book puts forward several conceptual models and propositions for further theory building on this emerging field as the time for moving from earlier styles and types of leadership has become ripe. I hope both the leaders and academicians would take the propositions forward through practice, further action research and validation for the benefit of all, imbibing the seven cardinal traits of sustainable leaders.

Jacob Thomas, PhD
drjacobt@gmail.com

Sustainable Leadership Process

Are you influenced in your decisions and actions by any person who lived in the past and who had been a leader in some other country or field? It is highly probable that directly or indirectly, vaguely or clearly, you are influenced by someone whom you haven't seen, who is no more, and who is outside your organization, occupational field, or subject of study. Your current decisions and actions are influenced by someone who lived centuries ago or generations back and not related to your field!

You may have to struggle to find out one who satisfies these three conditions:

- Someone who influences your current decisions and actions
- someone who lived countries ago
- Someone not related to your field.

> **Insight Box 1.1**
>
> *Sustainable leadership is the art of influencing decisions of strategic significance, affecting the quality of life and prosperity of present and future generations.*

You are likely to identify gods, sons of God or prophets, founders of religions, great explorers, great authors, great humanists, and great philosophers. If one more condition is added (a person that enhances the natural resources that we enjoy or use directly or indirectly today in our daily lives or the person who significantly enhances the quality of life of masses), the list shrinks further. You may start wondering, is there anyone who satisfies these four conditions? Probably there aren't many.

Here comes the opportunity for you to become one for future generations. Probably, the people who can satisfy the first three conditions in your life today lived during a time when nature was pristine and there was no need for anyone to enhance the quality or quantity of natural resources. If you want to influence others not only in this generation but in future generations as well by your actions today, there is a method.

Just as you searched your mind today to identify a person who influences your current decisions and actions, 50 or 100 years from now, many are likely to identify you as the person influencing them. Why not become a leader for the future with your actions today?

1.1 Are you a sustainable leader?

Journey of a thousand miles starts with a smile.
adapted from: Lao-tzu

A leader is one who has followers. It may be a physical following or a following of intangible things. Socrates had a physical following of persons in search of answers, participating in his debates at Acropolis. Jesus had a following of twelve disciples in his journey toward salvation, and Alexander the Great had an army following him in his conquests for territory and wealth. Leaders who have followers in intangible things may be followers of ideas, dreams, salvation, dogmas, discoveries, philosophical questions, spiritual well-being, a blog of an eminent person in any field, or ideas of writers. It may also be a fan following of star performers in sports, cinema, music, and art.

A researcher publishing his/her articles in one scientific journal will have followers, the readers of that journal or those using her article as citation. Those who do not read that journal are not her followers even if the impact of her research outputs is far and wide. She would be a sustainable leader if she makes significant, lasting contributions to her chosen field of study through publishing her results and thoughts in the journal and if the results contribute to the economic, social, and environmental well-being of present and future generations, not adverse to them. This includes unleashing the energy and talents of people in the present and future generations such as the leadership initiative that Abraham Lincoln and Nelson Mandela did for freedom of people, thereby contributing to the long term well-being of hitherto dissatisfied segments of the population.

People follow another person for many reasons. It may be for security reasons, economic reasons, emotional reasons, psychological reasons, normative or legal reasons, or spiritual reasons. When any of the reasons to follow becomes nonexistent, the follower walks his/her way. The leader has the strength to provide security, means to provide prosperity and sustenance, legal or normative authority to take decisions that affect others, or special capabilities that are attractive to others or that fulfill the special needs of others. Are these people sustainable leaders? Some are, but many are not.

1.2 Theoretical framework

There are many theories of leadership that explain what it is or how it happens. Many of these theories have roots in psychology and sociology.

1.2.1 Elements of sustainable leadership

You have the power to make a better world for the future.

Influencing is at the core of any leadership. This core aspect can occur only if two other elements are present, which are the answers to the following two questions:

- Who is influencing? The leader.
- Who is influenced? The follower.

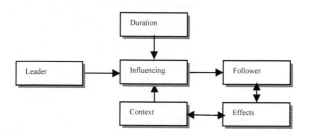

Fig. 1.1: The basic elements of a sustainable leadership.

Jacob Thomas, PhD

This core sociopsychological action of influencing occurs in a context or a situation. The contexts or situations where this influencing action occurs can be varied: military action, which is called military leadership; political action, which is called political leadership; commercial action, which is called business leadership; influencing action in an organization, which is called organizational leadership; influencing action within a religion, which is called religious leadership; and so on. The followers of a military leader are the army men, those of a political leader are the masses, those of a business leader are the people and firms in the value chain of the business organization, and those of a religious leader are the laity.

A leader has both an internal environment and an external environment to scan, understand, address, and embed. The internal environment involves the leader's mental, spiritual, and physical traits, habits, orientations, ambitions, aspirations, capabilities, strengths, and weaknesses. These elements of leadership, which are inherent to any leader, significantly impact the entire leadership process.

Insight Box 1.2

Temporal leadership

Leaders differ in their orientation toward the past and future. Leaders' orientation toward the future influences their strategic planning horizon, the shape and size of the vision, and the transcendence involved. The orientation toward the past provides a leader the strength from values, virtues rooted in a culture, ideologies rooted in philosophical traditions and the trajectory of social, political, economic, or environmental change from an evolutionary perspective. Ancona, Goodmen, Lawrence, and Tushman (2001) coined the word 'temporal leadership' as leadership challenges faced in work organizations adapting to changing environments.

Time is also viewed in terms of how long it takes to influence the followers, the duration of the effects of leadership being visible, how long it takes for followers to see certain characteristics in leaders, how the leader's vision alters the followers' time orientation, the time chosen by the leader to start his influencing. The times for certain initiatives are also dimensions of time factor in leadership (Liden and Antonakis 2009; Shamir 2011; Hambrick and Manson 1984; Day and Lord 1988; Das 1991; Bluedorn and Jaussi 2008).

The external leadership environment consists of the interpersonal and resource exchange relations. Since leadership is essentially an influencing process, people and resources, which constitute the surroundings of the leader, held by others individually or commonly are involved.

The impact zone of any leadership action is both the internal environment and the external leadership environment. Both the leader and the led change through a web of reciprocal interactions and managing expectations.

Another element of leadership is the time span. There are leadership actions that are temporary, short term, or enduring and lasting. Leadership actions in certain situations end when the situation changes, transformational leadership ends when the change or transformation is completed, team leadership ends when the team's purpose is fulfilled, and transactional leadership stops when the transactional relationship between the leader and the follower ends.

> **Insight Box 1.3**
>
> **Boundary conditions of sustainable leadership**
>
> *A sustainable leader is authentic, transformational, and transcendental and formulates a strategy to address the needs or aspirations of a set of followers, becoming a provider to the resource system that benefits the present and future generations. The positive expectations the followers have on environmental pristineness and quality of life linked to environmental aspects is a boundary condition under which sustainable leadership unfolds.*

Sustainable leadership is a type of leadership that is not limited by any context and time frame. When a leader's 'influencing' goes beyond one context and the time span involves multiple generations, he or she is a sustainable leader. Such people may have a unique method of influencing and a unique need or cause in the context. He or she influences both the internal environment and external environment, or the internal environment indirectly influences the external environment.

There are effects of this influencing by the leader on both the follower and the context. These effects on followers are changes in the attitude, perspective, actions, and relationships. Sustainable leadership effects are positive for the environmental and social contexts.

There are other elements, such as how the leader is influencing (method), what he or she is influencing (the needs, wants, hopes, ambitions of the followers), the resources that are used, and the attributes of both the follower and the leader.

1.2.2 Needs addressed by a sustainable leader

A journey of a thousand miles ends with joy.

A sustainable leader exists in an ecosystem. He or she is connected not only to the followers but also to many other elements in the ecosystem in complex ways. The elements of the ecosystem in which a leader sustains his/her leadership depends on the nature of the ecosystem. Ecosystems are complex, dynamically stable, open, and resilient systems in the environment, in which all people are also an essential component. Leaders evolve when there arises a need for a leader to address certain issues, solve problems, or meet certain felt needs. Leaders perform this role by drawing on the resources from an ecosystem which has the appropriate or befitting resource units. The leader's job in satisfying the needs of followers, as per a leadership strategy, while drawing on resources is depicted in Fig. 1.2.

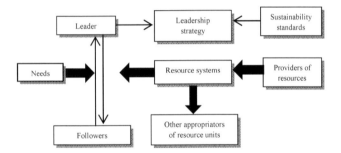

Fig. 1.2: Mechanism of the workings of sustainable leadership.

Can there be competing leaders to satisfy the needs of the same followers? If so, how can you differentiate from competing leaders with a view to remain the most attractive choice for the followers? Remaining attractive for the followers means many things in leadership. It may be through the attractiveness of the strategy proposed to meet the needs. The strategy may not be using many resource units from the resource systems so that there is no threat of scarcity of resources at any future date. The personal and interpersonal characteristics of the leader may also be factors of attraction.

Can any leader sustain herself or the position of leadership if there is a sustainable strategy? A sustainable strategy is not likely to sustain the leader who crafted the strategy, but a sustainable leadership strategy sustains the leader. Sustainable leadership depends on the needs it addresses and how the resources required for need satisfaction are drawn. The needs of the followers and the needs of the leader should match, which gives momentum to sustainable leadership.

The needs of followers also have no permanence as an effective leader would satisfy the needs of his or her followers within a time frame. Once the needs are satisfied, what is the role of the leader, and how can the leader sustain himself or herself? Or will the needs ever get satisfied? Even the physiological need for food expands in terms of quality, variety, flavor, nutritive value, and taste and whether it's ready to cook, ready to eat, fortified, value added, organically grown, locally sourced, etc., as depicted in Fig. 1.3.

Fig. 1.3: Physiological needs escalating to different levels.

In an organizational setting, by taking employees or staff as followers, the needs for job security, increasing pay, affiliation, identity, self-actualization by expressing one's potential, etc. are in different degrees, and none of the needs get fully satisfied. If there are more resources and the strategy permits to provide more to the followers, the needs expand themselves.

The needs of followers that sustainable leaders address are:

- needs that matter to many people and significant for dignified living

- needs that are nonsubstitutable and are essential to be fulfilled
- needs that are unique to a group of people or culture yet has generalizability across cultures
- needs that if not addressed are likely to impact the entire human race
- needs for maintaining and enhancing the resource system that supports the followers.

A sustainable leader is differentiated from other leaders in his or her ability to choose the needs that matter and influence the followers to consider issues holistically in an integrated manner. Sustainable leadership also ensures, through creating awareness among followers, the enhancement of the quality and quantity of the resource system whose units are used to meet the needs of the followers.

A sustainable leader fixes his or her own standards of performance as the road less travelled as part of the leadership strategy. These standards are likely to be above and/or different from the prevailing economic, social, and environmental sustainability standards, compliance requirements, benchmarks, and best practices. These standards are developed as a composite and holistic purpose of the organization sustainable leader leads or of the mission he or she is pursuing.

> **Insight Box 1.4**
>
> **Leadership types**
> - *autocratic leadership*
> - *aristocratic leadership*
> - *bureaucratic leadership*
> - *theocratic leadership*
> - *democratic leadership*
> - *communist leadership*
> - *military leadership*
> - *political leadership*
> - *narcissistic leadership*
> - *social leadership*
> - *business leadership*
> - *environmental leadership*
> - *visionary leadership*
> - *sustainable leadership*
> - *strategic leadership*
> - *tribal leadership*
> - *team leadership*
> - *primal leadership*
> - *spiritual leadership*
> - *resonant leadership*
> - *constructive leadership*
> - *destructive leadership.*

> **Insight Box 1.5**
>
> **Leadership sustainability**
> *'The ability of leaders to recognize the intricate systems, interwoven with human values that promote sustainability'*
> *(Grooms and Martinez 2011).*

1.2.3 Sustainable leadership strategy: From leading people to leading resources

A journey of a thousand miles starts with a decision.

A leadership strategy is formed initially as an idea about some desired effects either in the context or in the followers. The idea is formed from certain insights about either the context or the followers. For every effect, there is a cause going deeper into causes, which finally is likely to reach the resource system that nurtures life.

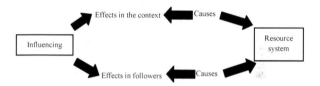

Fig. 1.4: Cause-and-effect orientation of influencing.

The resource system includes the tangible and the intangible aspects of the surroundings where the leader and the followers are embedded and enmeshed in complex relationships. The tangible aspects are perceivable and visible, such as natural forces and natural resources, whereas the intangible aspects are experiential, such as the energy and talents of the followers, cosmic energy, grand design, experience of transcendence, and many other invisible, unknown aspects in the followers, universe/multiverse. The causes of many of the effects are unknown to science and rationality, yet it is logical that every effect on a person and context must have some cause. A sustainable leadership strategy conceives such a holistic perspective about the resource system to be influenced for the desired effects.

Sustainable leadership is a process of mobilizing and harnessing resources to accomplish something of significance without depleting or degrading the resource system. The sustainable leadership process can start even without any direct physical followership of people even though eventually followers would flock to the idea of the leader. The influence process starts with investigation and introspection, leading to insights and then imagining an action with a purpose, catering to an enduring interest.

For example, Bittu Sahgal from Himachal Pradesh in India started *Sanctuary* magazine on his own in 1981 for the purpose of protecting and preserving India's wildlife. The readership became the followers of this leader. His inspection and introspection of the state of forests and wildlife, followed by the insight that preserving wildlife is a good way for protecting forests, led to starting this magazine. The magazine is a product of his fertile imagination and is his method to influence people into preserving the forest, which he believed would enhance the quality of life and prosperity of the present and future generations. He influenced resources and people as eventual followers are only instrumental in his purpose. When the resource system is seen as the primary factor, not the followers, the leader will have a positive impact on the well-being of the followers.

1.2.4 Influence strategy of sustainable leadership

> *A journey of a thousand miles starts with the first step. Adapted from: Lau-tzu*

Even though influence is at the core of leadership, the influencing process starts from a comprehensive understanding of the context, situation, and interconnections among elements of the ecosystem and stakeholders. This understanding is achieved by influencing the first step of *investigation* of the event, issue, or problem in their context to collect the required information.

While investigation collects data from the external environment,

> **Insight Box 1.6**
>
> Leadership *is the lever that a person (leader) uses to shift or move a system. The system can be an ecosystem, business system, social system, political system, or integrating all, the development system.* Strategy *is the idea and decision on where to put the other end of the lever, on where the shifting or moving should go (direction of movement), and on the quantum of shaking to be given to the internal configurations of the system during the shifting.*

introspection collects information from the internal environment. The internal environment can be the arena and hidden space of a self or the space within the boundary of an organization. The second step of leadership strategy is to influence the *insight* process using the data gathered to form inferences and meaning. The insights are likely to trigger an *imagination* process. Instead of a wandering and wanton imagination, the leader influences this imagination flow inside the head with the intention to get the correct choices among many options, methods, and paths to address needs or realize a vision. Fig. 1.5 depicts the flow of steps.

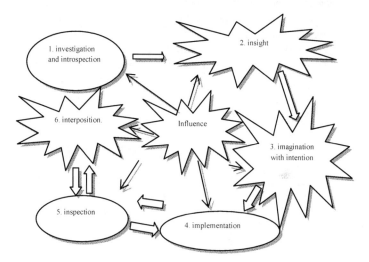

Fig. 1.5: Steps in the process of crafting an influence strategy.

In the first three steps, an influence strategy (a strategy to influence the followers) is formulated and is readied for *implementation* with the expectation that the intended followers are influenced by the leader. The leader develops the influence strategy so crafted with an action plan. The results of the influence strategy implementation—which can be measured as the number of followers, the degree or strength of influence, the direction of influence, and the time factor in influencing— are *inspected* periodically to assess the leader's effectiveness. The leader *interpositions* the feedback information so gathered during inspections to gain further insight to recraft the leadership strategy or to change some aspects of the implementation.

At the core of sustainable leadership is a strategy, a portfolio of choices to make, that determines the direction the led (the followers and their contexts) are going to take. The strategy consists of the mission, vision, and the model/framework designed based on the enduring interests of the organization and the core values (what he or she most values) of the leader. The leadership may be a single leader, a group of leaders (a board of directors, a trusteeship council, city council), or a dominant coalition that has the power to take decisions in a democratic, autocratic, participatory, bureaucratic, constructive, or destructive manner.

The influence strategy takes into account the different stakeholder groups to be influenced, the resources, the management, the technology, and the education that are related to the political, social, economic, and ecological systems. With the influence strategy at the core, how sustainable leadership results in sustainability is depicted in Fig. 1.6.

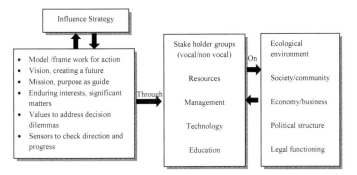

Fig. 1.6: Sustainable leadership strategy leading to sustainability.

The influence strategy is to make primary effects on the stakeholders, resources, technology, education, and management, which in turn are likely to make effects in the ecological environment, society, economy, polity,

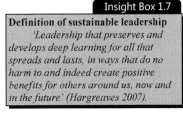

Insight Box 1.7

Definition of sustainable leadership
'Leadership that preserves and develops deep learning for all that spreads and lasts, in ways that do no harm to and indeed create positive benefits for others around us, now and in the future' (Hargreaves 2007).

and legal structure. The primary effects of the influence strategy are on the people and resources. Technology, education, and management are inputs combining people and resources that make effects on the economy, society, and polity, which in turn will result in sustainability with a focus on improving the community and quality of lives of future generations.

The influence strategy will be a clear direction to reach sustainability and comprehensive enough to create the future. It will have built-in sensors to check direction and progress (more details on influence strategy in chapter 6).

Even though the term 'sustainability' was initially referred by Lester Brown, the founder of Worldwatch Institute, it became mainstream along with the concept of sustainable development promoted through the report *Our Common Future* (the *Brundtland Report* of 1987) that was endorsed in the Earth Summit at Rio de Janeiro in 1992 through Agenda 21. The term denotes the ability of something to keep going ad infinitum (Brady 2005). After its confinement and hibernation in the ecology and environment domains, the term blossomed in the economic and social domains in the realms of sustainable cities, sustainable agriculture, sustainable tourism, sustainable businesses, and sustainable everything without fully understanding the interconnected, holistic, significant, and lasting aspects of the concept by most of the practitioners.

Sustainable leadership recognizes the dynamically stable, complex interconnectedness between different systems around human living, impacting life. There

---

Insight Box 1.8

Sustainable leaders' leadership initiatives that permanently improved a system at the global level

- *Abraham Lincoln—shift in a social system based on slavery*
- *Mohandas Gandhi—shift in a political system through peaceful methods (colonial rule)*
- *Nelson Mandela—shift in a perspective (apartheid)*
- *Rachel Carson—shift in the views on the impact of interventions on the ecosystem*
- *Buddha—dissemination of the value of nonviolence and the middle path*
- *Christ—the power of love and compassion*
- *Socrates—the courage to tell the truth on any subject, profound questions for the future generations to ponder*
- *Martin Luther King Jr—the power of dreaming for a better future*
- *Le Corbusier—urban planning and living, Levittown community housing*
- *René Descartes—laying of the foundation for modern philosophy*
- *Galileo—shift on the thinking about earth to heliocentric framework*
- *Mark Zuckerberg—shift on interactions through social media*
- *Steve Jobs—communication through a small gadget*
- *Bill Gates—shift in the way of doing business through software platforms*
- *Jochen Zeitz—shift in environmental profit–loss account, cochair of B Team, chief of PUMA.*

---

13   Jacob Thomas, PhD

are ecological, social, economic, political, and legal systems that are represented by different stakeholder groups. These systems can be enhanced by resources, technology, education, and management, provided there is a sustainable strategy crafted by the leadership. This strategy will lead to sustainability of the business, sustainability of development, sustainability of prosperity, sustainability of reputation, or sustainability of anything that human life desires and dreams of. Sustainability means continuous improvement with the community (group of closely interacting people) at the centre, living in socio-economic-ecological systems that need to be preserved for the future generations of the community.

Visionary leadership (Burt Nanus 1992), leader of the future (Drucker 1996), leader of leaders (Warren Bennis 1998), leadership sustainability (Hargreaves and Fink 2003), and sustained leadership (Hargreaves and Fink 2004) are concepts in different contexts, connoting the tenability of leadership.

1.3 Sustainable leadership process

A process has some inputs to drive it and some outputs in addition to certain catalysts, mediators, inhibitors, and a process owner. Leadership is also a process with several steps occurring sequentially and a few actions in parallel, catalyzed and mediated by a few aspects, as depicted in Fig. 1.7.

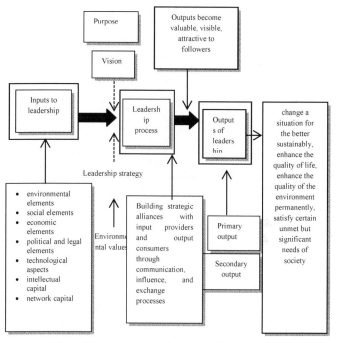

Fig. 1.7: Process map of sustainable leadership.

Integrating leadership theories into process-type models, identifying the mediating mechanisms of a proximal variable, intervening between a distal determinant and leader outcomes in a causal chain is a recent development (Antonakis 2011; DeRue et al. 2011; Judge and Long 2012; Lim and Polyhart 2004; Zaccaro et al. 2004). Most leadership research in management science takes the leadership of organizations as the macro level of analysis and the interpersonal influences in organizations as the micro level of analysis. There is also a self level or intrapersonal level, which is the domain of psychology. Sustainable leadership goes beyond the boundaries of a formal organization in its influence and outcomes. The leadership process elements of the three levels of leadership are given in Fig. 1.8.

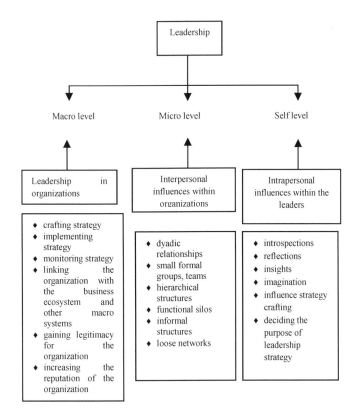

Fig. 1.8: The process elements of sustainable leadership at three levels.

1.3.1 Leadership inputs (distal predictors)

Sustainable leadership is a process with inputs provided from a context. Environmental elements provide both a context and the elements to spur leadership. For example, climate change in an environmental context can spur many enterpreneurial initiatives in measuring it, solving it, predicting it, mitigating it, leveraging it, and talking about it. Al Gore talked about climate change and got a Nobel prize for the effort.

Depending upon the elements mostly used as inputs to leadership and the context in which the leader operates, leadership can be classified as follows:

- environmental leadership (green businesses, ENGOs (Environmental non-govermental organisations), CER(Corporate Environmental Responsibility), UN organizational leadership)

- social leadership (social businesses, civil society, CSR(Corporate Social Responsbility))

- economic leadership (business firms, economy regulators, media firms)

- political leadership (nodes in governance stucture from local to global)

- legal leadership (courts, green tribunals)

- technological leadership (environment-friendly innovators, explorers)

- academic, intellectual leadership (academic leaders, professionals, artists, writers, filmmakers, urban eco-architects).

*Table 1.1 The antecedents, outcomes, and mediators
of the sustainable leadership process*

Antecedents (predictors)	Outcomes or outputs	Mediators
• ecological intelligence (Goleman 2009) • psychological capital (Jensen and Luthans 2006) • hope • optimism • ambition • social intelligence • climate change • extreme weather events • depletion of natural resources • high material use • fidelity of communication • high prevalence of diseases attributed to environmental causes • rising economic inequity • population beyond the carrying capacity • business firms pursuing profit-maximizing perspectives • globalization of educational institutions	**i. leader outcomes** • happiness • psychological well-being (Toor and Ofori 2009) • inspirational motivation (Spitzmuller and Illies 2010) • contingent self-esteem (Toor and Ofori 2009) **ii. follower outcomes** • empowerment • self-awareness • environmental awareness • ecocentric perspective • nature connection • work happiness (Jensen and Luthens 2006a) • environmental stewardship **iii. resource systems outcomes** • zero pollution • natural resources are used sustainably • zero waste • smart growth • less man-made disasters • internalizing all five types of external costs • sustaining organizational effectiveness	• followers' awareness about environmental aspects and issues and actual cause-and-effect relations • follower empowerment • identification with the leader • trust in leadership evolved from the positive outcomes of the leadership • academic outputs linking economic, health, and social well-being to environmental aspects • job satisfaction from work engagement

There are several predictors to the emergence and development of sustainable leadership, as can be seen in Table 1.1.

1.3.2 Leadership process

The leadership process is an influence chain linking the inputs of leadership to the outputs of leadership. Taking a few inputs from the external environment (be it ecological, economic, social, political, or technological), a person with leadership potential can add value tangibly in the eyes of certain others. These others who perceive value are consumers of products and services in the economic domain, local community, or larger society who get a better-quality environment in the ecological domain or a beneficiary group in the social domain. The value addition to the inputs is done by reconfiguring the inputs; discovering a new use or nonuse value to an input; packaging an input better; changing the shape, size, structure, and looks of inputs; transforming inputs; branding and bundling of inputs.

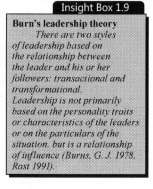

Insight Box 1.9

Burn's leadership theory
There are two styles of leadership based on the relationship between the leader and his or her followers: transactional and transformational.
Leadership is not primarily based on the personality traits or characteristics of the leaders or on the particulars of the situation, but is a relationship of influence (Burns, G. J. 1978, Rost 1991).

Insight Box 1.10

Transformational leadership
It is a type of leadership in the relational perspective proposed by Burns (1978). A leader transforms the state of affairs not only of the contextual factors but also of the aspirations and ideals of his or her followers. Such a leader attracts and inspires people to bring about strategic changes in the way things are in a situation and the way people deal with situations.

The transformation or reconfiguration or bundling process generates the primary outputs of leadership. With experience and leadership skills, a leader packages the primary outputs into sophisticated products attractive enough and irresistible to the leader's audience or customer segments (followers). In order to be a sustainable leader, he or she forges lasting alliances with input providers and output consumers. The leader also enhances the input base's ability to supply and the consumer's capacity to absorb the influences perpetually and irreversibly.

A sustainable leader may bundle environmental, social, economic, and political elements and package the elements well to change a situation for better sustainability. Another leader may

Insight Box 1.11

Transactional leader
He or she uses rewards and punishments to influence followers. The relationship between the leader and follower is one of command and control using formal power. By following the orders or expectations of the leader, the follower gets rewards, may lead to withholding of rewards or giving punishments.

Jacob Thomas, PhD

bundle technological elements, network capital, and environmental elements to enhance the quality of life. Yet another leader may reconfigure some economic elements and may bundle them with social and/or environmental elements to satisfy certain unmet but significant needs of society. The aspects and dimensions of the sustainable leadership process compared with two other well-researched types of leadership is given in Table 1.2.

Table 1.2 Comparing sustainable leadership with transformational leadership and authentic leadership

Transformational leadership	Authentic leadership	Sustainable leadership
• articulate a captivating vision for the future • act as charismatic role models providing inspirational motivation • facilitate acceptance of common goals • set high performance expectations • provide individualized support to followers • intellectual stimulation of followers or idealized support to followers • create a transformational leadership climate throughout the organization • mutual trust • facilitate candid communication • applicable to individual, team, organizational, and meta levels of analysis	• Focus on the development of self awareness and other awareness along with a development focus. • create high levels of trust built on a firm ethical and internalized moral perspective and the commitment to organizational success grounded in social values • lead with conviction in pursuit of a value-based mission or cause • do not fake their leadership but leads as an expression of their true selves • are originals, not copies, not driven by values imposed by others • are consistent in what he or she says and does • have balanced processing of information and unbiased or flawless processing of info • not an either/or condition as 100 percent fake or inauthentic leaders are rare • all authentic leaders may not be sustainable	• foster awareness about the interrelationships of environmental components for sustainability of quality of life • create trust built on environmental ethics and intra- and intergenerational equity • have commitment to ecosystem integrity and preservation with the ecosystem, nature, and planet as context • lead with conviction in pursuit of environmental value-based mission or cause • lead as an expression of man's embeddedness and true position in pristine nature • likely to build on the values espoused by indigenous people • are consistent in what he or she thinks, says, does, and believes • include information about the environment and quality of life while processing information

• transformational leadership's effectiveness dependent on the adoption of mechanisms to cultivate congruent follower perception through the processes of attraction, selection, and attrition; on newcomer socialization; on common experiences; and on mutual interactions	• use measures like ethical climate questionnaire or ECQ by Victor and Cullen (1988), ENTRESCALE, multifactor leadership questionnaire or MLQ by Bass and Avolio (1993), leader authenticity scale or LAS by Henderson and Hoy (1983), authentic leadership scale by Tate (2008), ALQ developed by Walumbwa et al. (2008), authenticity inventory by Goldman and Kernis (2001)	• are an either–or condition as there are non-sustainable leaders who are completely oblivious to their interconnectedness with nature • have qualities of authentic, transformational, and transcendent leaders • sustainable leadership score using SLS (sustainable leadership script) composite score from a group of ten-item scale (Thomas 2013)

1.3.3 Leadership output

Outputs of leadership can be in any domain, field, or activity. They can be new strategies, new knowledge, new methods, or new processes as innovations. They can be new or improved products and services, new technologies, books or research articles or ideas that can change a situation, a brilliant film, a campaign to save an environmental

Insight Box 1.12

Unsustainable leadership
- *failing to provide opportunity*
- *failing to provide direction*
- *failing to communicate a purpose*
- *failing to craft a good strategy*
- *failing to design a structure for a strategy*
- *failing to provide security*
- *failing to assure liberty*
- *failing to enhance dignity*
- *failing to provide growth prosperity*
- *failing to leverage resources*
- *failing to conserve natural resources*
- *failing to protect biodiversity*
- *failing to enhance resource systems*
- *failing to create ecological credit*

component, a new law, a farsighted judicial pronouncement, or a viral material in a social media network for an environmental or social cause, etc.

The characteristics of the output of leadership process are contingent upon the nature of inputs and the nature of the leadership process with several moderating variables—such as strategic alliances, purpose defined by the leader or followers, vision, and the process model—being chosen. Intangibles that do not enhance the resource system or quality of life of people are not outputs of sustainable leadership. Knowledge or ideas residing within the heads of several people, when expressed as coordinated and unified actions or tangible products or services that enhance the resource system as a result of the leader's stimulus, is sustainable leadership.

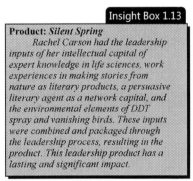

Insight Box 1.13

Product: *Silent Spring*
    Rachel Carson had the leadership inputs of her intellectual capital of expert knowledge in life sciences, work experiences in making stories from nature as literary products, a persuasive literary agent as a network capital, and the environmental elements of DDT spray and vanishing birds. These inputs were combined and packaged through the leadership process, resulting in the product. This leadership product has a lasting and significant impact.

1.3.4 Impact of sustainable leadership

The impact of the outputs of the influence strategy is positive, holistic, integrative, significant, and lasting. The impacts are good for the community, good for the health of people, good for the ecosystem, and enhances the quality of life of people in significant ways. The leader exercises his influence game with humility and compassion typical of level V leadership, and thus, there will not be envy or dissatisfaction in any stakeholder category.

1.3.5 Sustainable leadership process owner

The leadership process of converting/transforming the inputs to outputs, which has the potential to make significant and lasting impacts, can be leader centric, function centric, stakeholder centric, industry/sector specific, context specific, or issue specific. A leader-centric leadership process has the problem of the process coming to a halt when the leader burns out or is no more unless the leader makes a leadership succession plan from the very beginning. The commanders of an army unit or the captains of a ship are leader-centric leadership process owners. Industry-specific, context-specific, or issue-specific leaders are effective and significant in that specific context only yet can become sustainable leaders if they become stakeholder centric, ecocentric, and follower centric.

Ideally, the leadership process owner should be the primary stakeholder, and the leader acts only as an initial stimulus and facilitator, creating multiple leaders to carry forward the initiatives till the desired outputs and impacts are achieved. The stakeholder-centric leadership process makes the leader as a coach or mentor to other actors in the process.

1.4 Sustainable leadership practices

Leadership practices that meet the needs of the present followers and the current practices of the leader that enable the future generations to meet their own needs in equal measure or better are sustainable leadership practices. If the practices

> **Insight Box 1.14**
>
> **Fiedler's contingency theory**
> *A leader's effectiveness is contingent on how well his or her style fits the context. He classifies the contexts into three dimensions: position power, task structure, and leader–member relations. The contextual dimensions of leader–member relations are atmosphere, confidence, loyalty, and attraction to the leader (Fiedler 1974).*

initiated by a leader are profound, the leader is likely to be remembered by succeeding generations since the impact is lasting and the practices are sustainable. The characteristics of sustainable leadership practices are the following:

- They are enduring; another leader or the next generation will have no justification or reasons to stop this practice.
- Resources that are renewable and can be replenished (for materials and energy) are used for the practice, and thus, the practice won't stop for want of resources at any time in the future.
- The challenges pregnant in any leadership practice are foreseen, and hence, resources are conserved for meeting the future needs when the challenges appear as issues or problems.
- They prepare self-mobilizing follower base so that followers become process owners.
- They respect the interlinkages of all decisions in the lives of other people, groups, communities, and ecosystem components. Thus, all decisions integrate well into a dynamically stable human nature system. They nurture diversity for hybridization of ideas; hence, hybrid vigor occurs in subsequent generation of ideas, technology, business cycle.

Jacob Thomas, PhD

- They identify and nurtur the weakest in the system with the understanding that the weakest also has some areas of strength in some measure that are yet to be discovered.
- They focus on the significant aspects of the system for leadership interaction that makes the largest impacts in the lives of followers today and in future generations.
- They foster self-learning, praxis, and adaptation.

1.4.1 Features of sustainability practiced by sustainable leaders

Sustainability is a perspective that guides sustainable leaders in their actions or way of thinking. Sustainable leaders' decisions, styles, and actions have certain features:

- holistic
- integrative
- interconnecting
- simple in appearance yet complex in function
- system focused, not individual focused
- dynamically stable
- have changes occurring in structure and function—but these are evolutionary, seldom revolutionary
- follow a design which is beyond the control of anyone
- project warmth and strength together before the followers.

> **Insight Box 1.15**
>
> **Leaders of tomorrow**
> - lead the life one wants to
> - mentor their children to find their calling
> - coach their employees to find meaning in what they do
> - contribute to make their neighborhood a better place to live in
> - initiate debate on issues that matter to the organization and the community
> - take decisions to enhance the quality of the environment
> - tell the truth even when that affects their comforts
> - think out of the box to create products or services that make the lives of others better without harming the environment
> - champion a social or environmental cause

1.4.2 Cost and benefit perspectives of sustainable leadership

Sustainable leadership involves mobilizing people and material resources to accomplish something today that has lasting and significant impacts in the future. Mobilizing people and material resources in a natural-calamity rescue operation is for accomplishing the goal of saving people today. Mobilization will not take much time, and the commitment levels of everyone involved in the effort is very high, the reason being their emotional attachment to the event. In such a situation, cost is never a relevant factor as lives are invaluable. So why is a similar value not accorded to nature when, in the first place, it has the potential to prevent many of the calamities faced by human life? A sustainable leader perceives nature as the primary component to be nurtured, and by nurturing nature, human life is conserved directly and indirectly. The cost of nurturing nature is thus always far less than the benefits accrued from nature to human life.

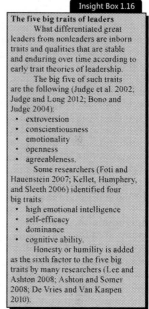

Insight Box 1.16

The five big traits of leaders

What differentiated great leaders from nonleaders are inborn traits and qualities that are stable and enduring over time according to early trait theories of leadership.

The big five of such traits are the following (Judge et al. 2002; Judge and Long 2012; Bono and Judge 2004):

- extroversion
- conscientiousness
- emotionality
- openness
- agreeableness.

Some researchers (Foti and Hauenstein 2007; Kellet, Humphery, and Sleeth 2006) identified four big traits:

- high emotional intelligence
- self-efficacy
- dominance
- cognitive ability.

Honesty or humility is added as the sixth factor to the five big traits by many researchers (Lee and Ashton 2008; Ashton and Somer 2008; De Vries and Van Kanpen 2010).

In the same situation of a natural-calamity rescue operation leadership, an ordinary leader will stop his influencing once the immediate rescue action is accomplished. A sustainable leader will continue his influencing in restoring the place to a much-better habitat, focusing on ecosystem interconnectedness and integrity, so that such calamities will never occur again. The people in that habitat will benefit immensely—not only in the short term, but in the long term as well. Similarly in the business world also each issue or problem can be addressed in such a way that, solution leads to durable system improvement.

1.5 Role of a sustainable leader

A role is the expected behavior from significant others, and hence, the role of a leader changes when the expectations from others change. However, a leader influences these expectations and makes or creates the role. The leader is also not satisfied with the existing people who give out their expectations but wants many more people to become significant to him and vice versa. A sustainable leader makes his role by creating expectations that enhances the resource system and makes many people who were hitherto unaware or uninterested in their capabilities into significant others. To perform such a role, he or she undertakes the following:

- identifying issues which need attention
- assessing the leader's competence to address the issue chosen
- assessing the means to become competent to lead different aspects of the issue and mobilizing people to support the issue and to become significant stakeholders
- communicating effectively the different dimensions of the issue
- generating solutions/ideas for change with the participation of stakeholders
- demonstrating the quintessence of the issue
- developing a mission and a vision as a direction to take
- making clear the interrelationships and interdependencies between the elements of the ecosystem where the issues are embedded.
- influencing others to see the big picture and to buy in to the mission

Insight Box 1.17

Authentic leadership

The etymology of the word 'authentic' is traced to 'authento' (Greek), meaning 'to have full power'. It involves being self-aware and acting in accord with one's true self by expressing what one genuinely thinks and believes (Lathens and Avolio 2003). It is related to ethics focusing on one's pursuit of higher goals achieved through self-realization when the activity of the soul is aligned with virtue to produce a complete life according to Aristotle and as deducted by Hutchinson (1995). It is not an either–or condition since people are never completely authentic or inauthentic. Whitehead (2009) defines an authentic leader as one who is self-aware, humble, always seeking improvement, aware of those being led, and looks out for the welfare of others. He or she fosters high degree of trust by building an ethical and moral framework and is committed to organizational success within the construct of social values. Walumbwa et al. (2008) defines authentic leadership as a pattern of leader behavior that draws upon and promotes positive psychological capacities and a positive ethical climate to foster greater self-awareness, an internalized moral perspective, balanced processing of information, and relational transparency on the part of leaders working with followers, fostering positive self-development.

- being flexible to diverse interests, needs, elements, and claims
- identifying all the stakeholders and each group's importance, influence, and interests
- developing plans that are acceptable, implementable, and widely agreed
- making strategic alliances with resource providers.

1.6 Sustainable leadership's differentiation and relevance

Leadership differentiation is 'reason to stand out', and its relevance is 'reason to adopt'. The leader will differentiate in terms of his or her choice of purpose, vision, strategy, value-addition methods, and intended impact on the larger environment and the community by the strategy. Followers should have reasons to follow, get influenced by, and adopt the paths, ideas, and outputs of the leader.

The world is looking toward leaders who can improve the quality of life of people without degrading the environment and the quality of life of people anywhere. Following the dispositional approach to leadership, the sevenfold traits of sustainable leaders would be:

- high ecological intelligence
- transcendence
- conscientiousness
- openness
- honesty or humility
- compassion
- equanimity.

People with this sevenfold leader traits are likely to have the required competence to shape the expectations of significant others for a sustainable leadership.

1.7 Sustaining the leadership position

A leader identifies and understands the forces that can sway, derail, and uproot the leader herself from the area of action. A sustainable leader needs to continue the influencing process from the investigation-and-introspection stage through implementation and interposition for the outcomes to manifest and the impacts to show up. Sustaining the leadership position till the leadership strategy is effectively implemented for the lasting change to manifest is an important aspect of sustainable leadership.

1.7.1 Sustainable leaders avoiding burnout

Many argue that a leader is like a candle burning itself to provide light to others and eventually sacrificing itself fully. A leader in an organizational context works hard, giving so much of oneself while dealing with the challenges. A good leader is perceived as one who puts the organization's needs ahead of his own and loses sight of everything other than the work, goals, and measures of success. While giving oneself to the challenges of leadership, the symptoms of burnout show up after some time. The journey of a thousand miles, which a sustainable leader undertakes, starts with the first step of developing the first leader from among the followers to implement the first step. And then he or she moves on developing the second leader for the second step, and so on, thereby lighting a thousand candles to scatter the light. The process of sustaining the leadership in perpetuity is depicted in Fig. 1.9.

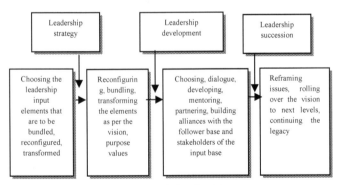

Fig. 1.9: Sustainable leadership process.

1.7.2 A sustainable leader influencing with warmth

Leadership involves influencing others to make them followers of the leader's point of view. Many are influenced by the charisma of the leader and many by the competence of the leader in solving a problem, addressing a need, or accomplishing a goal. A vast majority of leaders influence through the conduit of authority (the legitimized power one wields by virtue of the position one holds or the role one performs). There are a few leaders whose conduit of influence is warmth. Warmth leads to trust, and trust gets loyal followers. When the conduit of influence is warmth, there are less conflicts and interruptions in the march forward. Thus, the leader's influence is experienced by followers as a gentle breeze.

> **Insight Box 1.18**
>
> **A leaf's life**
>
> Will there be a tree without its leaves? Can the leaves be there without the tree trunk bringing nutrients and water to it? Can the leaves perform their functions without the branches displaying them for the sun's light to fall on them? Without roots, can leaves survive?
>
> Will there be beautiful flowers, nutritious seeds, fruits, and nuts without leaves? Without flowers, will there be honey bees and honey?
>
> Can the leaves forget the breeze that cools them when the sun energizes them during the day? Can the leaves ignore the rain that washes them clean and the moon that soothes them? Will there be leaves without the sun, moon, rain, and wind?
>
> For the healthy-performing life of leaves, soil, water, space, and air are also essential. Without the leaves, will there be butterflies, birds, animals, and human beings? How many leaves are required to sustain a human life?

1.7.3 Leading like a coach or counselor

Coaches may not be the best players, but coaches bring out the best in players. Players trust a coach, listen to them, obey them, and share their feelings with them. However, coaches are tough disciplinarians, timekeepers, and progress monitors. The coaching done on players nowadays are to enhance the value of a player in the market in order to sell him to another sports club in addition to winning games. Sports coaching are thus shorter in duration, whereas career coaching, life coaching, business coaching are more enduring. The principles and procedures are a hybrid between coaching and counseling. Counseling is a method to allow the follower to find the right path, with the counselor acting as a mirror, guide, and sounding board.

Jacob Thomas, PhD

1.7.4 Sustainable leader upholding enduring interests

In the business world, a firm or organization has certain enduring interests, such as sustained growth, legitimacy, increasing brand value, maintenance of strategic alliances, customer satisfaction, good-quality products, and innovative, productive employees. The strategy of every business firm is to sustain competitive advantages by satisfying these interests. The enduring interests of a nation that a national leader upholds are national security, prosperity for its people, and assuring fundamental rights to every human being.

Upholding the enduring interests of an organization is the primary goal

> **Insight Box 1.19**
>
> **Unsustainable leaders**
> - *dishonest*
> - *mean*
> - *greedy*
> - *stingy*
> - *uninteresting*
> - *self-obsessed*
> - *vacuous*
> - *lame*
> - *lying, cheating*
> - *stealing*
> - *evading tax*
> - *self-centered*
> - *appear as strong*
> - *arrogant*
> - *superficial*
> - *proud*
> - *short-sighted*

of a sustainable leader, and this is done by using all the levers and tools at his or her command. A sustainable leader builds and renews the required capabilities to serve well these enduring interests, investing in assets and capabilities to meet the future unforeseen challenges, including shocks or evolutions in the technological, operational, or strategic spheres.

Identifying correctly the enduring interests of the organization or community and committing resources and rebuilding capabilities to serve exceedingly well these few interests are part of the long-term vision and strategy of a sustainable leader.

1.7.5 Sustainable leader solving problems

A sustainable leader identifies issues as problems to be solved forever rather than viewing the issue as a way of life. People wear shoes that are made of leather to protect their feet from the cold. To make leather shoes, animals are killed for their hide, or after animals are killed for their meat, the by-product—that is, hide—is used for shoemaking. This is taken as the normal way of life in the shoe industry. When population increases, sourcing enough hide to make more shoes becomes a problem. As a way of life, killing as many animals as required to make shoes is normal, but it upsets the food chain in an ecosystem, and thus the ecosystem services are affected.

A sustainable leader in the shoe industry would solve this problem by making shoes with a special treatment on the hide so that the shoes will last longer, requiring fewer animals to be killed, or by finding out substitute materials for shoemaking. Additionally, the leader would take back all the leather shoes that are discarded by consumers after their use to reprocess the materials and make new shoes from the recycled old shoes. Such a shoe industry leader would forge a strategic alliance with animal rights activists, become a member of WBCSD (World Business Council for Sustainable Development), and make a reverse logistics chain for product take-back.

1.8 Levels of sustainable leadership

Considering the outer dimension or external environment of sustainable leadership, there are four levels:

- organization level: an institution, a firm, an NGO(Non-Govermental Organisation), a government department, an SBU(Strategic Business Unit)
- city level: a city, a town, a community, an urban settlement
- country level: sovereign states
- global level: regional grouping of countries, global markets of an MNC(Multi National Corporations), UN member states, global NGOs, global religious and spiritual organizations, global publishing houses, and the media.

The sustainable leadership arena and leadership challenge at the organization level can be in business firms, educational institutions, health-care institutions, government departments, charitable organizations, resident associations or gated communities/neighborhoods, religious congregations, media groups, etc. Each of such organizations, while embracing sustainable leadership principles and practices, would cover the entire population as each organization has a follower base that are different but overlapping.

Jacob Thomas, PhD

Are there any organizations in which the need for sustainable leadership is more important than others? Can organizations be graded based on the need for sustainable leadership? Educational institutions come on top, followed by business firms and government departments, considering the degree and spread of the impacts each of them can make.

The sustainability of a business firm is measured through the Dow Jones Sustainability Indices, which started in 1999. Those firms that are low in the grades need a robust sustainable leadership regime to catch up with those firms on the top of the list. Similarly, cities and countries are also graded on sustainability by many indices and measures.

Leadership can be conceptualized at five levels based on the type of leadership as follows:

- *Doing the long term, lasting things in all situations and problems, with the pristine-ness of the environmental components and the needs of future generations, guiding all decisions.*
- *Doing the right things in all situations, connecting a situation to a higher, transcendental wholeness.*
- *Doing things ethical in all situations and problems, by internalizing a moral perspective among followers.*
- *Doing the right things to transform the current way of doing things or state of affairs with the power of a strong vision and inspiring example.*
- *Doing things right in situations and problems; using rewards and punishments to motivate the followers.*

Jim Collins (2005) identifies five levels of leadership evolving from a level 1 leader, a highly capable individual, through to a contributing team member at level 2, a competent manager at level 3, an effective leader at level 4, and to the level 5 leader who builds enduring greatness through a paradoxical combination of personal humility plus professional skill and will. At level 4, the leader catalyzes commitment with a compelling vision and stimulates the followers.

Levels of leadership can be conceived in several ways in the three dominant theories of leadership: dispositional theories, process theories, and network theories. Within business organizations' boundaries, leadership levels can be viewed as lower level, middle level, senior level or unit/SBU level, functional level, and HQ/corporate level. In social organizations, the levels depend on geographic spread and the nature of the work. There are unit-level coordinators, regional coordinators, and apex-level trustees.

1.9 Evolution of leadership constructs

An attempt to understand 'good' and 'effective' leadership dominated the history of leadership research. The relevance of the constructs is related to the state of social organization and the economic contexts.

i. Sustainable leadership (2010s)

This concept of sustainable leadership first came to leadership literature during early 2000s, mostly in the education sector. The concept did not catch the attention of elite management institutions or journals. True to most of the concepts and theories in management that first evolved from practitioners and later popularized by academicians, sustainable leadership remains in the practitioner's domain. However, the antecedent conditions for its development are observed to be ripe.

ii. Authentic leadership (2000s)

The construct of authentic leadership has its origins in management literature during the 1990s, but it developed during the 2000s with more than fifty-five research articles. The scams and the scandals in the corporate world gave impetus to more research on authentic leadership. The concept of destructive leadership also gained currency during this period in the wake of immense financial and social losses in organizations in the energy and financial sectors.

iii. Transformational leadership (1990s)

With the popularity of reengineering and strategic change initiatives during the 1990s, transformational leadership was viewed as appropriate to reengineer organizations. The concepts of transcendental leadership and spiritual leadership also evolved during this period. Empowerment of followers was a unique feature of this era.

iv. Transactional leadership, team leadership (1980s)

The 1980s viewed teams and projects as the best method to improve productivity and thereby growth of organizations. Team leadership is essentially transactional leadership.

v. Bureaucratic leadership (pre 1980s till Max Weber)

Bureaucratic leadership is the conventional form of leading social organizations based on impersonal rules, which is assumed to be a rational mechanism. Command and control, rewards and punishments, chain of command, span of control, and clear roles based on rules and norms are the aspects of leading related to bureaucratic leadership. This is also a type of transactional leadership where the formal position is given the authority to command and control the followers.

vi. Charismatic leadership (prehistory)

Certain personality traits are believed to bestow on certain individuals the ability to influence others. Such charismatic leaders may be benevolent or autocratic, authentic or narcissistic, constructive or destructive depending on the sense of belongingness, the sense of power that the leader possesses, and the context of leading. Rulers, philosophers, religious leaders, artists, revolutionaries, military leaders, and social reformers who have a large following are categorized as charismatic leaders.
The above distinction in chronological order is purely based on the periods when academicians got more preoccupied with one construct over the other. Otherwise, all these types of leadership have been coexisting in some places as leadership practices.

1.10 Leader skills script (LSS) What skills make your influence more lasting?

What skills will make your influence more lasting? Please rate yourself on the following statements (1 is for low, 2 is for medium, 3 is for strong).

1. I have strong investigation skills on aspects happening in my surroundings.

2. I have strong self-awareness and introspection skills on the why of other's behavior toward me.

3. I have high degree of imagination with intention that leads to novel influence strategies in pursuit of sustainable development goals.

4. I have strong implementation skills with high levels of participation of others.

5. My monitoring initiatives induce progress and results.

6. I excel in coaching and bringing out the best in others.

7. I am good at communicating with warmth, leaving a lasting glow on others.

8. I am fully aware of all ecosystem services, and all my actions are designed to enhance the capability of such services.

9. I understand well the interconnections of all environmental components, and all my actions strengthen those connections and interdependencies.

10. I am conscious of my responsibility to preserve nature and provide inspirational motivation to others to preserve the pristine state of nature.

11. Honesty and humility are characteristic features of my personality and of all my actions in all circumstances.

12. I seek ideas from others and reconfigure them for all my actions, which are always in pursuit of improving the quality of life of the present and future generations.

Total score
Rating 30–36: sustainable leader
24–29: authentic leader
18–23: transformational leader
12–18: transactional leader

Leading with Insight

People follow their self-interests, not any leader.

Followership is mostly an illusion as people follow their self-interests. Identifying the self-interests of the followers and then developing a strategy to address those interests to their satisfaction without depleting the resource system and without sacrificing the growth needs of other stakeholders of the resource system enables leading with insight. Insight is seeing inside or the power of seeing into something with the mind. A sustainable leader sees the inside of events, symptoms, people, problems, and issues. She also has the power of seeing into different dimensions, seeing into the future, and seeing into the interactions. With insight, the leader distinguishes matters of significance and matters that have lasting impact. A conceptual framework of leading with insight is given in Fig. 2.1.

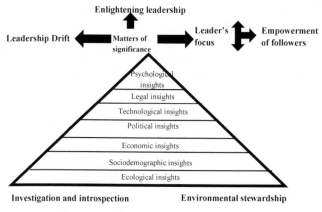

Fig. 2.1: Leading with insight, empowering followers through partnership.

There is a sevenfold path to getting insights in a systematic manner, as depicted inside the pyramid in Fig. 2.1, starting from ecological insights and ending with psychological insights. Investigation and introspection are a system of intense observation, reasoned attention, analytical thinking, and critical reflection and thinking by way of causal relation.

A psychological insight that can come up from *investigation and introspection* can be that greed and selfishness cause scarcity and that scarcity leads to overexploitation of natural and common resources and

Insight Box 2.1

Leadership mindset *is a continuum of complex levels of mental, social, emotional, ecological, and technological awareness, thoughts, and decisions.*

Insight Box 2.2

Vision*: your picture of the future*
Mission*: your fundamental objectives for yourself and/or the organization*
Purpose*: why you and/or your organization exists*

several unethical behaviors. Greed and selfishness are problems with the human mind and are the psychological causes of the environmental problems of today. Since the environmental problems have psychological causes, technological and material solutions alone may not restore the environment to its original state or even conserve the resource system. The sevenfold path is a guide to probe every aspect in a systematic manner, and the final output will be an integrated, holistic, balanced insight that is enlightening and empowering.

The insight gained through investigation and introspection on the incidents, events, and trends in the environment leads to identification of matters of significance. Correct insight about matters of significance leads to a focus on the substantive matters or issues or the significant need of the followers in their surroundings. With the leader becoming enlightened with extraordinary insight and focusing on a real matter of significance, the light is scattered among the followers, and they in turn tend to become willing partners. When the focus is lost or the leader is not pursuing matters of significance, *leadership drift* will result, and in such a situation, empowerment efforts will remain a weak tactic.

2.1 Matters of significance

With the insight gained from the processes of investigation and introspection, a sustainable leader articulates matters of significance to the followers, his or her organizational members, or the constituency. Leaders do four things in 90 percent of their waking time.

- Meetings—one-on-one or group meetings
- Taking decisions—in meetings, in files/ documents, in thoughts, or while listening
- Communicating—oral or written, direct or indirect, from top to down, from bottom to up
- Thinking—the mind never is free of thoughts except during meditation or

> **Insight Box 2.3**
>
> **Styles of leadership**
> - *Nomadic leadership (shifting bases)*
> - *Tramping leadership (destroying everything on the course like a warlord)*
> - *Pilgrim leadership (preserving and respecting the ecosystem)*
> - *Marching leadership (heady, power exuding growth)*
> - *Hiking leadership (nondestructive excursion)*
> - *Ranging leadership (both appropriators and providers flourish simultaneously with long term coexistence)*

mind-stilling exercises and mostly with the thoughts on matters of insignificance if the leader is enlightened with the right insights.

Leaders are expected to engage themselves in matters of significance in the four transactions: conducting meetings of significance, making significant decisions, engaging in significant communication, and thinking about matters of significance. Even though 90 percent of the waking time is engaged in these four activities, 90 percent of people may not be doing matters of significance because of not knowing the common thread that should connect the four: the purpose of the meeting, the purpose of decision-making, the purpose of communicating, and the purpose that guides the thoughts. Purpose is why the organization exists and why the leader exercises his or her influence on resources (human, material, natural and technological resources).

Most of the meetings, decisions, or thinking are also not connected to a mission and a vision. The distinguishing features of a mission and a purpose in the context of sustainable leadership are given in Table 2.1.

Table 2.1 Distinguishing the features of a mission and a purpose

Organizational purpose	Mission
♦ defines the end values	♦ defines the strategic objectives
♦ clarifies why profits or wealth are created	♦ aligns stakeholders' interests
♦ has a moral quality	♦ has a physical quality
♦ appeals to the higher instincts of human beings	♦ is linked to the organization's strategy
♦ connects with the universe	♦ connects with customers
♦ is a guiding concept that unites people with nature	♦ is a guiding concept that unites internal customers with the vision
♦ is a common cause	♦ is a common cause for employees
♦ is aligned with the essential nature of a human being	♦ is aligned with the organization's founding interests
♦ is immutable	♦ changes when environmental conditions permanently change

2.2 Starting from investigation and introspection

Leading with insight starts from understanding the paradigm that guides the leader's thoughts. While looking inside one's mind is introspection, seeing into something outside with the mind is a process of investigation. The external environment or surroundings of a leader is investigated thoroughly to gain understanding of systems, processes, interlinkages, interdependencies, trends, and challenges.

There are three *I*s in the process of investigation.

- identification of incidents, especially unplanned or undesired events of significance.
- information about evidences
- interpretation for inferences.

A leader will not go after all incidents and events occurring in the surroundings but will identify those incidents that are relevant for the followers. Then information that has the value to prove or disprove a hypothesis about the incident (why, what, how, when, and who of the incident) is collected and collated.

This collated data is interpreted for inference. The inferences trigger the thought process of an inspection about one's ideas, concepts, beliefs, and assumptions about people and aspects of the environment and the desirability of a future state. The process of getting insights with its inputs, outcomes, and mediating factors are given in Fig. 2.2.

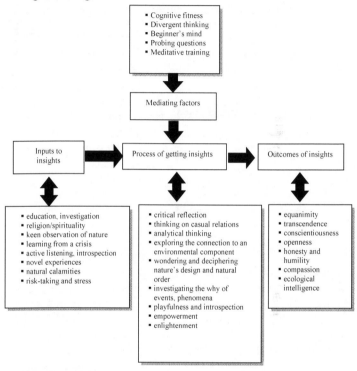

Fig. 2.2: Leading with insights by learning to get insights.

2.3 Leadership drift: Shifting the sights

Identify your innate desire and then make bridges to the desires of others.

A leader mobilizes people and resources to reach a destination. This may be in terms of a new product launch, a certain market share, a particular EBIT, sustainability score, or CAGR for a business organization. In the case of a nation, it may be a certain percentage of GDP or a measure in HDI, transparency index, or pollution ranking. Some leaders even mesmerize people, and a few may manipulate people in order to make a following and let the leader have his or her way. An ordinary leader's destination is visible and easy to reach or accomplish,

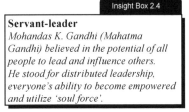

Insight Box 2.4

Servant-leader
Mohandas K. Gandhi (Mahatma Gandhi) believed in the potential of all people to lead and influence others. He stood for distributed leadership, everyone's ability to become empowered and utilize 'soul force'.

and hurdles on the way are surmountable. However, sustainable leaders have purposes that are not easily visible, hurdles en route are unknown, and the destination is not easily reachable. It is more like a voyage to the limits of human ingenuity and the limits of the beauty of nature.

Insight Box 2.5

Instrumental leader
Aristotle (354–322 BC) is an early example of an instrumental leader. His book A Treatise on Government *states that all citizens should take their turn of governing and being governed and that kings have no marked superiority compared to their subjects.*

Taking the followers into limits of their ingenuity is an inward journey, whereas taking everyone to the limits of the pristineness of nature is an outward journey. The beauty of nature in its pristineness, the rhythmic changes in seasons, the vastness of its diversity, and the integrated design of its elements make it not easily comprehensible, let alone attainable. In such voyages, losing focus, getting distracted by something more immediate and physical, and ending up somewhere else far away from the targeted destination is normal; this is called leadership drift. Sustainable leaders are constantly on vigil to stay on track in their inward journey through leading by insight and their outward journey of scattering light among the followers from the insights gained. The attributes of a sustainable leader compared with an authentic or business leader that enable focus on the purpose of sustainable

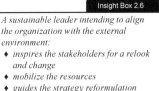

Insight Box 2.6

A sustainable leader intending to align the organization with the external environment:
♦ *inspires the stakeholders for a relook and change*
♦ *mobilize the resources*
♦ *guides the strategy reformulation*
♦ *facilitates implementation of new strategy through an action plan*
♦ *monitors impacts and adapts the strategy for a better fit.*

leadership in all leader–follower interactions without drift is given in Table 2.2.

Table 2.2 Attributes valued in interactions

Sustainable leadership	Ethical leadership	Business leadership
Steward	Joy	Hard work
Love of nature	Trust	Sacrifice
Harmony	Love	Speed
Interconnectedness		Hierarchy and control
Peace		Accuracy
Integrity		Efficiency
Adaptation		Top–down
Tacit knowledge	Respect	communication
Partnership	Wholeness	Effectiveness
Dialogue	Justice	Productivity
Followers are leaders	Empowerment	Excellence
	Bottom–up	Growth
	communication	Competency
	Leaders need followers	Knowledge
		Safety
		Followers need leaders

2.4 Leader's focus

Everyone desires to be cared for, to be wanted, and to feel special.

The focus of leaders can be on many things or on one thing at a time. What is focused gets done as more attention is paid to that aspect, and more resources and time are allocated. Focusing on many things simultaneously dissipates attention and resources. Aspects people usually focus on in an organizational setting are as follows:

- focus on people (followers)
- focus on profits
- focus on the planet
- focus on results for the self or others
- focus on reputation, image, status
- focus on issues, problems
- focus on opportunities, possibilities
- focus on legitimacy
- focus on emotions (avenging an injury)

- focus on the future, present or past
- focus on costs
- focus inward (self-interest, self-actualization, self-growth)
- focus on differentiation (the road less travelled)
- focus on making a difference
- focus on social capital, networks
- focus on shareholder wealth
- focus on socio-emotional wealth (family business leaders)
- focus on customers (giving value)
- focus on innovation, creativity
- focus on employees (enhancing the knowledge, commitment, hard work, and cooperation)
- focus on quality
- focus on product market
- focus on succession
- focus on capital market
- focus on spirituality.

Focus itself is described as a generic strategy by Michael Porter (1980) for business organizations, especially focus on price leadership or focus on differentiation to gain sustainable competitive advantages. However, two changes occurred afterwards; first, the information and communication technological advances has made knowledge a major source of competitive advantage, and second, there has been a convergence of economic, social, and environmental forces in the early part of the twenty-first century. This situation has resulted in confusion about what to focus on. When land, capital, people, technology, or management systems were the sources of competitive advantage, deciding on what to focus was fairly easy.

> **Insight Box 2.7**
>
> **Nomadic leadership**
> *This is a leadership that appropriates and uses resources at one place and, once the resource system dries up or gets degraded, moves on to another location to continue the unsustainable actions. A business firm relocating the polluting industries to developing countries, coupled with the alluring FDI to such countries, is an example of nomadic business leadership.*

In this scenario, the leader's focus is shifting to value creation in the economic, social, and environmental assets by leveraging knowledge resources and the economic, social, and environmental capital in an integrated, holistic manner. There is a five-action framework as a guide for the leader to focus and lead by insights.

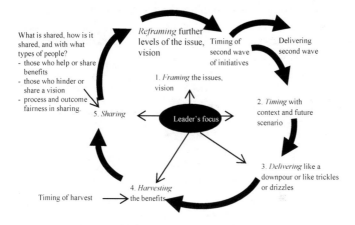

Fig. 2.3: The five-action framework of leading with insight.

Sustainable leaders focus on five actions (Fig. 2.3) in an integrated manner, starting with framing the issues or a vision based on the insight gained from investigation and introspection. There can be many choices as paths to take and methods to adopt. The integration of even the fifth action of sharing occurs at the first stage of framing— how to share the benefits. A sustainable leader does not use

coercive, manipulative, or mesmerizing tactics in getting people on board or while sharing the benefits. Even those people who hinder progress are attempted to be brought on board by sharing the vision.

The second action is timing, which is a choice based on the insight gained about the context and about the future scenario.

Jacob Thomas, PhD

There is a time to start delivering as per contextual factors and also a time to reach the future scenario. Too early or too late in starting and arriving will result in encountering challenges which are unnecessary and avoidable if the timing is right. An initiative needs to conserve the energy, spirit, and resources to reach the destination rather than filter away the energy and resources on the way, facing unnecessary and avoidable challenges. The great-man theory and situational theory base their concepts on this aspect of timing. A great man arises from nowhere when the situation is ripe, usually called a crisis situation. There would have been many of his predecessors who attempted the same initiative but faded, losing the energy while facing the insurmountable challenges.

Insight Box: 2.8

Theories of leadership
- *great-man theory*
- *trait theory*
- *situational theory*
- *contingency theory*
- *behavioral theory*
- *dyadic theory*
- *participatory theory*
- *relationship theory*
- *neo-charismatic theory*
- *transactional theory*
- *transcendent theory*
- *social-network theory*
- *complexity theory*

Source: various authors.

Once the timing is right, the next action is implementing the strategy formulated to reach the vision state. The delivery can be all of a sudden to overwhelm or awe the followers; this has the advantage of overcoming any resistance. Nothing stands against a downpour, whereas trickles and drizzles may germinate resistance to change.

The delivery of leadership inputs is for harvesting the fruits for a very long time. The timing of the first harvest is important as too early a harvest may jeopardize the robustness of future harvests. Harvesting of benefits should ideally start after a period of growth and stability. The time for harvesting the outputs of influencing is when a threshold number of followers are achieved and the follower base is stable. The outputs of leadership need to be shared with people who contributed to the harvest.

The cycle continues by reframing the vision based on the insights gained during the first cycle of five actions by interpositioning the new inputs to leadership. This leads to improved strategy, better timing, and better delivery methods. Sustainable leaders are not leading for a single harvest but for prolonged, repeated, and better harvests.

Focusing on one thing with devotion is the best way. This is usually done by professionals, scientists, writers, and social activists who are not pulled by the pressures of an organization. However, most of the business, social, and political organizations are constantly impacted by the changes in the external environment, and therefore, there are tendencies to shift focus. The five-action framework enables the integration and interposition of the inputs from the external environment in the subsequent cycles by reframing the issues/vision without losing focus.

2.5 Environmental leadership

It is an approach to leadership having two dimensions: an inner psychological dimension and an outer nature-oriented dimension. Environmental leadership in the first dimension nurtures a culture that excites and stimulates individuals to do what is required for the benefit of all. This type of leadership approach cultivates an environment or setting that develops cooperation and participatory qualities and brings out the best in other people so that each one is motivated enough to carry others. Benefits to all and carrying one another will benefit nature, which will carry forward to well-being of human beings. A psychological support system is created, leading to the flourishing development of individuals rooted in nature. Insight about the inner, emotional, and development needs of individuals will enable an environmental leader to craft a strategy to influence and mobilize resources to create the befitting, nurturing surroundings for their fulfillment.

> **Insight Box 2.10**
>
> **Lord Buddha on environmental leadership**
> Siddhartha Gautama was born 2,500 years ago under a sale tree, enlightened under a bodhi tree, and died under a sale tree. He taught people the following:
> - consume less
> - live in harmony with nature, understanding the natural laws, and use nature wisely
> - learn from nature to improve the mind and behavior.
>
> The precepts of Buddha's living are the following:
> - abstain from taking the lives of living forms
> - prohibit disposing of wastes to water; as all lives depend on water, polluting water is a sin
> - show respect for trees, which provide food, canopy, and protection
> - harmony between living things sharing the planet, denouncing human conquering of nature
> - connectedness with the environment near and far, past and present.

Leaders who identify the ecological challenges and actively promote sustainable development initiatives comprehensively and holistically for ecosystem health and human well-being are environmental leaders in the second dimension. Such leaders influence the socioeconomic system to make it more harmonious with ecosystems through environment-friendly products, technologies, and policies. Environmental leaders leverage their capabilities, expertise, and authority to lead new business models and solutions to global environmental challenges. The CEO of PUMA footwear, a sports goods company, has introduced the full costing of the environmental externalities in the company's balance sheet, which is an environmental leadership policy initiative.

> **Insight Box 2.11**
>
> **Power of purpose**
> *Purpose motivates and guides people to:*
> * *Cooperate in efforts*
> * *Co-exist in peace*
> * *Flourish in harmony*
> * *Endure hardships*
> * *Preserve nature*
> * *Value life*
> * *Value connectedness*

2.6 Empowerment of followers

> *Everyone gets more power when connected to one end of a lever.*

Identifying the appropriate lever that can enable a person to gain more influencing ability is an insight leaders need to have. This lever can be the purpose of the leadership that aligns the followers. Mobilizing followers through this purpose as the lever and creating conditions to bring out the best in everyone is a process of empowerment. The initial followers develop into collaborators first and graduate to partners when leader–follower relations are transformed into a harmonious partnership with dialogue as the mode of communication.

The term 'empowerment' connotes two sides: a side with power and the other side without power who are to be given power. This concept has evolved in the management field during the 1950s when bargaining—a competitive, adversorial process—

> **Insight Box 2.12**
>
> '**Empowerment** *is a process of acquisition of an inner drive and direction to do things the way one likes, through successive goal setting and goal achievement' (Thomas 2006). This definition explains that empowerment is externally mediated (acquisition), intrinsic to a person, involves freedom and ability to do the chosen things, and involves goal setting and goal achievement.*

was in vogue. The scarcity hypothesis involved was the underlying process of bargaining, which was also a form of empowerment that at least concedes the opportunity to the other side to bargain. Empowerment evolved as a strategy to reduce conflicts and to optimize performance. The concept was existing in practice as delegation of powers and opportunities for self-determination before academicians started theorizing.

During the 1960s, the construct of involvement developed, which means involving the other side in decision-making. The next stage was the participation model of empowerment that moved one step ahead of the accommodative phase of the involvement type of empowerment. Participation is more cooperative than accommodative, wherein opposing interests are brought together. Empowerment works on the coexistence principle based on the expansion hypothesis than the scarcity hypothesis (Barnett 1999). Empowerment is both an objective reality and a subjective experience. During 2010s, the construct of partnership and 'co-creation' have gained currency, viewing followers as partners.

2.6.1 Power and the empowering process

The word 'power' has several meanings. In a legal sense, power can mean authority so that empowerment can mean authorization. Power also may be used to describe capacity, as in the self-efficacy definition of 'empowerment' (Conger and Kanungo 1988). Power also means energy; thus, to empower can mean to energize (Thomas and Velthouse 1990). Through formal authority, cultural norms, technical expertise, and organizational politics, individuals with power attempt to influence others (Mintzberg 1983). Managers' incentives and discretion and subordinates' dependencies define the use of power in an important organizational issue (Vredenburgh and Brender 1998).

> **Insight Box 2.13**
>
> **Five stages of empowerment:**
> - *enlarged empowerment*
> - *enriched empowerment*
> - *threshold empowerment*
> - *conscientized empowerment*
> - *emancipatory empowerment.*
>
> *Source: Jacob Thomas (2006).*

Herzberg (1984) stated that individuals pass through stages of externally and organizationally oriented power stages before moving to internally and globally oriented power stages. The stages are the following
- powerlessness characterized by manipulation

- power by association characterized by dependence on mentors, supervisors, etc.
- symbol-dependent perception of power
- power through self-reflection with resulting influence
- visionary power or empower others
- power by gestalt, which is associated with wisdom characterized by service, ethics.

Power distribution can be viewed from one of two basic viewpoints: fixed sum or expandable pie. When viewed through the lens of influence tactics, programmatic empowerment confirms with an expandable-pie view of power that the more one gives away, the more one has. Programmatic empowerment, called a mechanistic form of empowerment (Quinn and Spreitzer 1997), tends to empower followers by sharing information, providing structure and process, offering relevant training opportunities, and rewarding initiatives and risk-taking. According

---

Insight Box 2.14

Development of empowerment construct:

- *reduced alienation (Seeman 1959)*
- *self-regulating English coal miners (Trist et al. 1963)*
- *semi-autonomous teams in Scandinavia (Bolweg 1976)*
- *US team experiences (Walton 1982)*
- *to empower is to authorize or delegate or give legal power to someone (*Webster's Dictionary*)*
- *'empower' means 'to enable' (*Oxford Dictionary*)*
- *job enrichment (Hackman and Oldham 1980)*
- *participatory management (Lawler 1988)*
- *employee involvement (Bowen and Lawler 1992)*
- *power and control are the root constructs of empowerment and involves motivating through enhancing personal efficacy (Conger and Kanungo 1998)*
- *quality circles (Sundostram et al. 1990)*
- *empowerment, the process which enhances intrinsic task motivation (Thomas and Velthouse 1990)*
- *'empower', the belief that one has control, the belief that one can influence decisions (Parker and Price 1994)*
- *four dimensions of team empowerment: potency, meaningfulness, autonomy, and impact (Kirkman and Rosen 1997)*
- *two types of empowering: programmatic/mechanistic and organic empowerment (Quinn and Spreitzer 1997)*
- *four dimensions of empowering, corresponding to four dimensions of power (Hardy and O'Sullivan 1998)*
- *personal influence, self-efficacy, meaningfulness—the dimensions of empowerment (Corsum and Enz 1999)*
- *empowering, a matter of personal belief (Lee, 1999)*
- *empowering practices for women (Crampton and Mishra 1999; Loy 1999; Markson 1994).*

---

to Lukes (1974), manipulating workers wants in the form of programmatic empowerment in order to prevent conflict is an insidious exercise of power.

Power is a complex concept having many dimensions (Luke 1974). The four dimensions of power related to four ways of empowerment as follows was postulated by Hardy and O. Sullivan (1998).

- the ability to mobilize and acquire resources by managing resource dependencies
- the ability to gain access to the decision arena through overt or covert conflict
- consciousness-raising and delegitimization strategies to create the will to resist; when fully aware of the issues, legitimacy of the status quo is confronted
- creating more positive experiences by embedding power in the system; empowerment in the sense of freedom from power effects is not possible, although local struggles may produce more positive experiences.

Empowerment practices appear to rely on the increased use of the third dimension of power by management, such as an emphasis on selection and socialization, socializing to legitimate organization goals (Barker 1993). Empowerment terminology reduces conflict by emphasizing consensus and cooperation through such terms as 'associates', 'team members', 'partners', 'colleagues', 'vice presidents', etc. Empowerment programs reduce the necessity of having to use more visible or coercive forms of power to ensure that organizational goals are met and resistance is quelled (O' Conner 1995). Dissenters may be marginalized as uncooperative or in need of additional education or training.

Monica Lee (1999) defined 'empowerment' as a matter of personal belief rather than an externally measurable quality. It is about the ability to set and achieve goals that are valued by the organization. This value belief is created by the organization. When one loses one's self-responsibility to the needs of the organization, one becomes impotent as a questioning, reflective, and potentially disruptive individual.

In business organizations, empowerment practices transfer some resources to employees, and the senior managers often retain control of many important resources, especially the right to hire, fire, promote, hand out rewards, and control budgets (Bernstein 1992; Eccles 1993). Even if the empowered employees secure access to some decision-making process, from which they were previously excluded, the ultimate control of these processes usually rests with the senior managers, who set the parameters within which subordinates may operate (Stewart 1989).

2.6.2 Empowering process

Empowerment is fundamentally a motivational process of an individual's experience of feeling enabled (Corsun and Enz 1999). To empower is to give power (Thomas and Velthouse 1990). Hence, empowerment as a concept presupposes that somebody gives power with a certain objective.

Nancy Foy (1996) writes that total empowerment is a fairy tale. It does not belong to the real world. This presupposes that empowerment in organizations are partial and incomplete. And there will be scope for further doses of empowerment. Thomas and Velthouse's (1990) notion of the process of empowerment (that it is an individual's work context and that personality characteristics shape empowerment cognitions, which in turn motivate an individual's behavior) exposes the fact that when work context changes, the process of empowerment changes. In a fast-changing business organization context, both the work context and personality characteristics, to fit into that changed-work context, have to be different. Since empowerment is a process, it may never end as the control of one individual on all organizational decision-making affecting his or her self-efficacy and job performance may not be complete at any given time, especially when the work context and environment will be changing. Empowerment reflects the ongoing ebb and flow of people's perceptions about themselves in relation to their work environments (Bandura 1989). Thus, empowerment is a continuous variable; people can be viewed as more or less empowered rather than completely empowered or not empowered.

Viewing from another dimension, true empowerment will not be achieved without a radical metamorphosis of the system, which cannot be achieved by actors who are entwined within it (Hardy and O'Sullivan 1999). Prospects for empowerment in the sense of freedom from power effects are limited.

2.6.3 Models of empowerment

Literature so far exposes three major models of empowerment.

2.6.3.1 Revolutionary model

Karl Marx (1844) first documented the dehumanizing aspects of work through routinization in the business organizations. Routinization and de-skilling of workers strip workers of the power associated with the thinking and planning aspects of work (Braverman 1974). To put an end to the dehumanization and alienation, Marx had proposed a revolution and capturing of power by the disempowered workers, which was one model of empowerment. The revolutionary model of empowerment is defined as a process or a mechanism by which people, organizations, and communities gain mastery over their affairs (Rappaport 1987). Advocates of this perspective argue that empowerment has to be taken and not given since the very act of empowering someone else creates a dependent relationship, which by definition is disempowering, particularly when the empowerer has significant power over the empoweree (Gruber and Trickett 1987; Simon 1990). The political dynamics of this more radical form of empowerment is thus different from business empowerment. Business empowerment programs are in contrast designed to achieve organizational goals more effectively and more smoothly.

Business empowerment practices are the practices observed in both motivational and relational models of empowerment. It was evidenced that power and effectiveness of the management increase with the sharing of power and control (Tannerbaum 1968; Kantar 1979). Several studies have demonstrated that empowerment is positively associated with an organization's effectiveness (McClelland 1975; Kantar 1983; Bennis and Nanus 1985). This presupposes that empowerment is a process of sharing of power.

2.6.3.2 Motivational model

Realizing the danger involved in the revolutionary model of empowerment, another model emerged, called motivational model. Different practices and theories of motivation of employees emerged after the Russian Revolution of 1917. Business organizations put into practice many of these motivational theories in the form of empowerment programs. The stronger such unobtrusive cultural controls are, the less likely that the organization norms will be transgressed and the more comfortable the top management will be in delegating power (Westley 1990). Empowerment programs, though often packaged as management efforts to return power and control to the workers, may be viewed as a weak tactic of influence (Kipnis 1984).

In this model of empowerment, there is less delegation of power, but the emphasis is on open communication and inspirational goal setting to increase commitment and involvement (Conger and Kanungo 1988). Attainable objectives that employees can achieve are set in order to provide opportunities for enactive attainment, give words of encouragement and feedback to verbally persuade individuals that they are capable, and provide emotional support to offset stress and anxiety. Alderfer (1969), Maslow (1954), and McClelland (1961) considered employee motives and needs as factors which affect work behavior.

2.6.3.3 Relational model of empowerment

In this model, dependencies that make it difficult to get the job done are reduced by delegating more power and authority (Burke 1986; Lawler 1992). Such empowerment practices decentralize power by allowing employees to take part in decision-making (Stewart 1989; Bowen and Lawler 1992). Employees are typically permitted to take decisions only within specified policies and procedures set by the management (Eccles 1993; Humphrey 1991). These controls are referred to as strategic alignment, which is reinforced by rewards that provide a clear link between individual and organizational goals, communication of a shared vision, training, and education. Allthese are designed to heighten employees' awareness of strategic business objectives (Eubanks 1991; Fleming 1991).

The support-based relational model of empowerment is also called the organic form of empowerment, wherein the creation of a supportive work environment is the focus. It is also a weak tactic of management influence since it is a creation of the management for effectiveness and sharing of power. The organic form of empowerment is a process of risk-taking, trusting, and personal growth, where the management creates the context, which is more empowering (Quinn and Spreitzer 1997). It is a process of identifying and removing the conditions which cause powerlessness while increasing feelings of self-efficacy (Conger and Kanungo 1988). Thomas and Velthouse (1990) defined it as a process which enhances the intrinsic work motivation by positively influencing impact, competence, meaningfulness, and choice. The organic form of empowerment also is an attempt to reduce alienation and powerlessness by increasing motivation to work and be effective.

From a leader–follower format with hierarchical structures, empowering leadership reaches a leader–leader form with collaborative structures. The communication style also undergoes a change in the empowerment process from directing to dialogue.

Directing

↓

Consulting

↓

Discussing

↓

Dialogue

Dialogue is the main communication method when the leader–follower relationship reaches partnership mode, where the two side's positions have fully vanished.

Jacob Thomas, PhD

2.6.4 Empowering forces

Job and organizational characteristics may act as antecedent conditions to empowerment (Kirkman and Rosen 1997). Four thematic areas have been identified: external leader behaviour, production/service responsibilities, human resource policies, and social structure. Karl Marx (1844) identified frustation arising out of alienation as the driving force for throwing away the dehumanizing structure. Social exclusion, referred to as a state or situation or process or mechanism by which employees are excluded, may be another force for empowerment (Haan 1998). Exclusion will generate forces for inclusion in decision-making and planning in organizations and thus results in empowerment. The same empowering forces are not likely to empower everyone equally due to the mediating role of empowering attributes, as depicted in Fig. 2.4

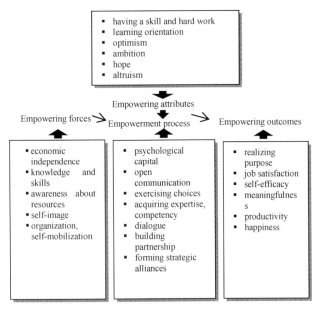

Fig. 2.4: The mediating role of empowering attributes in the empowerment process.

Hapke (1992) stated that the empowering process results from several mutually reinforcing forces beginning with economic independence. When recruited to a managerial position, a person can achieve this level, which is an incomplete one. The second empowering force is knowledge and awareness about oneself and society, personal needs, legal rights, availability of social and economic resources, and how to take advantage of them. The third force is self-image, which includes realization of one's capabilities and potential and the confidence to take action in one's life. The fourth force is autonomy. Women's empowerment can happen when gender relations within family, workplace, and society at large are reconstructed, and autonomy may act as a driving force for this. The fifth force is likely to be organization and collective bargaining and pooling of resources and lending moral support to one another.

> **Insight Box 2.15**
>
> **Environmental profit-and-loss account**
> *Jochen Zeitz, CEO of PUMA, a sports goods company, broke away from the herd of business leaders by first preparing an environmental P & L account, assigning monetary value to PUMA's use of ecosystem services across the supply chain.*

2.6.5 Consequences of empowerment

The consequences of empowerment is the gaining of power by those who were hitherto disempowered in order to be effective in realizing their purpose (Block 1990). Empowerment facilitates fuller applications of human potentials, spontaneous commitment of people to organizational goals, and innovative responses to unexpected organizational problems (Brown and Brown 1995).

Empowerment was considered as an elixir in the 1990s (Burdett 1991) and an indispensable device for accomplishing a competitive edge in a globalized and liberal economy (Goksy and

> **Insight Box 2.16**
>
> **Maintain leadership by any means necessary**
> *Machiavelli (1469–1527) wrote* The Prince *while he was in exile, stating that a leader needs to employ coercion and collaboration to stay in power depending on the situation. It is what the leader appears to say or do that is more important than what a leader actually does. Leaders can find people who are willing to be duped into seeing what they want to see whether real or not. It is based on the assumption that individuals are governed solely by their present needs. He also wrote* The Art of War, Discourses on Livy, Florentine Histories.

Belfry 1991). Various authors have identified productivity, quality, low costs, safety, job satisfaction, and organizational commitment as the consequences of empowerment. Literature is abound with intended consequences of empowerment, and all these consequences are contributing to the survival and growth of the organizations.

The consequences of empowerment described in management literature so far demonstrates that empowerment is an influence by the leadership in order to produce positive outcomes for the effectiveness of the organization. It is an observation that the best practices of empowerment, as seen in the Microsoft headquarters in Seattle or the Infosys campus in Bangalore, still leaves employees with intellectual capital disempowered (Thomas 1999). The employees are seen glued to computers, chained to the machines, and all their hidden resources still not being expressed even with the best forms of empowerment mechanisms, such as reward system, self-managing teams, comfortable work environment, and welfare facilities. Empowerment is seen as a mechanism to exploit the intellectual capital of the employees fully. The unintended consequences of empowerment in some situations far outweigh the intended consequences.

> **Insight Box 2.17**
>
> **Transactional leader**
> *Plato (428–347 BC) states that some individuals have innate abilities to control and lead. To control and to be controlled, to lead and to be led are innate needs of mankind. Democracy leads to tyranny, and some individuals balance the tyranny by being mindful of the needs of the population and by guiding people through challenging situations.*

2.6.6 Joy of empowerment

By helping employees feel that they have power over significant aspects of their work and by enabling them to develop a sense of pride and ownership in their work and in the organization, empowerment is thought to leave employees optimistic, involved, committed, able to cope with adversity, and willing to perform independently and responsibly (Conger and Kanungo 1988; Thomas and Velthouse 1990; Block 1990). Through the many practices of empowerment (those that grant autonomy, provide variety and challenge, relax formal controls, enhance the opportunity for personal initiative, generate an emotional attachment to collective goals), the subjects believe themselves more highly valued, feel more excitement and passion in their work, and derive a more rewarding work experience (Hardy and O'Sullivan 1998). In other words, individuals may enjoy being empowered. While empowerment may contain a risk of exploitation, it also encompasses changes in the organizational environment that may improve the experience of the working life for some, even if not all, employees.

2.6.7 Empowering attributes

Why some individuals do not experience the joy of empowerment when empowering forces are existing needs some explanation. There may be individual traits or attributes which enable people to be empowered, while some others who lack these attributes are left out. Age, gender, and education are described by Spretzer (1996) as attributes which affect empowerment. Gender relations at the workplace may have an important role in affecting the empowerment of women (Bailyn 1993). J. Thomas (2006) identified the following empowering attributes as individual attributes that will enable a person to gain more influencing ability and self-determination:

- having a skill and hard work
- learning orientation
- optimism
- ambition, aspiration
- hope
- altruism.

2.7 Environmental stewardship

Stewardship is careful and responsible holding and management of something entrusted to one's care. The steward assumes the responsibility of taking care of something that belongs to someone else. The environment and all resources in it are viewed as a common heritage, and no individual or generation has any exclusive right of ownership over it. Environmental stewards strive to sustain the resource system of the planet and its expanse without degradation for the future generations to enjoy in the same, if not better, quality and quantity.

Businesses that gather financial rewards by appropriating the resource units from the earth in many ways (as energy resources, as raw materials, as sink of wastes and pollutants, as medium of communication, etc) have an added responsibility of caring for the environment. A business leader can transform into an environmental steward by focusing on any of the following:

- improvement in the efficiency of operations to reduce waste of resources
- use of less toxic and nontoxic chemicals
- responsible use of natural resources in a manner protecting the ecosystem integrity
- participation in cleanup programs
- self-assessment of the compliance with all environmental regulations
- self-assessment of the adherence to the twenty Aichi Biodiversity Targets, WBCSD principles, and best practices in environmental management for insights
- report of environmental actions to each stakeholder categories in a form tailored to the expectations and interests of each group.

Environmental stewardship's focus can further be disaggregated into water stewardship, forest stewardship, energy stewardship, biodiversity stewardship, and stewardship of a water body, land area, a particular species, etc.

2.8 Enlightening leadership

Sustainable leaders themselves are enlightened, and they in turn scatter far and wide the new light, new vision, new perspectives, and new methods. Enlightenment is a process of gaining a new or altered insight based on the investigation and introspection processes.

2.8.1 What is enlightenment?

Light enters the mind that was darkened by dogma or faith emanating from exposures and indoctrination. The fresh mind that a person is endowed with at birth is progressively clouded with repeated exposures to the surroundings. The person gets fully attached to the society and its faith, its god, its norms, its celebrations, and its rituals. Such a person gets answers to his entire existential and life's question from the scriptures or society and probably be contented with those answers. For some individuals, such answers from the dogma—be it religious beliefs, social dogma, ideologies, and philosopher's answers—may not be satisfactory. They will be in a quest for answers. Certain events, crises, or stimuli act as a spark to enlighten the darkened space in their minds, and then their lives change.

2.8.2 Why some people get enlightenment

The insightful mind of a leader evolves in phases due to the particular social, ecological, economic, and intellectual surroundings in which one progresses through life stages. They are enlightened by shaping certain questions arising from certain events, crises, or situations. The surroundings, events, and crises they are exposed to and the evolution of the insightful mind are unique to individuals, and those make some people enlightened.

2.8.3 What is it that distinguishes some enlightened persons from others?

Enlightened persons are distinguished by the intensity and depth of insight that they have gained on the purpose of their own lives, the purpose of all lives, the purpose that they should bestow all their energy and the actions they should take. The purposes and actions or ends and/or means are different for each one. Can Lord Christ be equated with Lord Buddha? Can Gandhi be equated with Swami Vivekananda? Can Mata Amritanandamayi be equated with Sai Baba of Puttaparthi; Can Mother Teresa be equated with Saint Ignatius of Loyola? Can Sankara be placed on the same pedestal as Martin Luther? Can René Descartes, David Hume, Schopenhauer, Santayana be on the same pedestal?

The strength and stability of the light that entered the minds of enlightened persons, how much of that new light is scattered, how far and how long it is scattered, and how many people in how many generations have benefited from that light determines the ranking of enlightened leaders.

2.8.4 Enhancing leading with insights competence

Building mental capacity as one ages from childhood through adolescence to old age so that you are more open to new ideas, alternative perspectives, and new ways of seeing the world and its phenomena is a necessary condition for leading with insights. Leading with insights is both a physical and a cognitive activity simultaneously. As the leader observes any event or information, the left brain is automatically activated, stimulating the analytic neural networks. Instead of quickly taking decisions followed by action (as a result of the action of the constellation of neurons called attractors based on pattern recognition), the leader needs to introspect and reflect on the inputs or signals.

Reframing the initial automatic response to the external stimuli by asking probing questions to oneself in a playful manner, by sitting or walking in a different environment than the normal place, and engaging in a pleasant but totally different activity/hobby will enable the brain to not depend on the stored experiences and the existing mindset. Sleeping over an idea or gaining twenty-four hours of thinking time before taking a decision will throw up many alternatives and possibilities. The mirror neurons (a dedicated neural system in the brain) take its course to internally reflect on the experiences, events, or objects of the external world. Let the imagination wander wild, exploring farther and wider, by stepping back from prior knowledge and existing norms. Simultaneously raising doubts about the alternative solution or perspective that crops up automatically in the mind will guide one to see things in a fresh and new perspective, as in a beginner's mind.

2.9 Leader's script: How I will be perceived by my circle of influence?

Score the appropriate response to the following questions

i.   I am the same person to everyone I am directly interacting with.

ii. I am influenced by others rarely against my interest.

iii. I am able to implement my decisions.

| 1 | 2 | 3 |

iv. Each day is a beautiful, memorable experience to me.

v.   Other people are always happy when they are with me.

| 1 | 2 | 3 |

vi. People with whom I studied or worked ten years before still send me greetings on every occasion.

| 1 | 2 | 3 |

vii. Every day, at least five people seek my opinion and views.

| 1 | 2 | 3 |

viii. I am known as a person who always gets what I aim at.

ix. I schedule my week and stick to the schedule always.

x. I have a major goal to achieve five years from now, and for this, I seek the support of many people actively and earnestly.

1	2	3

1. Strongly agree: Score: 10-12: You are a sustainable leader

2. Not always: 13- 15: You are an authentic leader

3. Strongly disagree: 16-20: You are a situational leader

Carrying self while leading

*People should have two objectives; to improve
the community in which they live and to improve
themselves as they live- but majority fail on both
counts.*

Goethe

A person is born into a community that draws its resources from
the ecosystem for its growth needs. He or she is expected by the
community to be an asset by growing with the virtues and values
of the community. In the course of time, the person develops
a self-schema based on the unique configuration of his or her
character strengths and self-image. The self becomes the person
that a community values or despises.

The self is the reflexive perception of oneself as an object
of consciousness and the subject of one's own experiences,
emotions, and thoughts. The self is the experiences of phenomena
and constitutes a person's uniqueness or essential being. The
conditions and attributes of the self are not static and finite but
are altered by the external environment.

There is a superficial self or false self and a real self for many
persons, and the differences between these two identities can
be wide. This concept of the self enables a person to look back
on themselves as both an object and subject and who one truly
is. There is also an ideal self, and everyone strives to become
more like this ideal self. Each person develops a schema about
themselves as to who they are, which is conditioned by social,
cultural, environmental, and occupational experiences. The scripts
so formed activate specific cognitive, verbal, and behavioral
expressions of the self on different situations.

Self-schemas lead to self-concepts of who you are. However,
there are at least two levels of self-concepts: a personal identity

and a social identity. There are classifications of the formed identities of persons, such as refuser, drifter, searcher, guardian, and resolver (Cote and Levin 2002); as strategic manipulator, pastiche personality, and relational self (Kenneth Gargen); and the master–slave identities (Hegel 1817). A sustainable leader carries an ideal self in the eyes of the followers, and the bases of her power and influence are different from other types of leaders. Being in this ideal self gives happiness or joy to the leader, and this joy spreads to the followers as an emotional contagion.

A sustainable leader has only one self and her mind, soul, and body are integrated into one whole. There is also integration of her thoughts, words, and deeds.

3.1 Bases of influence of a sustainable leader

No one is influenced for nothing. A person who tries to influence and the person who is thus influenced identify a base that acts as the platform or subject. Even in a master–slave relationship, the influencing need not be absolute as the thoughts of the slave can be beyond the control of the master. However, Machiavelli's base of love can control even the thoughts. The bases of influence of a sustainable leader are given in Fig. 3.1 as a series of five questions from the perspective of the leader and the follower.

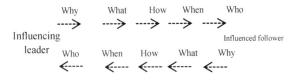

Fig. 3.1: Bases of influence.

The influencing leader has an answer to why he or she wants to influence and on what subject or area. He or she selects a method of influencing, a time, and who to influence. The answer to the who question gives the universe of the potential follower.

In the same fashion, a potential follower who is exposed or wants to be exposed to the influences of another person (the leader) has a reason to get influenced. For example, the hundreds of thousands of people who gathered to listen to the I Have a Dream speech of Martin Luther King Jr in Washington DC had a need for equality or a reason to support the move for a society based on equality and fraternity than a society based on skin color and race. In this case, the potential followers of Martin Luther King Jr had the subjects of discrimination, unequal opportunities, and social exclusion. The method chosen by the followers was showing strength and solidarity by appearing on the day of the speech and demonstrating their trust toward King junior as one capable of leading them.

When there is a match or best fit for the what and the why of the leader and the follower, the process of influencing begins. If there is a good fit, then the leader can influence further about the method (how), timing (when), and place (where).

You are likely to buy a book on self-development from a bookstore only if you have a felt need or desire to improve yourself and thus get influenced by the author of the book. If you have the desire to improve, then your eyes will fall on the section for self-improvement books of the bookstore, and you'll get influenced to buy one that best suits you and then probably follow the author's suggestions. Thus, the a priori need is the primary base of influence of a sustainable leader unlike influence based on reciprocity. In reciprocity-based influence, exchange of favors and generation of a partnership framework continuously can sustain a relationship but fades when the exchange stops. In reciprocity-based influence, answers to the following two sets of questions are the bases of influence:

Insight Box 3.1

Bases of power to influence others

Power is a relation among social actors and represents a potential for influencing others (Dahl 1957). John French and Bertram Raven (1959) identified originally five sources of social power as the bases of influencing other people.

i. *legitimate power   place in hierarchy*

ii. *referent power   personal relationships*

iii. *expert power   knowledge and skills*

iv. *reward power   based on inducements*

v. *coercive power   based on fear.*

Researchers such as Morgan (1986) identified fourteen bases, and Handy (1976) identified three bases. Leadership theories point to seven bases of power that includes French and Raven's original five plus the following two:

• *information power   access to information*

• *connection power   networking.*

Raven and Krualanski identified these seven bases. One more base resource power, the gatekeeper of resources was added by some researchers. Machiavelli identified two bases: personal power, which is based on love, and positional power, which is based on fear. Cumming (1981) gave a scale to identify a power base.

Jacob Thomas, PhD

<u>Set 1</u>
  i.   What will I lose if I do not follow?
  ii. What will I lose if I follow?

<u>Set 2</u>
  i.   What will I gain if I do not follow?
  ii. What will I gain if I follow?

The loss and gain may be tangible or intangible aspects, temporary or permanent things, and an influence will be successful if there is win-win situation for both the influencer and the influenced either in the short term or long term. Sometimes one may lose in the short term in order to gain in the long term. The influence will be sustained only till the loss–gain exchanges are significant to both sides.

In contrast, the speech of Martin Luther King Jr inspires people even now, and thus, he is a sustainable leader. Mohandas Gandhi's methods influence many, and thus he is a sustainable leader.

Fealty, loyalty, community, locality, and personality are the other bases of influences, which complement the leader–follower need congruence in sustainable leadership.

3.2 Difference at the top

A leader is the one who has an overview of matters and is able to see the views at the far distance. He is able to do this not by climbing over a hilltop but by elevating his mind and soul all above others to perceive the larger picture and the distant picture. In a meeting situation, normal people are engrossed in the details of the agenda, whereas the sustainable leader will be seeing the overall purpose of all the agenda put together. She leaves the details to the followers and guides everyone to the interconnection

> **Insight Box 3.2**
>
> **Emotional contagion**
> *Emotions have a great role in the context of leadership. The emotions of leaders impact the emotional states of followers. Salovery and Mayer (1990) first defined emotional intelligence as the subset of social intelligence that involves the ability to monitor one's own and other's feelings and emotions to discriminate among them and to use this information to guide one's thinking and actions. The word 'emotional contagion' was coined by Barsade (2002), describing the influence of a leader on the emotional state of followers.*

among the agenda items and between the meeting's agenda and the outside world and beyond.

Any leadership has a hierarchical situation with at least two layers: the leader and the led, the influencer and the influenced, the dominant coalition and the subservient aggregate of people, the rulers and the ruled, decision-makers and the subjects of decision, experts and laymen, priests and laity, and so on. When the number of followers increases, more layers come in, and when people organize themselves for achieving certain objectives, a structure of relationships, roles, and functions develop.

Expectations from significant others define the role of a person. Leadership is also a role created from the sum total of the expectations of followers. The base of power of the leader is thus this sum total of the expectations. Does this force of aggregate expectations create a leader out of anyone? The concepts of self-schema, real self, and ideal self are useful in answering this. People project their selves for others to see, and if that self

> **Insight Box 3.3**
>
> **Ethical leadership**
> *Ethical leadership is respecting and appreciating the entire person of the follower, considering the functions of both the head and heart. Unlike the capitalist approach of viewing people as a means of production, ethical leadership involves valuation of the entire human being, the wholeness within individuals, each one with immense potential to blossom, flourish, and add to the beauty of nature.*

is a best fit to the expectations of many people, the self gets a base for influencing those people whose expectations potentially match the self-schema. This self is different, unique, valuable in the assessment of followers in terms of the ideal self (who), her vision (what), her purpose (why), and methods (how). A sustainable leader's ideal self has roots both in the ecological realities and in the socioeconomic realities, and her self is shaped by the expectations from her ideal self, as depicted in Fig. 3.2.

Jacob Thomas, PhD

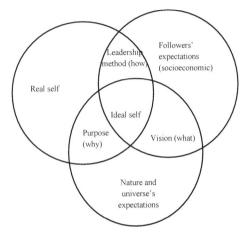

Fig. 3.2: Shaping of the ideal self from expectations.

Follower's expectations are mostly in the socioeconomic sphere and less on the ecological sphere. These expectations act on the real self of the leader, influencing him to become the ideal self. In addition, the purpose and vision crafted by the leader and agreed upon by the followers while considering the needs of the leader, followers, and nature or the universe in a harmonious, holistic manner also impact the real self. This purpose and vision mediate the expectations; thereby, the leadership methods are shaped subsequently. Thus, a sustainable leader transforms himself through an intelligent crafting of the widely acceptable purpose and vision. Thus, these factors are in a dynamically stable condition, with the ideal self of the leader getting differentiated.

A sustainable leader understands the need for her vision to be realized, which would benefit the followers not only in the

> **Insight Box 3.4**
>
> **Getting people on board a *sailing ship***
> *The preconditions to get people on board are the following:*
> - *The ship should be demonstrated as stable and durable.*
> - *The ship should have sails of adequate size and strength.*
> - *The ship should have a captain of competence and integrity.*
> - *The ship should have a destination and knows the purpose of the journey.*
> - *The captain should know the way.*
> - *The captain should know when to raise the sails and how to catch the wind.*
> - *The destination should be shown as a better place than the present place in terms of attractions and offerings.*

present generation but also in the future generations, whereas the current followers' interests are mostly in the present world. Future generation's interests are only an estimate and projection. The top leaders are the ones in the organization nurtured by the sustainable leader who are different from others in understanding the interests and needs of future generations and are capable of rolling the vision forward in an adaptive manner and of absorbing the successive generations also into the vision and purpose.

3.3 Being on one side always

Sustainable leaders subscribe to most of the universal virtues or live by those virtues and values. They will never cross over to the evil side or the opposite side of any of the character strengths or traits related to the virtues under any temptation or situation. There are many leaders who abandon or postpone personal interests and privileges for the sake of the group's welfare. Such sacrifice can be partial or full, temporary or permanent. Mohandas Gandhi and Mother

> **Insight Box 3.5**
>
> **Universal core virtues**
> *Peterson and Seligmon (2008) identified six universal core virtues after a thorough search in the ancient cultures of India, China, and the West along with twenty-four character strengths (given in brackets) related to each virtue.*
> - *wisdom and knowledge (curiosity, open-mindedness, love of learning, creativity, perspective)*
> - *courage (integrity, vitality, bravery, persistence)*
> - *humanity (social intelligence, love, kindness)*
> - *justice (fairness, citizenship, leadership)*
> - *temperance (forgiveness, humility, modesty, prudence, self-regulation)*
> - *transcendence (hope, appreciation of beauty and excellence, gratitude, humor, spirituality).*

Teresa abandoned fully and permanently their self-interests and privileges. The antecedents of such sacrifice are the leader's sense of belongingness and the leader's sense of power. If the leader feels fully included in the group and perceives that he or she has got high capacity to influence others, he or she is more likely to go beyond self-interest and take on personal costs to benefit the group or organization (Van Prooijen, Van den Bos, and Wilke 2004; Conger and Kanurgo 1987; Choi and Mai-Dalton 1999, 1998; Van Knippenberg and Van Knippenberg 2005; De Cremer 2006).

Jacob Thomas, PhD

3.4 Leading without conflicts

Contradictions and uncertainties in the social or economic systems throw up leaders who in turn promise to remove those contradictions or end the uncertainties. Sustainable leaders bring certainty in uncertain, ambiguous, unstable context by their unwavering approach to the situation and articulating a clear way forward which is the best-fit option.

Conflicts arise when there is a mismatch in any one of the five bases of influence, as depicted in Fig. 3.1 in two ways.

> **Insight Box 3.6**
>
> **Petter Stordalen puts humanity before profits**
>
> *Petter Stordalen, the owner of 171-strong hotel chain Nordic Hotels, replaced pornography TV channels in the hotel rooms with contemporary art. He took this decision with a conviction that pornography reduces women into sexual objects rather than as precious members of the human family. He understood that pornography has links with human trafficking, which is dehumanizing, degrading, and corrupting. Pornography deflects and deviates young people from achieving love that is liberating and fulfilling. Pornography is considered a social plague that deceives the public, even though it's supported by many hotel chains, including Hilton. Nordic Hotels was the first hotel chain that banned smoking also. He is a sustainable leader scattering light in the world (CNA/EWTN NEWS 6.9.2013)*

i.   misfit between the elements among themselves in one direction—for example, there is a mismatch between the why and how of the leader's influence in the forward direction or between the what and when of followership responses in the reverse direction

ii. misfit between the same element or base in the forward and backward influence– response chain of Fig. 3.1—such as what the vision is or where to act.

> **Insight Box 3.7**
>
> **Sustainable leaders are:**
> - *introspective and reflective*
> - *authentic*
> - *more empathic*
> - *less anxious*
> - *morally developed*
> - *responsible*
> - *fulfilled*
> - *innovative, creative*
> - *flexible*
> - *self-directed*
> - *effective*
> - *committed*
> - *ethically sensitive*
> - *motivated and motivating*
> - *inspired and inspiring*
> - *consensus oriented*
> - *participatory*
> - *able to cope with stress*
> - *manages anger*
> - *wise and observant*
> - *happy and spirited*
> - *more intelligent.*

A sustainable leader has to constantly be aware of these two types of potential mismatches in order to lead without conflicts.

When slavery was accepted by everyone and there was no uncertainty about the system, there were no worthwhile leaders.

However, when the political system started speaking of equality, fraternity, freedom, and democracy, contradictions crept into the socioeconomic system that threw up leaders such as Abraham Lincoln and Martin Luther King Jr in the USA, who chose to be on one side always on a large issue which has a lot of uncertainties.

A leader who is pioneering as a savior of a contradiction to a socioeconomic system needs to carry himself always on one side of a divide, on the strength of virtues and values to be sustainable.

3.5 Knowing one's boundaries

		Leader	
		Known	Not knowing
Follower	Known	**Arena-** a space in the leader's personality and self that is fully expressed and visible	**Ideal self:** there is a chasm between the real self and the ideal self. Ideal self is an arithmetic sum of the expectations from all the followers, what their leader should be.
	Not knowing	**Unfelt needs realm:** The followers have both felt and unfelt needs. Also there are needs of future generations. A sustainable leader knows these, whereas the current followers may not realize.	**Unknown realm:** Within the self of both the leader and the follower, there are characteristics of the self, such as soul, connect of self with the cosmic forces that impact a self's thoughts etc.

Fig. 3.3: A leader's arena of action.

Everyone has a personal boundary when viewed by others into which access by outsiders is restricted. Since the personal boundaries of a person vary with the views of others in his or her surroundings, there are multiple boundaries. The Johari Window (Joseph Luft and Harrington Ingham 1955) attempted to define this boundary as the arena based on the two factors or aspects of a person: known to self and known to others (Fig. 3.3). The arena's area is expanded through feedback from others. For a sustainable leader, this arena's area will be enlarged, and the unknown blind spot and hidden areas of the personality will be very less in the ideal self. The expected character strengths of a sustainable leader define her boundary of thoughts, words, and deeds. With a clear boundary for the self, the leader develops an

Jacob Thomas, PhD

identity which is defined as the sense of a continuous self (McEwan 2003). Sustainable leadership identity has five elements:

- purposeful: the resource system is enhanced for the well-being of the present and future generations.
- process oriented: the why, what, how, when, and where are acceptable to the followers and are achieved through effective communication and influence process as part of the leadership influence chain.
- inclusive: the vision and the needs that are addressed in the leadership strategy do not exclude any category of people and are meaningful to all.
- enlightening and empowering: the process of leadership is through enlightening the followers to become leaders and empowering each one to take the required steps toward the vision.
- transcendental: appreciation of the beauty and excellence of the follower base and nature or the universe is part of the leadership strategy.

The development of the sustainable leadership identity occurs in steps which are both linear and cyclical in the sense that each stage ends with a transition phase which is a period of introspection and exploration. The stages are:

i. self-awareness about one's ideal self: the leader-to-be has a real self based on her experiences and thoughts so far, and when the sustainable leadership inputs (as shown in Fig. 2.4) are experienced, the ideal

---

Insight Box 3.8

Spiritual leadership

Every society and group is likely to seek spiritual solutions to ease tumultuous social, political, and economic changes. Anderson (2000) describes a person's spirit as the vital principle or animating force that gives the life-affirming energy in oneself and all human beings. Spiritual leaders strive for values and beliefs that transcend physical existence (Maddock and Falton 1998; Mitroff and Denton 1999). Global and local changes brings a growing social spiritual consciousness. Spirit is the fundamental yet intangible feature of what it means to be human (Duchon and Plowmen 2005). Fry and Slocum (2008) argues that spiritual leadership that accelerate employee well-being and sustainability without sacrificing performance is immanent. Spiritual leadership emerges from the interaction of artistic love, vision, and hope/faith in organizational members (Fry 2005a). Spiritual leadership satisfies the fundamental needs for transcendence and connection.

---

self is likely to be revealed in an awakening or enlightening experience.

ii. exploration/introspection phase: with exposure to the leadership inputs, the leader-to-be becomes aware of the ideal self and then starts an exploration process through critical reflection, thinking on causal relations, wondering about and deciphering nature's designs, and exploring connections.

iii. imagination/visioning phase: the leader-to-be adopts new ways of being and thinking, acquiring knowledge and new insights, and from the insights gained in the exploration phase, a vision is crafted based on the enduring interests and her own values as part of an influence strategy with due consideration of the stakeholder groups, resource system, and technology (as depicted in Fig. 1.4); the leader-to-be becomes an authentic leader.

iv. leader's differentiation and blossoming: the leader-to-be believes strongly that she is a leader armed with an influence strategy and purpose, which builds confidence in taking initiatives and operating from personal influence; this is a phase of self-authoring corresponding to the fourth order of consciousness (as defined by Kegan 1994) and the fourth stage of leadership identity (as defined by Komives et al. 2005), and this phase can be equated to the transformational leadership level described in section 1.8.

v. transcendent leadership phase: the leader develops an ability to look beyond herself and express a passion for all her engagements with transcendent purpose; the passion for true causes that affect humanity or community gets articulated, leading to the development of personal philosophies of leadership, such as an act of service or developing/coaching other leaders.

vi. sustainable leadership phase: the leader builds solid boundaries for herself with clear and visible character strengths, and her real self becomes the ideal self, corresponding to the sum of expectations of all her followers; the ideal self is not an average or mode of the expectations of all the followers but the arithmetic sum inclusive of all their expectations.

Jacob Thomas, PhD

3.6 Knowing one's arena

> *The foundation of science is that yesterday's truth is*
> *likely to be falsity today.*

When you are playing football, the playing field and its conditions, the position of other players, and the demarcated zones are observed before the start. There are also rules of the game. Football cannot be played in a football ground with the rules for basketball or volleyball even though the balls look almost alike. The bases of influence (as developed through Fig. 3.1) will define the arena of each sustainable leader, and the leadership steps given below will unfold between the leader and the follower—the who at both the ends in Fig. 3.1.

i. efficacy of self (leader) and the self of the followers to progress, flourish, collabrate, cooperate and coexist
ii. delegating, empowering, enlightening
iii. harnessing resources from the resource system without degrading and depleting
iv. cobbling together, like a gear, all selves and their energies and strengths
v. predicting the outcomes of each step in the direction of the vision
vi. being in charge of the process with an overview, like the force that propels the wind sweeping across a landscape, swaying all trees.

3.7 Artistry and orginality

Leadership is more of an art than anything else combining the essence of different types of arts, such as performing arts, fine arts, visual arts, negotiation arts, and communication arts. Leaders bring people out of their usual selves in order for them to see the aesthetics of life and nature. It is thus a superior skill that is learnt by studying people, practicing virtues, and observing phenomena.

Superior skill means it is more than the ordinary ability, realizing prowess or mastery, as is observed in an experienced sculpter who brings out a beautiful statue out of an irregular rock or a music composer who combines different elements of music, such as dynamics, harmony, beat, and meter produced by a set of instruments. Artistry involves three types of knowledge—experiential knowledge, conceptual knowledge, and directional knowledge—which guide and inform mutually for mastery with a purpose and focus.

Orginality refers to generating new knowledge through perception, openness, flexibility, creativity, and innovation. Imagination, creativity, and spontaneity make orginals that surpass the status quo. Superior artistry is achieved through the integration of capabilities of mastery and orginality and when the characterisitcs of indeterminancy, instability, complexity, ambiguity, immediacy, intensity, and uniqueness are present in the context of the leader and followers. When the vision and the means of reaching the vision are open, complex, and uncertain, artistry is essential for the leader to craft the strategy and guide the followers to the destination.

3.8 Leader's differentiation and distinctiveness

Leaving footsteps in the sands of time.

Sustainable leaders are different and distinct from other leaders in their perspectives that guide their decisions, the methods chosen to achieve the future state, and their approach to resource use. The resource pool is decreasing, which compels resource appropriators to go to unexplored areas in oceans, deeper inside the earth, other ecosystems, and artificial intelligence. When the resources become scarce, the extraction turns to places that should have been left untouched, and the damages done to humankind's long-term interests are thus multiplied. Here the role of a sustainable leader comes in to reverse this process of appropriation that's unmindful of mankind's long-term interests. Similarly when evil and unethical practices darken the lives of most people of an area, sustainable leaders emerge to lead the people to ethical courses. Sustainable leaders differentiate by saying what is to be said at the correct moment, standing up to the principles and values that govern their personality and their cultivated selves. They believe that if you do not stand up for something, you will fall for everything. They believe in one right way and do not waver. The distinctiveness of sustainable leadership is given in Table 3.1.

Jacob Thomas, PhD

Table 3.1 Distinctiveness of sustainable leadership

Sustained leadership	Leadership sustainability/ sustaining leadership	Sustainable leadership
• The successors of a leader will continue the initiatives, and all the leaders in succession will act in a common thread without disruption.	• A leader maintains her relevance and influence ability for a long time among followers in the present generation. • The leader wants to continue to be in a leadership position. • Mostly, influence is based on the position or authority. • Power is anchored on reciprocity. • The same leadership is sustained to continue or be prolonged for an extended period without interruption.	• Leaders influence on matters that are significant for future generations as well. • Leadership is not necessarily based on authority. • The human potential of followers are enhanced. • The natural resource system is preserved. • The self flourishes, scattering light among followers. • Power is anchored in universal virtues and values. • Power is also anchored on the strength of the vision and purpose.

3.9 Communication authenticity: Being whole with a soul

There will not be any dissonance in the communication from a sustainable leader as their instant decisions and actions speak for themselves, who they are, and what they aim for. There will be consonance and harmony between the why, what, and how between the leader and the followers. The souls are the scales that connect each of the followers among themselves, with the leader and nature or the universe also being in consonance as sublime communication. This three-way connection (as depicted in Fig. 3.4) illustrates the communication authencity.

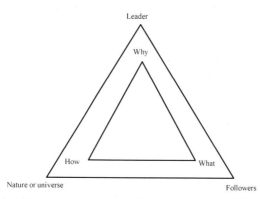

Fig. 3.4: Three-way connection for communication authenticity.

There is an inner three-way connection between the why, what, and how of the leadership influence base, which forms the basis for the communication between the leader and the followers. This occurs within the sublime, transcendental three-way communication between the leader–follower system and the wonders and elements of nature or the universe.

3.10 Soul connect: Embracing peace and cooperation

The methods employed by sustainable leaders are not those that lead to competition or conflict but to cooperation, peace, and harmony. They seek aesthetic experiences, discovering the commonalities among the responses to man-made objects, such as works of art, architecture, engineering, and those induced by natural wonders. Vladimar Konecni (2011) in his aesthetic trinity theory proposes three levels of experiences in terms of intensity, depth, and frequency.

- aestheic awe: a unique and fundamental emotional product of fear and joy, occuring as a response to unexpectedly encountered natural wonders and human artifacts; this is the experience one has when watching Niagara Falls from close quarters or what a follower feels toward a sustainable leader.
- state of being moved or touched: a person is being moved by aesthetic stimuli in theater, film, painting, poetry, books,

Jacob Thomas, PhD

etc. while witnessing certain acts of forgiveness, generosity, nonkin sacrifice, pure beauty, and boundless love.

- thrills or chills: these are archaic physiological responses of short duration to aesthetic stimuli, such as music, movies, stories, visual arts, roller-coaster rides, etc.; with joy, awe shares the experience of thrills, and the emotion of awe with fear is felt as chills.

Physical grandeur, rarity, and novelty offer sublimeness to natural and man-made wonders that evoke aesthetic experiences. The vast expanse of an ocean, a pristine forest or landscape, a clear night sky with numerours blinking stars, a serenely flowing river with dense forests on both sides, snowcapped Himalayas, and sights of horizons with the rising sun, etc. evoke aesthetic experiences depending upon the proximity, immediacy, and salience. These experiences often move into the observer's soul, evoking a feeling of connection between herself and the external aesthetic phenomena being experienced at the moment. Some such experiences of soul–nature connections are transient, while some shape the selves to become more virtuous in terms of the six universal core virtues. The essential being of a sustainable leader is thus evolved through such aesthetic experiences, acquiring the universal virtue-related character strengths along the way.

3.11 Influence script: How I will expand my influence circle?

1. What percentage of your followers fully understand the why of your leadership?

Less than 50 percent	50 to 90 percent	Greater than 90 percent

2. How much percentage of your followers participated in designing and deciding the why of your leadership?

Less than 50 percent	50 to 90 percent	Greater than 90 percent

3. How much percentage of your followers fully understand the what of your leadership?

Less than 50 percent	50 to 90 percent	Greater than 90 percent

4. How much percentage of your followers are considered by you as partners and collaborators in your leadership process?

Less than 50 percent	50 to 90 percent	Greater than 90 percent

5. How much percentage of your follower's personality traits, character strengths, and self-interests are fully known to you?

Less than 50 percent	50 to 90 percent	Greater than 90 percent

6. In your perception, what percentage of your followers know your intentions, virtues, and values very well and correctly?

Less than 50 percent	50 to 90 percent	Greater than 90 percent

7. In your perception, how many of your followers will carry forward the agenda with equal vigor if you are not there in the scene?

Yes	Undecided	No

8. Do you firmly beieve that 'if you do not stand up for something, you will fall for everything'?

Yes	Undecided	No

Jacob Thomas, PhD

9. Do you like to prolong the tenure of your leadership in the arena or aim at prolonging the agenda and the why and what you set in the arena?

Yes	Undecided	No

10. In your perception, is there a mismatch between your real self and your ideal self (the person you want to be)?

Yes	Do not know	No

Looking Ahead:
Leading with an Intention

Our intention creates our reality.

Wayne Dyer

A sustainable leader's major role is to have clear answers to the following five questions:

- Why do I require followers? (*To accomplish a social project, to discover a new drug formulation, to sell more of a product to carry out a significant social change, to get readers to a book, and so on.*)
- Where am I now?
- Where am I going?
- What do I do to make progress?
- Who are following me, and who are not?

To find out the answer to 'Where am I now?' the leader has to understand the context or the environment in which he and his followers are rooted. The characteristics of the environment are:

- information overload from multiple sources, leading to decision dilemma
- diversity of followers with different needs and aspirations
- followers themselves empowered to varying degrees
- different choices for the followers to meet their needs
- opportunity costs of choosing one path
- cultural melting pot within the organization and outside.

The answer to 'Where am I now?' depends to a great extent on the answer to 'Where am I going?' The information that is relevant, the needs of followers that are chosen to be addressed, further doses of empowerment of followers, and opportunity costs are different for different destinations.

Articulating 'Where am I going?' is the most complex aspect of a leader's task. How far you are able to see is an important element in looking ahead. If the leader is looking from the top of a hill, he can see farther but will miss the details of the terrain to be traversed. If he is looking from the bottom (Fig. 11.1), he cannot see much ahead.

Fig. 4.1: A leader's viewing horizon.

The planning horizon in today's complex, diverse, and dynamic world has shortened considerably. A destination that is desirable today may not look so attractive after a month due to changes in both the environment and the follower's needs. In such a situation, looking ahead is more of looking inside through a reflective, imaginative, inventive mind and identifying the images of the future that can raise the hope of the followers. While looking ahead in this fashion, through mixing mental images, the aspirations and ambitions of the leader and the followers are likely to match. 'What do I do to make progress?' is answered by the different leadership styles and methods, such as high-ambition leadership, aesthetic leadership, servant leadership, and quantum leadership.

The busiest place for most people is their head, where hundreds of thoughts and ideas flash each day, leaving very little time for a still state. The frequency will be much higher if the different levels of the conscious mind are accounted for their processes. Leading with an intention is the existence of a specific purpose or mental image of the end destination in performing a series of actions by the leader and the followers in a leadership ecosystem.

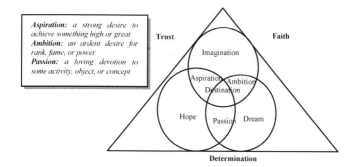

Fig. 4.2: Leadership destination triangle.

Apiration is a self-oriented desire to achieve something higher than onself, which is perceived as high or great on a social and ethical perspective, whereas ambition is a comparative view to rise above others in terms of rank, fame, or power. A combination of these two elements in a leader-to-be requires a loving devotion to where he is going and what he has to do to make progress. The leader demonstrates to his followers a firm determination to reach the destination, trust in the abilities of the followers, and faith in the motives of the followers. The destination is defined by a combination of the three primary environment–leader interface factors (imagination, dream, and hope) and the three of a leader's psychological/ personality factors (aspiration, ambition, and passion). Imagination, dream, and hope are triggered and shaped by the environmental conditions even though they are mental processes occurring within the leader's head. While imagination is a process of

Insight Box 4.2

Quantum leadership
It is an interactional field of leader–follower engagement leading to the followers' self-actualization. It is a leadership concept with four gifting principles, giving others love, power, authorship, and significance, weaving hearts into a sense of shared identity and celebrating successes.
Quantum thinking expands a leader's capability beyond serial and associative thinking, looking for a higher calling in life and releasing the potential in others (Ercetin and Kameet 2008).

forming mental images about the future destination, a dream is a free flow of ideas, concepts, and connections to the destination, and hope is the state of mind that the destination imagined and dreamed of is better and is certain to materialize.

4.1 Leading with imagination

Imagination will often carry us to worlds that never were. But without it we go nowhere.
Carl Sagan

Imagination takes one beyond the real and beyond the obvious—in unrestricted movements and in all directions—toward impossible realms. It is the ability to form images, pictures, or stories as if they're true and to experience their enactment. Leading with imagination involves thinking oneself away from the familiar courses of thoughts, perspectives, and actions. Even though imagination happens within the mind, a leader projects it outside and envelops the outside world within the boundary of his imagination.

4.1.1 What fires up imagination

Imagination is fired up by occurrences which are not routine and by observations that lead to nonroutine insights as they occur in unfamiliar contexts or at altered frames of mind. The process of image formation in the imagination integrates the self and the world. A threat or a challenge to survival catches the attention of people first as humans are genetically wired to identify threats, bad things, lack, crises, what does not work, and fear instead of opportunities, good things, abundance, solutions, what works, and love. Threats to survival fires up the imagination automatically on a

> **Insight Box 4.3**
>
> **Strengths and weakness of leaders**
> *In 1983, Oprah Winfrey was a young television person trying to take her career to the next level. She applied as a host to the television show AM Chicago.* The Phil Donahue Show. *By 1986, the show was renamed as* The Oprah Winfrey Show *and was broadcast nationally with high viewership rating. During the 1980s, when talk shows and auditions were dominated by white males, she established herself with her plain-spoken curiosity and robust humor. She went on to become a leader with a worldwide following even when she did not have the journalistic toughness.*

fear-based future, whereas imagining on abundance, solutions, good things, and what works by reframing the mind on a possibility-based life requires voluntary development of skills.

4.1.2 What fuels imagination

Emotional connection with the goals, the clarity of the image of the future, and the scope for growth of that future image will fuel a possibility-based imagination. Be curious about everything while widening your world by reading about new things, discussing new things with professionals, and listening to diverse aspects of a subject in relation to the goals. This cultivates the mind for a harvest of great images.

4.1.3 Applied imagination

> Insight Box 4.4
>
> **Aesthetics of leadership**
> *Leadership is management of meaning by stimulating the intellect into meaning creation using symbols and images and by appealing to feelings and emotions through an inspiring vision about future.*
>
> *Charismatic image leaders engage in personal image building that produce favorable perceptions of themselves to followers.*
>
> *Leaders craft a vision of what is needed in the organization's story, like a creative artist. Leaders act as artists by designing the organization as per the strategy and designing their actions as per the plan, thereby conveying meaning to followers. Aesthetics, even though synonymous with art and beauty, involves meanings that get constructed based on feelings about what followers experience via their senses (Dobson 1999; Strato 1999; Manson et al. 2007; Murphy and Ensher 2008).*

> *Imagination is everything; it is the preview of life's coming attractors.*
>
> Albert Einstein

The mental images of something are formed in an open-ended, unlimited mental process which is not present to the senses. If what is imagined as the images of something is transformed into something tangible in generation of new ideas, such a type of imagination is called applied or creative imagination. Imagination is put to productive use.

> Insight Box 4.5
>
> **Imagination** *is a process through which the world is made and, at the same time, through which the self emerges to experience the world (Vygotsky reputed by Connery et al. 2010 and Nilson 2010). Imagination is the process of resolving and connecting the fragmented, poorly coordinated experience of the world so as to bring about a stable image of the world. (Pelaprat and Cole 2011).*

Seeing something that is not yet there in the form of mental

Jacob Thomas, PhD

images, concepts, ideas, scenarios, and solutions to problems is the faculty of imagination. Seeing a future and a path to the future that is not yet there is the primary role of a leader. The purpose of a leader is to tell compellingly to others that which he or she can uniquely imagine further—a clearer, larger, better future—and carry them toward that better future.

4.1.4 Creative imagination

A leader gives a vision that is expected to sustain the organization during times of crises, turmoil, change, stability, and calamities. When imagination is intended to galvanize the followers into reaching the vision amidst chaos and crisis, it is creative imagination. Creativity is a natural result of imagination. A creative act is defined by Koestler as something 'that combines, reshuffles and relates already existing but hitherto separate ideas, facts, frames of perception and associative contexts'. This creative act is both a cognitive and emotive process in the journey to discover the end of possibilities. To prevail over complex challenges of the environment and engage the follower's imagination is the skill that leaders use to navigate this complexity.

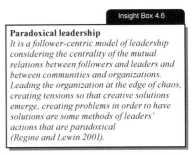

Insight Box 4.6

Paradoxical leadership
It is a follower-centric model of leadership considering the centrality of the mutual relations between followers and leaders and between communities and organizations. Leading the organization at the edge of chaos, creating tensions so that creative solutions emerge, creating problems in order to have solutions are some methods of leaders' actions that are paradoxical (Regine and Lewin 2001).

4.2 Leading with ambition

> *They did not define themselves by money, fame or power. They defined themselves by impact and contribution and purpose.*
>
> Jim Collins and Morten T. Hanson

Collins and Hansen describe level 5 ambition as a passion for a cause or company that is larger than them. The impact and contribution that people make on others and how the impact benefits others define great leaders. Striving for the greatest purpose or goal or the grandest imagination is the ambition of a sustainable leader.

The inner drive that pushes one to advance tends to be destructive if it is used to focus on the self, and it is constructive if it focuses on the advancement of the organization or community or society to a great destination.

4.2.1 Relationship of the extent of ambition and the ability to lead lives

A man's worth is no greater than his ambitions.

Marcus Ayre

If the leader has a high ambition, whether he will be a better, more effective leader is the question. Ambition means where one sets one's sight—whether at a higher level or lower level. Ambitious leaders not only aim high but also try to sharpen their skills by seeking out opportunities to lead.

4.2.2 Factors that promote setting one's ambition at a higher level

Keep away from people who try to belittle your ambitions. Small people always do that but the really great make you feel that you, too can become great.

Mark Twain

Having ambition in mind alone is not likely to get followers, but using the ambition to lead will. This is contingent on the following factors (McClelland 1961):

- confidence in one's abilities
- clarity about the future as to where he is trying to make the organization or society reach
- attitude of risk-taking and innovativeness

> **Insight Box 4.7**
>
> **Five core disciplines of high-ambition leadership (Beer et al. 2012):**
> - *forge a strategic identity for the firm*
> - *build a shared commitment to excel*
> - *create a community out of diversity*
> - *lead with clarity and consistency*
> - *consult to collective leadership.*

89   Jacob Thomas, PhD

- entrepreneurial orientation
- high achievement motivation.

4.2.3 High-ambition leadership

Advice is judged by results, not by intentions.
                                                                            Cicero

Nathaniel Foote and his colleagues (2014) identified that a leader's ability to unlock the full human and business potential of an organization to excel in creating long-term economic value, producing significant benefits to the community and building robust social capital within the focus, makes him a high-ambition leader. He draws on an expansive view of the firm's heritage, cultural, organizational, and social assets. He also develops a community of practice with emotional connection, trust, and respect that enables him to gain faith in the vision.

4.3 Leading with a dream

Whatever you can do or dream you can, begin it.
Boldness has genius, power, and magic in it.
                                                          Johann Wolfgang von Goethe

Martin Luther King Jr could have started his 1963 speech in Washington with 'I have a goal', 'I have an aim', or 'I have a vision', but he chose 'I have a dream'. A leader's ambitions and destination are connected to things of higher importance, embracing the most-cherished longings. Dreams are positive, uplifting, and achievable aspirations unlike a fantasy, which cannot be realized. Dreams are more than the goals, objectives, mission, and vision of the organization. 'What is your dream?' is a more powerful and more transforming a visual of the future than the narrative of a goal or vision.

4.4 Leading with hope

A leader is a dealer in hope.
                                                          Napoleon Bonaparte

Hope is a state of mind believing firmly that the future is going to happen soon; it is near, and it is better. Leaders are operating in a highly uncertain, fast-changing, and complex world now, and thus, leading with hope is necessary to infect the followers with hope. The followers of any leader have lives that go beyond the shadow of the leadership, and the hope that is kindled among the followers makes the vision a lustrous entity beaming its rays on the path of advancement.

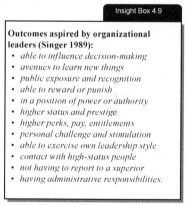

Insight Box 4.8

Seven ages of a leader:
- *infant leader*
- *schoolboy leader*
- *lover leader*
- *soldier leader*
- *general leader*
- *statesman leader*
- *sage leader*

This is from Warren Bennis (2004), adapted from the seven ages of man from Shakespeare's As You Like It.

4.5 Leading with passion

Passion is a strong feeling and enthusiasm toward the destination making a person fully immerse in an activity with devotion. Passion comes from the confidence that the destination chosen is the right one and is achievable. Confidence is a state of being certain that a proposed or predicted course of action is the best. Self-assuredness in one's personal judgment, power and ability with an attitude of positive and realistic views of themselves and their situations is the characteristic of a leader with self-confidence.

Insight Box 4.9

Outcomes aspired by organizational leaders (Singer 1989):
- *able to influence decision-making*
- *avenues to learn new things*
- *public exposure and recognition*
- *able to reward or punish*
- *in a position of power or authority*
- *higher status and prestige*
- *higher perks, pay, entitlements*
- *personal challenge and stimulation*
- *able to exercise own leadership style*
- *contact with high-status people*
- *not having to report to a superior*
- *having administrative responsibilities.*

4.6 Leading with an aspiration

While aspiration is a strong desire, longing, yearning, or inner urge to achieve something, ambition is an earnest desire for some type of achievement or distinction such as power, fame, or wealth. Past success in interpersonal influence is likely to make an individual more desirous of being in a leadership role. A person with a leadership aspiration places more importance on leadership roles and are likely to embrace one.

4.6.1 Approaches to leadership aspirations

Personality traits approach and cognitive approach are the two major approaches that explain leadership aspirations. The expectancy valence model, self-efficacy model, vocational self-concept theory, and attribution theory are the four theoretical frameworks in the cognitive approach. The perceived instrumentality of leadership in providing certain outcomes and the perceived desirability (valence) of these outcomes to the leader (Mitchell 1980; Vroom 1964) provide aspirations a shape.

The self-efficacy theory (Bandura 1977, 1982) postulates that the efficacy of success varies with differential socialization processes, and thus, the leaders' self-efficacy expectancies would be higher. Vocational self-concept theory is developed by Super (1963, 1969), accounting for the decision-making process. The attribution theory explains the links between cognition and behavior (Ross 1977), explaining that cognitive schemata about the concepts of leadership are formed due to previous relevant learning or socialization experiences.

Eden and Leviatan (1975) suggested an individual's implicit leadership theory as the beliefs held by an individual about what is the expected behavior of a leader. The required attributions of leadership are intelligence, personality traits, competence, favorable organizational characteristics, followers' support, and several other factors beyond his control.

4.7 Leading with determination

The self-determination theory suggests that people are very active organisms with natural growth tendencies, seeking out challenges, novelty, and opportunities and integrating the social practices and values surrounding them (Ryan and Decirpol,2006). These inherent natural growth tendencies are dependent on three psychological needs—autonomy, relatedness, and competence (Ryan et al. 2006). Determination is to act in a certain way to reach the destination.

4.8 Leading with faith

> *Follow me and I will make you fishers of men.*
> *Adapted from: Mathew 4:19*

Faith is a part of the culture and is mostly 'assumed', and faithful leaders in this sense exhibit God's or an ideology's power and presence through their gentle demeanor, loving service, and sacrifice of comfort, wealth, and status while walking the path for others to follow them to the destination. Faith is belief that is not based on proof and confidently believing in the truth, value, or trustworthiness of a person, idea, or thing. In the arena of leadership, followers are expected to have faith in the ability of the leader and the leader's intentions, and the leader in turn is expected to have faith in the value of the followers in realizing the vision. Good leadership is leveraging the faith that followers have in the vision to reach the destination.

4.9 Leading with trust

> *Trust happens when leaders are transparent.*
> Jack Welch, former CEO, GE

Trust is an element of certain leadership styles which is defined as a psychological state comprising the intention to accept vulnerability based on positive expectations or behavior of another (Rousseau et al. 1998). Trust is an expectation or belief that one can rely on another person's actions or words and that the person has good intentions toward oneself. Trust is meaningful in situations where one party is at risk to or vulnerable to another party. There are two perspectives of trust in leadership.

i. relationship-based perspective: trust in leadership operating in a social exchange process and issues of care, consideration, and mutual obligations in leader–follower relationships
ii. character-based perspective: how the perception of a leader's character influences a follower's sense of vulnerability in a hierarchical relationship (Mayer et al. 1995).

Jacob Thomas, PhD

Trust is a perception held by the follower and is not a property of the relationship or the leader per se. A framework for trust in leadership is given by Dirks and Ferrin (2002), considering trust both as a belief expectation and a behavioral intention. An integrated multilevel framework of trust in leadership is given by Burke et al. (2007) with several antecedent factors and outcomes of trust. Many researchers have suggested that a higher level of trust in a leader leads to higher levels of performance both in direct-leader (supervisor) or indirect-leader (organizational) relations.

4.10 Defining the destination

Almost all conflict is a result of violated expectations.
Blane Lee

The leader, through his imagination and/or dreams, gets an image of the goal and hopes that this goal is the best one for himself and his followers. How can the leader be sure that this is the best goal or is the right destination for him to lead others to? The destination that has come up as a result of mental processes interacting with the leader–follower eecosystem (as depicted in Fig. 4.2) has more accuracy, clarity, reliability, and acceptability. A destination which is as per the imagination, as per the dream, as per the aspiration, as per the ambition, and raises hope will be a better destination trusted by everyone involved.

4.11 Future script: How I will be remembered by future generations?

1. My ambition is to mainstream the organization where I work.

Yes	No

2. I engage everyone in the organization in a process of imagination to find new solutions as part of a large dream.

Yes	No

3. I would like to lead the organization on the edge of chaos.

Yes	No

4. I recall the four gifting principles in all my decisions in the leadership role.

Mostly	Sometimes	Seldom

5. I share the full meaning of the decisions and the impact of those decisions to the followers.

Yes	No

6. I pursue dreams that serve the larger interests of society and nature rather than my fame, money, or rank.

Yes	No

7. The expectations, I raise among my followers is centered around a clear destination, and sum total of such expectations give momentum in advancing towards the vision.

Yes	No

5

Looking Back:
Leading in a Context

You cannot lead the world when you are away from it.

Asustainable leader not only looks to the distant horizon but also investigates the terrain where he or she stands and the terrain where his or her potential followers are spread out. The context of influencing by a sustainable leader is the intersection between three overlapping systems—social, economic, and ecological systems (as depicted in Fig. 5.1).

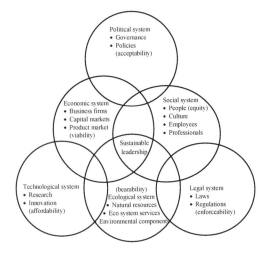

Fig. 5.1: The arena of sustainable leadership.

Both the economic system and the social system flourish and grow according to the carrying capacity till the limits of the ecological system even though most of the actors in the above two systems are not fully aware of the interconnectedness and interdependencies. In here comes the role of the sustainable leader, who is not only conscious and knowledgeable about the interconnections between the three systems but also has the competence to influence actors in any of these systems. A sustainable leader can emerge and influence either from the economic system or social system, which are directly in interaction with the ecological system. Since the ecological system is nonvocal, it communicates its reactions to interference with it often through violent means, such as extreme weather events, climate change, natural calamities, and scarcity of natural resources. The scarcity occurs when either the quality or quantity, or both, of the natural resources are depleted or degraded due to the interference, inputs, or outputs of economic and social activities.

There are three other main subsystems from where there are possibilities of a sustainable leader emerging. They are subsystems as they consist of people, procedures, and policies with a subculture embedded within the larger socioeconomic ecological systems. Political, legal, and technological subsystems contribute immensely if the leaders in these domains are ecologically aware and sensitive to the needs of sustainable actions in both economic and social systems by enacting laws, regulating activities through rules and standards, assuring process fairness and equity by the legal subsystem, and making environment-friendly technological innovations by the technological subsystem. The political subsystem is more active in the interface of social and economic systems, whereas the technological subsystem is more active in the interface of economic and ecological systems. Most of the research and technological exploratory studies are guided and funded by economic interests, and the resultant technology impacts the ecosystems directly or indirectly. There is a strong legal framework available at the interface of the social system and ecological systems with the eight UN principles (such as polluter pays, common but differential responsibility, principle of cooperationguiding national and local laws.

97   Jacob Thomas, PhD

5.1 Dimensions of sustainable leadership

The context in which a sustainable leader undertakes her role has many dimensions. Seeing one or a few dimensions alone will not lead to the sustained well-being of the current and future followers.

5.1.1 Time dimension:

Sail away from the safe harbor when the winds are to your destination.

The historical events that shaped the present situation are an important dimension to be considered for anchoring the effort in context. There are fragmenting adaptations and flourishing phases in the social economic and ecological systems. These three phases are cyclic, as shown in Fig. 5.2.

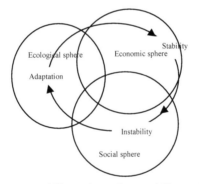

Fig. 5.2: Instability–adaptation–stability cycle traversing the social, economic, and ecological systems.

The instability may occur in one of the systems at a point in time, leading to fracturing, fragmenting, or changes, and then the other two systems adapt eventually to the changed or altered situation. Although adaptation is a time-consuming process, when the systems are fully adapted, a balance or integrated intersystem functioning occurs, which will result in a period of stability and growth. The growth that automatically occurs when there is stability leads to fracturing or fragmentation or changes, leading to a further cycle of instability in one of the systems. If an instability such as global warming occurs in the ecological system in the first cycle and the other two systems eventually adapt to the altered state, in this system, the instability in the second cycle that may occur can be predicted through a mapping of the IAS (instability–adaptation–stability) cycles for each of the three systems throughout history.

> **Insight Box 5.1**
>
> **Dimensions of leadership**
> *The concepts that can potentially help transition a leader to a celebrated status, as proposed by Peter Fuda (2013), are:*
> - *showing ambition (a fire inside)*
> - *accountability*
> - *reflection (motive)*
> - *authenticity*
> - *use of tools and frameworks*
> - *internal and external support (coach)*
> - *organizational context.*

5.1.2 Natural resources (ecosystem services)

Entrepreneurs and leaders in the business or economic sphere have a goal of maximizing value to the customers and shareholders through their strategic leadership. Maximizing value perspective unlocks a never-ending quest for growth in terms of net worth, market share, profits, sales revenue through a portfolio of products, using resources. This perspective is depicted in Fig. 5.3.

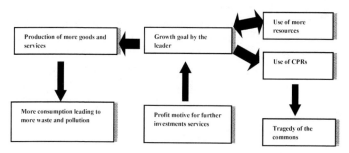

Fig. 5.3: Impact of the goal of growth by a leader.

Every leader aspires to promote the growth of the organization one leads or the development of the region or area where one focuses. Growth and development occur through the production of

Jacob Thomas, PhD

more goods and services, which in turn drives more consumption. More production and more consumption necessarily deplete the natural resources, such as water and minerals, and consumption will degrade the environment by way of pollution and wastes. A sustainable leader assures growth and development not by depleting the resources but by enhancing the resource system, which is a challenging task.

5.1.3 People

Leadership is the influencing process of leaders and followers to achieve organizational objectives through change (Lussier 2001). Thus, it is a people process, and people include supporters and resistors, the affected and unaffected, the relevant and irrelevant, present and future generations, employees and customers, leaders and followers, the near and far, organized and unorganized categories of people. Influencing the attitudes and actions of people is the role of any type of leader. People generally need to sense progress in how they are doing and what they are doing. No one likes stagnation and depletion. This sense of progress is in relation to other people in the surroundings of a person, using measures such as independence, freedom, reputation, recognition, attention, importance, and prestige. A leader attracts followers by providing this sense of progress. Abraham Maslow (1943) proposed a hierarchy of needs in his paper *A Theory of Human Motivation*. This concept is based on the organismic theory of personality proposed by Kurt Goldstein (1939). The human needs are addressed layer by layer, and one layer is likely to get all of one's attention at a time. Majority of the people have deficiency needs, and leaders who address the four deficiency needs (lower four needs in the Maslow's needs hierarchy) get more influencing ability. A leader is likely to become potent and sustainable when the three dimensions of the people aspect of leadership are addressed, as depicted in Fig. 5.4.

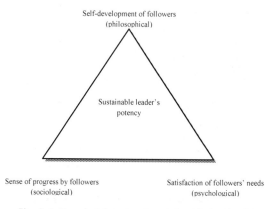

Fig. 5.4: People triangle of sustainable leadership.

Self-actualization is the fifth need Maslow has proposed, which means 'what a man can be, he must be'. The search for truth, religious interest, and artistic expression and mastery are considered expressions of the fifth level of need by Maslow. The need satisfaction is a personal achievement as needs differ from person to person. There is also an aspect of diversity; individuals are unique not only in their orientation and needs but in many other ways. A leader should be attractive and significant to the diverse followers. People also have concerns other than their needs or about themselves. What is the purpose and meaning of life? Why is one undertaking this journey of life? These are not psychological or motivational aspects but philosophical and metaphysical. A leader who correctly identifies and understands people aspects gains the potency to be sustainable.

5.1.4 Ideologies

The perspectives that guide the leader determine the strategy and the actions that flows from it. The ideologies that help sustainable leadership are:

- ecocentrism
- enlightened anthropocentrism
- biocentrism
- humanism.

Jacob Thomas, PhD

The ideologies that hamper sustainable leadership are:

- profit maxim
- anthropocentrism
- materialism.

Dominant Western ideology is anthropocentric and materialistic, and globalization spread this to the Eastern world, which was fundamentally ecocentric. Thus, the concept of sustainable leadership was alien to the Western culture even though it was more relevant and applicable in cultures having anthropocentric ideologies. There is a three-way path to liberation according to Indian philosophical thoughts. They are *knowledge* of the illusory nature of life, including the concept of life beyond death; *action*; and total *devotion* to the leader's purpose or even surrender to an ideology or one's personal god. Both the leader and her follower need to follow these paths simultaneously to become sustainable, leading a life with insights and purpose. This is one of the ideological dimensions of sustainable leadership that can be used as a framework (as depicted in Fig. 5.5), assessing the interaction of each path of both the leader and the follower.

The leader should have more of these three than the followers as a model. Knowledge of self and others alone is not enough. Knowledge should lead to actions that are in line with a purpose, and actions should be with total devotion. In a business organization context, knowledge can denote knowledge about the job, vision, purpose, objectives, and subject. Actions are the activities and performance indicators, and devotion is organizational commitment and accountability.

		Leaders		
		Knowledge	*Action*	*Devotion*
Followers	*Knowledge*	Vision	objectives	accountability
	Action	activities	strategy	ideology
	Devotion	commitment	equity	purpose

Fig. 5.5: Three paths leadership strategy.

The leader's knowledge will lead to designing a vision, which all followers should know. Followers also contribute to vision development with their knowledge. From the vision, the leader's action is to make objectives, which should be known to all followers. Both the leader and the followers are devoted to a common purpose, and both enact the same strategy. Followers have commitment to the vision, which is devotion, whereas leaders are devoted to an ideology or perspective that defines the boundaries of the action of the followers. Followers perform activities which are monitored by the leader.

5.1.5 Inter- and intragenerational equity

Leadership uses time and other resources not only of the self but of the followers. The time spent on efforts benefitting the present as well as future generations is a mark of sustainable leadership. Similarly, other resources also need to be used by considering the needs of the future generations, with due considerations on the trajectory of technological innovations that might replace certain resources or enhance efficient use of resources, such as dematerialization, energy efficiency, and zero waste. A sustainable leader will act as a vocal steward and trustee of the resources and talents of the present and future generations focusing on fair and equitable sharing, with due care.

5.1.6 Technological dimension

The technologies one values and therefore adopts for actions is an important dimension of sustainable leadership. Technologies that use a natural resource more than its replenishment rate are unsustainable. Uses of traditional technologies that coevolved with nature and are well embedded in a culture–nature context are sustainable. Since a sustainable leader focuses equally on the resource system and the people and people become instrumental in enhancing the resource system, attention to technologies that enhance the resources that people need now and in the future becomes a pillar of sustainable leadership. Innovations that enhances the quality of life of people and which are rooted in a particular culture-nature context are initated and promoted by the leader.

Jacob Thomas, PhD

5.1.7 Cost–benefit dimension

There are five types of costs for all developmental (deficiency removal) and growth-related actions.

- type I costs: direct costs that include costs of raw materials, wages, interest, rents, utilities, packaging, and transportation
- type II costs: potentially hidden costs, such as corporate, manufacturing site, or overhead costs (reporting, monitoring, oversight costs)
- type III costs: future and contingent liability costs, such as cleanup costs, potential compensation
- type IV costs: internal intangible costs, such as damage to consumer loyalty, worker morale
- type V costs: external costs borne by society, which is hard to quantify, including degradation of habitats, biodiversity loss, pollution of water and air, landscape value erosion, increase in housing costs and food costs and health-related costs of the population.

Similarly, there are five types of benefits from any developmental action.

- type I benefits: the benefits the leader and her immediate circle of influence get in material and monetary terms, satisfying the deficiency needs (for examples, profits, material wealth, and modern comforts)
- type II benefits: the benefits of development actions by a leader that extends to all the followers but not equitably, with the unequal distribution of benefits being on account of the variability and diversity in the people dimension
- type III benefits: the benefits that are equitably distributed to all followers, including those in the sphere of impact, with the leader guiding her influence strategy in such a way that the benefits of actions are enjoyed by everyone
- type IV benefits: the benefits that are not only equitably distributed among people in the sphere of impact but are also good for the ecosystem, the benefits that start moving

from the people domain to the ecosystem in which the people are embedded

- type V benefits: the benefits that will go more than proportionately to the providers of the resource systems and will be advantageous to the future generations in equal measure to the current followers, the benefits of today's actions that will flow to the future generations as well since followers at this stage tend to become providers than appropriators of the resource system.

The analysis of all the costs, including type V, and an orientation to focus more on the benefits beyond herself and her immediate circle of influence are marks of a sustainable leader. A sustainable leader brings more benefits in type IV and V while minimizing type IV and V costs.

5.2 Leader context analysis

To make your dreams come true, wake up and walk toward the dream.

In the force field of influence, be it unidirectional or reciprocal between a leader and her follower, there are three direction-giving lights similar to traffic signals that guide their actions: green, amber, and red. The process of influencing starts with the green light shown by the leader, which is visible (similar to a road junction where many vehicles wait for the green signal with arrows marked to different directions).

A leader–follower context is like this traffic junction with many potential followers waiting for guidance toward a direction that should be taken. Usually, the vehicles wait for the signals to proceed toward their planned destination, as decided earlier. However, a traffic signal can show that one of the roads in the junction is closed now and all should take another route. At this moment, the follower may not be happy, and in the next traffic junction also, if a green light guides them to a different path than what was decided earlier, then there are chances that some may start thinking of new opportunities, like visiting a friend living along the new routes or finishing another task which can be accomplished in this new route.

It is likely that the light in the passenger's mind also becomes green, which was red or amber all this while. From the initial mad and sad state, the passenger realizes that there is a method in the madness and a reason for the sadness. This is the amber stage in the followers, from which the followers can be turned green by creating self-awareness about the why, what, how, and for whom, as illustrated in Fig. 5.6.

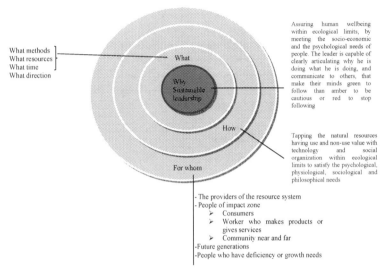

What methods
What resources
What time
What direction

What

Why
Sustainable
leadership

How

For whom

Assuring human wellbeing within ecological limits, by meeting the socio-economic and the psychological needs of people. The leader is capable of clearly articulating why he is doing what he is doing, and communicate to others, that make their minds green to follow than amber to be cautious or red to stop following

Tapping the natural resources having use and non-use value with technology and social organization within ecological limits to satisfy the psychological, physiological, sociological and philosophical needs

- The providers of the resource system
- People of impact zone
  ➤ Consumers
  ➤ Worker who makes products or gives services
  ➤ Community near and far
-Future generations
-People who have deficiency or growth needs

Fig. 5.6: Leader context analysis cascade.

The how question of sustainable leadership is answered by the processes he or she adopts to realize the vision. The processes have the following principles:

- cooperation (avoiding conflict of interests)
- coordination (developing harmonious systems)
- integration (unity of all stakeholders' voices, actions, and ideas)
- participation (inclusion of all stakeholders' voices, actions, and ideas)
- adaptation (evolutionary cycle approach).

The people context (for whom) of sustainable leadership ranges in a continuum of slave to partner, as depicted in Fig. 5.7. In a leader–follower relationship, the slave is the follower with the least power and influenced maximally by the leader or master. The control of the leader or master on a slave or follower is more or less absolute and total.

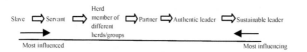

Fig. 5.7: The influenced follower–influencing leader continuum.

Then there are categories of people in varying degrees of being influenced by others (servant, unemployed, employee, worker, staff, subordinate, assistant, secretary, etc.) who are relatively powerless in taking decisions and are therefore influenced by others more. These people, in order to become leaders, need to first get empowered and become skilled to be consulted in decision-making and treated at an equal level with the ordinary leadership level. Those who are neither slaves nor servants are at some level of leadership in some roles that they perform, but they are in a herd among equal leaders, influencing and getting influenced simultaneously, being leader and follower alternatively.

> **Insight Box 5.2**
>
> **Different ideologies followed by a sustainable leader**
> - *ecocentrism*
> - *biocentrism*
> - *environmentalism*
> - *bioregionalism*
> - *enlightened anthropocentrism*
> - *ecofeminism*
> - *eco-friendly technocentrism*
> - *humanism.*

This herd or equal-leader level is a level of transactional leadership. The communication patterns and styles of slaves, servants, and transactional leaders are characteristic. Slaves show obedience, servants show acceptance of commands, and herd or equal transactional leaders show familiarity and friendliness in communicating. Sustainable leaders have all these types of people as potential followers, but all of them need to be brought to the level of partners with dialogue as the main mode of communication. The providers of the resource systems will be the first set of readily accepting followers of a sustainable leader.

Jacob Thomas, PhD

Many of such partners or followers in the course of time become authentic leaders, who replicate and multiply the work of the sustainable leader when initiated.

5.3 Environmental situation of leadership

Tools such as ETOP analysis, SAP gap analysis, SWOT analysis, PESTELD framework, scenario planning, gap analysis, Delphi technique are useful to understand the environmental situation of leaders within organizations. The opportunities and threats to a sustainable leader from the external environment are analyzed in the SWOT analysis. The strengths and weaknesses of the leader based on his personality traits and dispositions are also captured in the SWOT analysis.

Conventionally, PESTELD analysis and ETOP analysis map the political, social, ecological, technological, legal, and economic situation in the macro environment of a business. Thus, PESTELD analysis gives all the required inputs for any organization to plan sustainable development initiatives or business plans. The ecological component in PESTELD and ETOP itself has multiple dimensions, such as political, economic, technological, social, cultural, legal and demographic.

A sustainable leader has a three-way PESTELD analysis to plan her methods: the first from the economic-sustainability angle, the second from the social-sustainability perspective, and the third from the ecological-sustainability angle (as depicted in Fig. 5.8).

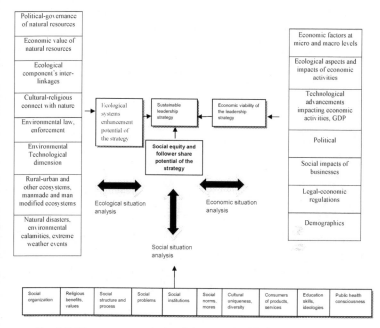

Fig. 5.8: Three-way analysis of the sustainable leadership arena.

A holistic situation analysis of a leadership strategy requires looking equally to the ecological, social, and economic imperatives as sustainability of the leadership strategy in the long run is dependent on all three arenas in equal measure. A cradle-to-cradle approach to all products and services, more environmental consciousness among consumers, more quality of life orienatation in development, more focus on good governance principles, more health consciousness among the general population, and linking public-health issues and calamities to environmental causes, etc. will give rising opportunities for sustainable leadership.

5.3.1 SWOT analysis of a sustainable leadership situation

The internal strengths and weaknesses of the leader with respect to attracting, retaining, and developing followers and the opportunities and threats from the three-way sustainable leadership arena (as depicted in Fig. 5.8) are assessed as part of sustainable leadership's SWOT analysis. An illustration is given in Table 5.1.

Table 5.1 Sustainable leadership's SWOT analysis

Strengths	Opportunities
• seven big traits of a sustainable leader • has a vision • has focus on type V benefits and type V costs • close real self and ideal self • has bases of influence • high degree of universal virtues • stage six of the sustainable leadership identity • has a sense of history • has overview skill. • Has knowledge of the principles of good governance • Has care for the quality of life of present and future generations.	• growing clout of MNCs, global NGOs, global media, and mobile technology in more countries • popular media linking natural calamities and extreme weather events to environmental degradation • growing green consumerism • environmental law enforcement becoming strict • product redesign for dematerialization • growing urbanization and vertical growth may leave more land for trees • imperative efficiency enhancement of of and reduction of wastes • start product take-back schemes and reprocessing • eco-labeling of products • paperless offices, paperless communication, work from home • people seek better quality of life • plant more trees • people demand good governance • social media creating awareness far and wide quickly • more diseases attributed to environmental causes
Weaknesses	**Threats**
• understanding local complexities, which is difficult, and thus sidelines local traditional knowledge • the mediating factors of the sustainable leadership process that may be absent or weak • ideologies such as profit maximization, anthropocentrism, and materialism, which are still very strong among the dominant coalitions of each society • manufacturing and selling defense equipments, warplanes, guns, naval ships, missiles, and nuclear materials, which are big businesses having high influence.	• growing consumerism on account of global presence of MNCs and sophisticated advertisements • global priorities being on market expansion, profits, and dominance • growing economic disparities creating sociopolitical tensions in many regions • local wars, insurgency • growing inequity between rich and poor • top 1 percent of the wealthy becoming more rich. • growing awareness of the corruption chain and the impact of corruption on quality of life and development.

5.3.2 Consciousness as context of leadership

There are various categories or types of consciousness described by scientists and philosophers, such as:

- human consciousness
- universal consciousness
- quantum consciousness (Hameroff and Penrose 1996)
- cosmic consciousness.
- environmental consciousness
- physical consciousness
- emergent consciousness (Zizzi 2004)
- altered consciousness—megahertz, gigahertz, terahertz consciousness (Chopra 2001).

How consciousness is produced by the brain is still not fully understood, even though the microtubules inside the brain neurons, dendrites, axonal firings, low-energy quantum process in neurons, etc. driven by metabolic, biochemical processes are proposed to create and maintain consciousness.

Consciousness is a process believed to be on the intersection between the quantum and classical material worlds that we ordinarily experience. Some scientists state that consciousness occurs at around forty hertz in the brain, and that, at quantum level consciousness in the brain, is a manifestation of the universe with particles, waves, mass, spin, charge, platonic values, and physical constants of a grand design. Grand design is the theory by Hawking and Mlodinow (2010), postulating a near-infinite number of parallel universes.

Sustainable leadership understands and acknowledges the reality of consciousness and the possibility that there is a quantum world, where atomic particles can

> **Insight Box 5.3**
>
> *Seven pillars of environmental leadership*:
> - *concentrating on growth and results, not blaming others or making others wrong*
> - *creating opportunities to make others successful and positively acknowledging others' actions*
> - *having a greater purpose and cause (mission)*
> - *having a methodology to make the change and coaching key individuals in this methodology (strategy)*
> - *speaking a common language, reinforcing the methodology for change*
> - *having a unified identity to distinguish those who are part of the great purpose with a clear vision*
> - *maintaining an internal supportive environment for emotional gratification of personal growth, achievement, significance, belonging, security, and diversity.*

Jacob Thomas, PhD

exist in two or more states or places simultaneously. Thus, there is a connectedness and flow between and among human beings and with other aspects of the ecological system in this universe.

5.4 Sustainability values guiding a sustainable leader

Profit is not the proper end and aim of management and it is what makes all the proper ends and aims possible.

David Packard,
founder of Hewlett-Packard

Values mean 'What do you stand for?' in simple terms. A leader can stand for many things. Reaching goals by whatever means emanates from the value of 'The ends justify the means'. Business leaders making profits through sustainable business practices emanates from the value of 'The means justify the ends'. Thus, profit maximization is a universal value for all commercial business firms and for many social business firms even though they're subscribing to different value systems.

Having happy shareholders and stakeholders may be a business value of some firms striving always to enhance share value and/or socio-ecological benefit value, paying higher dividends and higher CER/CSR contributions consistently. Efficiency, quality, innovation, employee happiness, work-life balance, and transparency are business values adopted by many reputed firms which help them to achieve their mission. Each leader will have specific values depending on the sector in which he or she is operating and the cultural context from where the leader and followers are coming.

> **Insight Box 5.4**
>
> **Leading for a cause: Radiation from mobile phones**
>
> *Permissible radiation levels vary between countries. The range is 450 milliwatts per square meter for 900 megahertz of frequency to 1,000 milliwatts per square meter for 2,100 megahertz in India, which is 400 times more than those in countries such as Austria and Belgium.*
>
> *Lowering the combined power output for an antenna, reducing the number of antenna for a site, increasing the distance between antenna and buildings, switching of telecom antenna, reducing the length of use of mobile phones, etc. are proposed to reduce radiation.*
>
> *Juhi Chawla along with Prakash Munshi formed an organization called Indians for Safe Environment in Mumbai, forming citizen groups to create awareness.*

Sustainability values are of relatively recent origin and primarily stems from the growing global environmental-security concern, as depicted in Fig. 5.9.

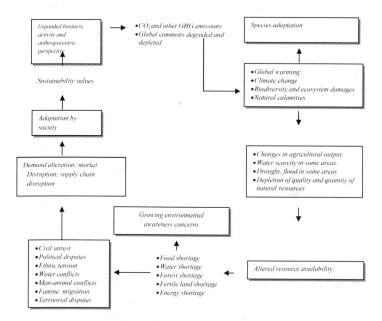

Fig. 5.9: Environmental-security issues impacting social organizations.

Overexploitation of global commons, such as atmosphere, oceans, polar regions, forests, groundwater, wetlands, underground minerals, shale gas, public lands, and biodiversity started with expanded business activity. The search for raw materials, new markets, and energy sources to expand the business and thus achieve economies of scale for cost leadership and market leadership led to faster depletion of natural resources not only in the host country of the industry but in many supply countries. Infrastructure development by way of roads, ports, airports, rail lines, and vehicles/vessels to move raw materials and finished goods faster and in great numbers further damaged the environment. There is a strong case that expanded business activity and transportation is the cause for global warming and climate change.

The global climate change as an environmental situation for a leader brings changes at three levels by virtue of the ecosystem's resilience and natural adaptation.

- first level—changes with changes in temperature and rainfall intensity and pattern
- second level—changes with the shifting of crop regions, longer growing durations, species changes, and migration of people
- third level—changes with the adaptation of humans, other species, and ecosystems to a new equilibrium of global climate and natural phenomena.

If the above is true, that even climate change will be absorbed by the global ecosystem (i.e. the planet), what will be the role of a sustainable leader? The second-level changes are a very painful transition to a new equilibrium, and the end result is not predictable. Will the new equilibrium be better than the past pristine nature or a worse situation for humans? Will it be more prudent to prevent a climate change and preserve the environment as it was, or is it wiser to leave it as such and endure the second-level changes? A sustainable leader becomes relevant in guiding people in this context whether she values the past pristine nature or a future uncertain state of nature.

The changes in the economic and social systems all of a sudden in a 100-year period in most parts of the world did not give the required adaptation time to the diverse ecosystems, which were in an equilibrium state. There were also many wars with large-scale destruction, including two world wars. Reactions from nature first documented by Rachel Carson in *Silent Spring* set the move for growing environmental consciousness and more strict environmental laws, which increasingly constrained business firms to accept sustainability values along with earlier competition-oriented business values. Even now at practice level, most of it is in the nature of greenwashing.

The sustainability values espoused by economic and social actors are emerging. A few of such values are:

- inclusive growth
- being carbon positive
- being water positive
- being eco-efficient, eco-friendly
- human dignity and human rights
- developing a sustainable business
- developing a social businesses
- being ecologically sensitive
- zero waste
- reducing ecological footprint
- social equity
- good governance
- producing and marketing green products and services.

Sustainable leaders are guided not only by environmental values but also by social and economic values, albeit in an integrated, holistic manner.

5.5 Different styles for different contexts of leading

A sustainable leader faces many contexts in her endeavor, and thus, she is expected to lead in different styles in tune with the context. A leadership situation can be viewed in different ways for the leader to shift emphasis from one style to another, depending on the context.

i.   leading like a captain of a ship

The captain is in charge of the ship and its people. He gives directions with his superior skills of navigation and knowledge of the waters. He avoids accidents and pirates and leads the ship, braving tempests to the port of destination. Reaching the destination while carrying the passengers or cargo safely is his mission. He is the steward of the ship, all its crew, cargo, and passengers as everything is entrusted to him once the ship leaves the harbor. He is also expected to leave the vessel last if it sinks. It is direct and indirect influence strategy. An airplane pilot, a tourist bus driver, and an exploration team leader are expected to be steward leaders, like a captain of the ship.

ii.   leading like a conductor of an orchestra

The conductor's job is to give signals to harmonize diversity. Diversity is the strength and value of an orchestra, and the role of the conductor is to streamline and channelize the strengths of each diversity category into a cohesive whole that benefits the audience as well as the participants to excel. It is a direct, on-time or concurrent influence strategy on stage. The conductor is a great coordinator using nonverbal communication.

iii.   leading like a novelist

A novelist is far removed from the followers physically but writes to sway, enthuse, and amuse a set of followers. A novelist attracts readers through the strength of the plot and the characters in the plot. The leader is invisible to the followers and the influence is indirect—through the medium of a book. Just as the saying goes, 'the might of a pen can move mountains', a writer can create lasting influence on many, far and wide.

iv.   leading like a teacher

A teacher has expert knowledge in one subject and has good teaching skills. She prepares for class, clears all doubts, and through the sincerity of efforts to develop the students, makes lasting influence on the pupils.

v.   leading like a fire fighter

A firefighter performs with a sense of urgency where agony is all around. A firefighter is skilled in leading in emergencies and guiding people to safety. When all others are watching, the firefighter acts decisively by virtue of the superior training and the equipment he or she commands.

vi.   leading like a commander

A commander leads a formation of people with arms, where disciplined marching forward is the norm. A commander has the full confidence that his orders will first be complied with by the followers before any complaints are raised. Showing formidability is his forte.

vii. leading like a film director

A film director has the craft of influencing a large audience through visual media, which is often used to stun, entertain, show, or inform rather than influence. However, there are documentary films and mainstream cinema with social, environmental, or sustainability messages intended to influence the thoughts and attitudes of people. A film director stays in the background and influences through the dialogue and actions of the actors.

viii. leading like a coach

A coach motivates and pushes a person toward excellence by guiding and bringing out the true potential of the person. The coach prods and prompts through constant preparation and training. The coach assists in overcoming physical and psychological hurdles inherent in moving toward excellence and charges with confidence on the match day.

ix. leading like a great mountaineer

A great mountaineer scales different hostile heights to finally experience the wonder and awe of an overview from the top. The mountaineer is, however, attentive to even the minutest signals from his body and movements outside during his climb and while at the top, but he gains an overview at the end of his trip to the top, which is his thrill moment.

x. leading like an architect

An architect designs and builds structures with beauty, function, and durability, filling the spaces. The structure should stand against rain and shine, tremors, and tedium fires while serving its function. Architects design structures in spaces considering how the space should be kept in relation to the surroundings. Some such situations are valued eternally as monuments, whereas many go unnoticed.

xi. leading like an entrepreneur

An entrepreneur has passion, a dream, and creativity to make his idea flourish like a seed growing into a mighty tree, producing many seeds for future harvest.

xii. leading like an activist

An activist has a cause to consume his energy, and he channelizes all his energy for the cause. Performance and the ability to face challenges and seek opportunities set apart an activist in addition to making his life as the example for others to follow.

xiii. leading like a priest

A priest performs religious rituals on behalf of his clients, who are the faithful followers of the religion. The followers do not question or doubt the competency of the priest in performing the rituals, which are instrumental in getting physical, spiritual, and psychological benefits to the believers. These rituals are performed to get relief from diseases and stress or to invoke divine presence at life stage ceremonies, such as deaths, births, marriages, etc. A sustainable leader also becomes like a priest, who is bestowed with the faith of his followers in satisfying the needs.

xiv. leading like a family doctor or traditional doctor

A family doctor and all doctors prior to the present-day specialist doctors considered the person holistically, whereas the specialists depend on machine-generated data for diagnosis and deciding on treatment. The past doctors used to understand the person in the patient, his occupation, habits, family background, history of life, food, and thoughts and intuitively arrive at a diagnosis from the insights gained about the person. Nowadays, specialist doctors focus on organs or parts of the person without much emphasis on the self of the persons and the relationship of the self to other selves and the surroundings.

xv. leading like a gardener

A gardener is expected to love all the plants in a garden. A garden has a place for each type of garden plant, such as flowering plant, foliage plant, grasses, shrubs, climbers, topiary plants, trees, annuals, perennials, and plants with different flower colors and growth or nutrient requirements. The gardener understands the needs of each plant and the characteristics of the garden space and has a picture or vision about the garden as an ideal shape toward which all his efforts are directed. Imagine if the garden is not tended for six months; it would lose its aesthetics, design, and vibrancy. To prevent this situation, a gardener who loves his garden engages another person, trains him, and gives clear guidelines if he is going away, which is in the nature of a planned succession.

The above fifteen contexts of leading gives insights about the different elements of leadership and different styles of leading. All of them demonstrate the process of leadership, the central position of the leader, the place of vision, the methods of influencing, the characteristics of followers, and the outputs of leadership. Each of them has the potency to become sustainable leaders but often falls short of becoming one.

An analysis of why these fifteen types of leaders do not become sustainable leaders will open up the various contextual factors that are to be addressed. Does every captain get the opportunity that Columbus or Shackleton got? Can every architect become like Frank Lloyd Wright? Does every coach become like Sergei Bubka or Sir Ferguson?

Table 5.2 gives a few distinguishing features of the four leadership types. In each of these types, a combination of the different contexts of leading listed above can be applied.

Jacob Thomas, PhD

Table 5.2 Looking back at different leadership forms

Sustainable leadership	Authentic leadership (transformational or ethical)	Transactional leadership	Situational leadership
• present and future generations • primacy to ecological considerations • ecocentric approach • seven big traits required for the context • purpose oriented • sustainable leaders are authentic and ethical • universal virtues, sustainability values, and environmental ethics guide decisions	• present generation • primacy to human considerations • enlightened anthropocentric • five big traits plus honesty and humility • mission oriented • all authentic leaders are not sustainable leaders • universal virtues and cultural values guide decisions	• short term • primacy to economic considerations • anthropocentric • five big traits • goal oriented • all transactional leaders are not authentic • material values and results orientation guide decisions	• episodical • primacy to problem-solving considerations • situation centric • self-efficacy • task oriented • situational exigencies guide decisions

5.6 Creating the overview skill

Imagine the difference between seeing the people around while walking along a road and seeing the same people from outer space. Both views are different. The components of nature and features of people are very distinguishable while walking, but from outer space, Earth is seen as a blue sphere. There are four levels of overview skill for a leader.

- overview from the ground level
- overview from the air (from an aircraft, helicopter, balloon, glider, or even a hilltop)
- overview from outer space
- overview rising above the stars and beyond.

The overview from the ground level is with details—the day-to-day life and its problems. In day-to-day life, there are many divisions of the world around and the world inside one's head or organization, as shown in Fig. 5.10. We see people of different colors, shapes, ages, and personalities. We also see the morning, noon, evening, night, storms, rains, trees, barren land, and water. We see births, growth, diseases, accidents, and deaths. This is the view majority of people have about life and living. Occasionally, a person looks up and sees the stars and so many other worlds scattered up above.

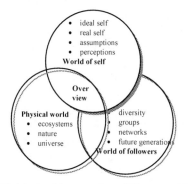

Fig. 5.10: Leadership overview skills at multiple levels.

At the second level, the distinction and divisions on the ground are visibly less distinct. The person still stays within the political boundaries created by people. However, the person rises above the social and ecosystem boundaries. At the third level, a person does not see the political, social, and ecosystem boundaries. A person experiences a worldview without the man-created boundaries and divisions. Universal brotherhood and unity with nature are experienced.

The fourth level of overview is an exercise of seeing within and outside in a harmonious manner, which is the transcendent view of nature. The significance and insignificance of human beings in the scheme of things are experienced while being anchored on earth. The overview is supreme at this level.

Jacob Thomas, PhD

5.7 Winning follower share

> *Try not to become a man of success, but rather to become a man of value. A man of value will give more than he receives.*
>
> Albert Einstein

Since leading is the process of influencing others and sustainable leaders lead on matters of significance for lasting and positive impacts on the present and future generations, winning the mindscape of followers is an imperative for effectiveness. Just as business firms market their products or services with a view to achieve market share, which consists of a number of consumers in different territories, leaders are to aim at a follower share, which consists of a number of followers.

The followers have many options and expectations. The options are:

- not to get influenced at all
- do things against the influencing current
- get influenced mildly and have no behavior change or action occurs as per leader's expectation
- get fully influenced and go along the line of the leader.

Even though sustainable leaders are not focused on winning a follower share, they influence many people to change their attitudes and behaviors toward other people and the environment. This influence is not only among the people of his or her own generation but is also among people in succeeding generations as the impact sphere of a sustainable leader extends across generations.

5.7.1 Leader's perception of followers

Leaders have a certain conception about the traits and behavior of followers, which are called leader's implicit followership theories (Whitely et al. 2012). Since followers are diverse, complex entities, categorizing the followers is an economizing strategy to simplify the complexity (Tajfel 1969). Leaders' mental representations of followers may represent ideal or central tendency prototypes (abstract, composite mental representations for particular cognitive categories). Leaders' central tendency (how followers typically are) conceptions of followers consist of six dimensions (Sy 2010), which are industry, enthusiasm, good citizenship, conformity, incompetence, and insubordination.

Leaders' perceptions about followers affect the performance as there is a perception–behavior link (Chen and Bargh 1997; Bargh and Williams 2006). For example, if the leader perceives that her followers are industrious, enthusiastic, and are good citizens, followers will be given challenging tasks and stretched goals and thereby higher performance results. Mirror neurons in the anterior cingulated cortex of the brain are responsible for this perception–behavior link. The reverse is also true; when followers perceive their leader as visionary, authentic, ethical, and competent, the leader's behavior likely to be as per the followers' expectations, proving the saying 'Every society gets the leader it deserves'.

5.7.2 Sustainable leader's perception of followers

Perceptions–behavior link is an insight used by sustainable leaders as a base of influence. The followers are perceived as benign, inherently noble creation of the same source of life, self-similar in more ways than self-dissimilar, and impregnated with a unique ability to make the community a better place. A sustainable leader gets the insight of the scale that is present in all the potential followers which makes each person similar in many ways to other human beings. He uses more of the needs, fears, emotions, and sources of happiness among followers. Studies have shown that the sources of happiness among people of different cultures in the ultimate analysis are similar.

5.8 Stakeholders of sustainable leadership's success

The success of sustainable leadership is defined in many ways, depending on the focus of the leader—whether the leader addresses a need or pursues a vision. The success may be defined by way of the extent or degree of impact, the size of the geographical area benefitted, the size of the following, and the significance of the output for future generations. Fig. 5.11 provides a framework to gain insights about the success factors.

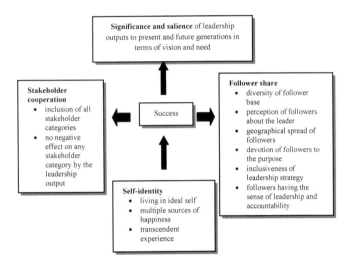

Fig. 5.11: The success matrix of sustainable leadership.

A sustainable leader achieves his outputs and positive impacts with the cooperation of many stakeholder categories. It is not easy to get the cooperation, let alone the support, of some stakeholder categories that are appropriators of common property resources and natural resources for their private benefit. The leader needs to identify categories of stakeholders who will be impacted or will impact the sustainable leadership strategy. A three-way stakeholder classification is given in Fig. 5.12.

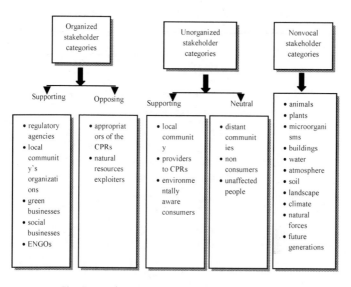

Fig. 5.12: Three-way stakeholder classification for the sustainable leader.

Truly sustainable leaders will be expected to get support from the local community, environmentally aware consumers, and providers of the local resource systems, whereas distant communities will be mostly neutral unless they are organized appropriators. She can expand her follower share by educating the local community about the impact and implementing the sustainable leadership strategy while engaging the nonvocal stakeholder categories, which includes future generations also. For each cause, strategy and vision, the stakeholders are likely to be different and each category's importance and influence are also likely to be different.

5.9 Leader-style script: How much of the leadership context are you likely to consider?

1. I usually connect and interact with people like a family doctor interacting with a patient.

Usually	Sometimes	Never

Jacob Thomas, PhD

2. I know very well the growth needs of all staff in my organization, like a gardener knowing each plant in his garden.

Usually	Sometimes	Never

3. I usually design projects, programs, and organizations like an architect designs buildings.

Very well	Some what	Not much

4. I usually handle the issues and problems of other people, like an activist dealing with a socio-ecological problem.

Usually	Sometimes	Never

5. I am usually successful in coordinating highly skilled professionals with everyone cooperating to achieve the goal, like different coordinating players in an orchestra.

Usually	Sometimes	Never

6. I am gifted exceptionally well in seeing the big picture or larger perspective of issues and in crafting a lasting solution to problems.

Always sees the big picture	Sometimes places issues in a larger perspective	Always attends to details

7. My preparation and perseverance on any mission or initiative are like those of a mountaineer going on an expedition to Mount Everest.

Usually	Sometimes	Never

8. People who are associated with me always sense progress from the situation that they were in months before.

Usually	Maybe when years are reckoned	Not sure

9. I usually go to the historical-evolution aspect of an issue or aspect that I handle.

Usually	Sometimes	Never

10. I usually assess the power of opposing, neutral, and nonvocal stakeholders of a project or issue who may spring up surprises at some time.

Usually	Sometimes	Never

6

Looking Sideways: Leading among Followers

The function of leadership is to produce more leaders, not more followers.

Ralph Nadar

Looking forward and looking backward are exercises performed by the leader, mostly alone, to craft the vision and strategy in an organizational setting, whereas looking sideways is the behavior from the leader.

In a conventional military formation, a commander leads from the front and the supreme commander leads with the strategy at the command HQ away from the front. Both in the conventional army and the modern army, a battle is fought by several units. The units of a conventional army consists of platoons of soldiers using different weapons and different animals and wearing different types of armor along with units for water, food for soldiers and animals, and provisions for communication, signaling, caring for the wounded, intelligence gathering, spying, repairing and sharpening of weapons, and ring-round security to the supreme commander.

If any one of the units works at cross purposes or if the timing of the performance is not in harmony, the battle may not be won. Thus, every unit leader needs to look sideways to assure good performance from other units in order for the war to be won. Even the supreme commander, who usually is the king himself wherever royalty rules or is the head of state in democratic countries, also looks sideways to the best kings or kings in the neighborhood for alliances, opportunities, copying, or competition for benchmarking.

6.1 Leaders are equal

Leader's don't create followers, they create more leaders.

Tom Peters

Leaders help the followers to follow what the leaders themselves are following in a fellowship. From a start-up stage of an organization, people are recruited as employees to perform certain essential functions. As the organization grows, more people are recruited to meet the different organizational needs, and thus the CEO gets many people to lead. Are any one of the persons who were recruited at different phases of the growth of the organization not essential for superior performance? All are recruited as per the need and thus are important elements

> **Insight Box 6.1**
>
> **Leadership**
> *It is 'the influencing process of leaders and followers to achieve organizational objectives through change'.*

(as role holders) in the structure of the organization. If any one person is removed, the organizational structure is likely to become weak and deficient. If we think of the reverse process, wherein the organization compulsorily retires or sheds people, many of the jobs are left unattended, which eventually leads to the demise of the organization (except in cases where the people retrenched were redundant or flab or not creating value or were wrongly recruited initially). The organization may survive up to a threshold level of shedding of the direct employees unless the same jobs are done through machines or by other organizations in alliance, provided the jobs themselves have not become nonfunctional or dysfunctional to the organization.

From the above structural analysis, it can be inferred that each job in an organization is critical to the long-term survival of the organization if each job is a unique and integral node in the organization structure. As each job is a critical, unique, and integral part of the organization, all organizational members have equal significance. Imagine a situation where all the organizational members have the same commitment, belief, and faith toward the mission, vision, and strategy and have the same level of aspiration, passion, and ambition to take the organization to that vision as if all are rolling together like a smooth ball toward the destination; a small dent in the ball will reduce the speed and make the progress wobbly. We see such a process in football and cricket teams.

Success has three dimensions for most of the followers based on the depicted roles in Fig. 6.1

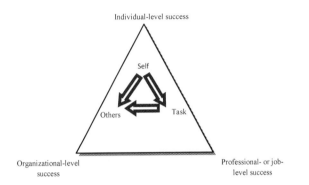

Individual-level success

Self

Others   Task

Organizational-level success   Professional- or job-level success

From the followers' point of view, success is achieved when the roles are fulfilled to the satisfaction of the fellow followers and the leader. However, the followers have roles which are not aligned or sometimes in conflict with the roles in the leader–follower ecosystem. These are individual-level roles at three domains.

- personal growth and sense of progress providing activities
- doing what one likes, which shifts in different life span stages
- activities that are performed for realizing certain special needs.

Professional- or job-level success is a task- and

Insight Box 6.2

The *A–Z* of leading

A—ardent, accountable
B—balanced, benefitting
C—curious, caring
D—devoted, decisive
E—enthusiastic, empowering
F—focused, fearless (fortified)
G—growth oriented, grateful
H—humble, harmonizing
I—inspiring, innovative
J—just, joyous
K—keen, kind
L—leveraging, learning
M—monitoring, motivating
N—Nurturing, Noble
O—organized, optimistic
P—proactive, persevering
Q—quaint, quick
R—resilient, reliable
S—sustainable, stimulating
T—trusting, transformative
U—undeterred, unifying
V—visioning, versatile
W—winning, wonderful
X—xenial, xenodochial
Y—youthful, yearning
Z—zealous, zestful

action-focused domain which changes as the external and internal organizational environment changes. Job-level success often has its own parameters of success. Organization-level success is based on participative, complex, and flexible role enactment of many followers collectively where leadership comes into play, coordinating and integrating the parts into the whole. Here the relational aspects gains significance. The individual follower has a self-orientation, task orientation, and other orientation while being in an organized effort.

6.2 Followers as signal posts

> *There are two ways of spreading light: to be the candle or the mirror that reflects it.*
>
> Edith Wharton,
> 'Vesalius in Zante' (1564)

A traffic signal post holds the signals red, amber, and green in the correct position relative to the track so that it is visible to everyone moving forward.

Signal posts or signal stations perform many functions. First of all, signal posts are visible symbols of the institution that it represents. For example, a signal station of an army unit is taken by the public as an integral part of the army's function. No less important is their role as a vital sense organ of the unit, collecting and transmitting information, signals, and changes in the area it scans or in the place around it. They have gadgets such as readers, binoculars, night-vision equipments, telescopes, radio transmitters, transponders, etc. Followers transmit the message of the leader to the people around each follower and retransmit the feedback to the leader. What a follower does is as per the influence of the leader and not based on the volition of the follower.

6.3 Influencing game: Fear, tear, gear, dear, near, peer

> *Authenticity is the alignment of head, mouth, heart and feet—thinking, saying, feeling and doing the same thing—consistently. This builds trust, and followers love leaders they can trust.*
>
> Lance Secretan

Jacob Thomas, PhD

How a leader gets into the brain and/or the heart of the follower and thereby influence the thoughts and actions of the follower is more like a game of emotions than rational actions. The influencing leader has varying effects on each of the follower, depending on how each one experiences the influence game. Combining emotions with capability, the leader creates fear (awe), tears (tears out of pure joy), a feeling of gearing up (empowerment), endearment, nearness (closeness), and peer (one-among-us identity or feeling). Awe and admiration about the actions of the leader attracts many, while many others may get a feeling that the leader is one among them. Followers then identify with the leader as a person who is dear to them and near to them when emotions such as joy, happiness, awe, love, and admiration are part of the leader's influencing actions.

6.4 Leveraging cumulative strengths: The strength of many without weakening

> *A follower shares in an influence relationship among the leader and other followers with the intent to support the leaders who reflect their mutual purposes.*
> Rodger Adair

Just as a flowing river consists of millions of water drops that flow in one direction as a single unit with formidable force when together, a leader–follower ecosystem becomes a social entity of great potential. What is individually not achievable becomes easy when cumulative strengths are considered. Thus, harnessing the cumulative strength is an 'expedient means' to create impact. But human beings who constitute the leadership ecosystem are not water drops devoid of feelings, emotions, ego, self-concept, and self-interests. Thus, a leader's job is to align the interests of many into one goal and to leverage the individual disparate strengths of many cumulatively, adding them up arithmetically at least, if not geometrically. The accumulation of strengths can happen geometrically if maximum synergy from the strengths of individuals is designed in the organizing logic.

The strengths of many can weaken below the arithmetic accumulation if the power of leadership is not inspiring, creative, motivating, and action oriented. The weakening forces are found from four sources: individual follower, the environment, the structuring of roles, and the leadership strategy.

6.5 Leader–follower ecosystem: Interdependencies, energy flows

> *It is the man behind who make the man ahead.*
> Mark Crowell

In a natural ecosystem, there are several species coexisting in a habitat in several types of relatively stable interactions in clearly defined boundaries. Across these boundaries, there is a flow of information, materials, and energy as natural ecosystems are open systems. The interactions are of various types—competition, cooperation, commensalism, symbiosis, predation, and parasitism. A typical leader also has a set of followers who are in stable interactions over the course of time, and nonfollowers are outside the boundary of this space of leader–follower interaction. The needs of both the leader and the follower are met in this bounded space, creating interdependencies. The leader energizes the followers toward action to reach the goals, and the followers in turn keep up the energy level of the leader by their support, feedback, and wins along the way.

6.5.1 Online followers and offline leaders

There are online leaders who post materials for others to like it, ignore it, imbibe it, dislike it, or post a comment on it. Those who share, like, dislike, or post a comment about the material are visible followers of the online leader. There are also invisible followers, who do not contribute online but imbibe the knowledge and transfer this knowledge to offline contents. Thus, the online community is a part of a larger polycontextual community or ecosystem having diverse online and offline contexts with several types of leadership roles in the ecosystem (Cranefield et al. 2011).

6.5.2 Multimodel communities and their interdependencies

The online communities, offline communities, backchannel communities, online–offline multimodel communities, and epistemic communities are different stable interacting collectives of people with clear boundaries of activities. Online communities use online tools for information exchange and exist in the context of bounded online spaces with interactions such as discussion groups and facilitated forums. Castro (2006) proposed a community of practice conversation space ecosystem as a model for today's technologically mediated online communities in which individuals may participate in some communities as a core member and in some other communities as a peripheral member. This ecosystem is made up of overlapping communities containing a set of people having a shared or common practice or interest and their conversations. These people in conversation in one can transmit the information straight or after reflection and adaptation in several ways across the conversation space.

The technology that enables online community conversation is now strongly merged into daily life, and hence, the boundaries of online–offline communication are very porous, creating a multimodel reality (Garcia et al. 2009). The online world, which consists of several interacting communities, and the offline world, including the leader–follower ecosystem, have become multimodel or polycontextual environments. Individuals easily move between online and offline communities, among online communities, and between public/private and formal/informal organizations. Some individuals who are very active participants in one online community may be a lurker in another online community, and the same person may be a leader in an offline community. Thus, leaders in today's multimodel communities have several interdependencies in their different roles across the larger online–offline community ecosystem (Cranefield and Yoong 2009; Nonnecke et al. 2004; Peerce et al. 2004; Arnold and Paulus 2010).

Epistemic communities are interactional coalitions of experts in a particular field of knowledge with reference to policy problems (Haas 1989).

6.6 Expanding arena, individual arena, and institutional arena

Nothing grows well without space and air.
Patricia Monaghan

An arena is the real or virtual space or place where different actions of the leader–follower system get enacted, generating a particular result and making effects on the followers. The characteristic feature of an arena is the visibility of an action or performance that it offers to a large number of spectators. The activities of the individual leader in the action arena produce a wide range of results that are viewed by the followers and others.

An individual leader has many action arenas which are separate processes and generating different results. Every impact can be traced back to an action arena, and every action arena of leadership has a leadership action. The result that is produced by the individual actor from inside the action arena interacts with the overall institutional context that surrounds the arena, resulting in the expressed impacts. Individual arena-based actions are onetime events, the results of which are not sustainable unless the leadership arena is expanded into an institutional arena.

Institutions are characterized by recurring functions, activities, roles, and the relationships between roles along with the different types of institutional entities, such as formal organization, informal organization, persons, collectivities, and social orders. Institutional actions by a leader are leader–follower exchanges that have evolved into a form with a norm. Thus, institutional arena has primarily a norm or a set of norms as rules of conduct which carries social meaning with a form which not only persuades and constrains but also charts directions and sets contexts.

When leadership expands to the institutional arena, it becomes a structural component of the social system with a network of information and resource flows and exchanges. Thus, a business leader who produces and facilitates flow of goods between persons or social units in accordance with social norms plays in an institutional arena. When the leadership becomes a normative formulation of the society, embodying a particular society's judgments about the desirability of the leader's messages, actions, and products or services, it gets an appearance of order, stability, structure, and system.

At this stage, the leadership as an institution is manifested through a set of activities that further the functions and roles, having a normative context and resource configurations. Roles constrain the variety of ways a particular functional activity can be performed through the force of expectations of a set of stakeholders of the activity or function.

An institutional arena of leadership consists of a combination of institutions having a particular resource configuration within a relatively longer period of time and engaged in exchanges. The exchanges are mostly actions of information sharing in the case of the leadership arena; information exchange is between the leader–follower ecosystem and leadership institution–other institutions ecosystem (defined by their own functions, activities, and roles). When the information exchanged acquires social meaning, the leadership becomes institutionalized.

Public policy-making arenas include legislatures, public executives, courts, regulatory agencies, semipublic bodies, and specialized committees of experts with decision-making or recommendatory autonomy in a particular domain, such as think tanks. These arenas are institutionalized rather than ad hoc as they acquire legitimacy from a diverse set of social actors, sensing the value of social policy leadership.

6.7 Shielding, exposing, protecting, and sharpening followers

> *Always recognize that human individuals are ends,*
> *and also do not use them as means to your ends.*
> Emmanuel Kant

Even though the leader–follower ecosystem has interdependencies, no component or link in this ecosystem is inferior to another, but it remains functional as a system that has the maximum edge to cut through challenges in realizing a vision. Just as the Macedonian king Philip (father of Alexander the Great) perfected a formation of advancing soldiers carrying big spears to channelize the momentum of a section or platoon of soldiers forward as an indefensible force for the army at that time, the leader–follower system has great potential in right formations.

The cumulative strength of each follower is harnessed to make the collection of soldiers formidable. Even though such a formation exposed the soldiers at the flanks, the very form and force of it shielded individuals from individual attacks. Even a weak soldier has value as he adds up to formidability of the formation by increasing the numbers carrying the big spear. The innate abilities of individual followers are sharpened by the messages from the leader, making them more effective and efficient.

6.8 Leadership ecosystem, leader webs, leadership pyramid

> *Be not angry that you cannot make others as you wish them to be, since you cannot make yourself as you wish to be.*
>
> Thomas à Kemps

The leadership ecosystem consists of many leaders across a set of online and offline communities, militating against the barriers of distance, time, knowledge, social norms, and professional isolation. Traditional social barriers of face-to-face followership and leadership are no longer applicable in the virtual arena, reducing the erstwhile psychological distances and promoting shared understanding (Baker-Eveleth et al. 2005; Hew and Hara 2007; Rovai 2002). The leadership ecosystems form part of a complex tiered ecosystem of overlapping online and offline communities. In such an ecosystem, leaders form a web with the same leaders in a particular COP (community of practice), while another is a leader in an online community, and a third leader may be active in an offline community, and so on.

6.8.1 Polycontextual leadership

There are overlapping leader–follower communities; some are in the virtual arena, and some are in the real world. For each community, there is a leader, and the leaders who have a shared understanding form a web of leaders who transmit similar messages to their own followers. Depicted in Fig. 6.2 is a leader web consisting of global leaders, connector leaders, and service-provider leaders.

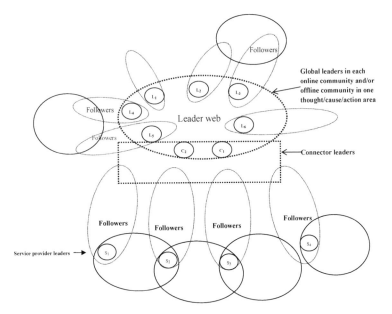

Fig. 6.2: Leader web.

6.8.2 Leadership pyramid

Just as there is a food pyramid in an ecosystem, there is a leadership pyramid in a leadership ecosystem. There are *global leaders,* who are thought leaders in their respective subject areas or causes or action arenas. Their reach is much wider in terms of geographical spread, number of followers who are inspired, and number of separate communities being influenced in multiple nodes. Examples are Socrates, Picasso, Karl Marx.

At the next tier, there are *leader connectors,* who are not leaders of any particular community specifically but influence several communities by interpretation and adaptation of the global leaders to suit each context. They are creative by innovating the thoughts, concepts, and ideas to suit specific contexts. Examples are Albert Einstein and Abraham Lincoln.

The third tier consists of *institutional leaders,* who effectively communicate and ignite passions among a set of followers and provide particular terms of access, structures that shape perceptions, and ways of acting. Examples are Lenin, Nelson Mandela, and Mother Teresa. While the second-tier creative leaders do not develop structures or forms but only norms, third-tier leaders establish specific structures for the followers.

Fig. 6.3: Leadership pyramid.

The fourth tier consists of leaders who are action oriented and are in offline communities in different action arenas as enablers and/or service providers. *Action leaders* produce the direct results in the action arena by performing the intended functions and activities exceedingly well. Action leaders are role models for others in spurring actions, whereas *motivational leaders* are mostly the people who develop the structure and systems that facilitate and motivate performance of activities.

In an organizational context, these four tiers can be equated with the board members as the inspirational leadership web at the first tier; the strategic planners, R & D experts, consultants, and innovators as the creative leadership web at the second tier; the functional leaders and SBU leaders as the motivational leadership web at the third tier; and the operational executives at the fourth tier.

All these leaders in the web of the formal organization context may have roles and activities in some other online or offline communities also, either as leaders or as followers.

Jacob Thomas, PhD

6.9 Connect script: How you will build more bonds and ties?

We make a living by what we get, we make a life by what we give.

Winston Churchill

1. My followers/staff in the organization are considered assets.

Yes	No

2. I respect and promote other leadership roles performed by my staff.

Yes	No

3. All in my organization, including me, are subjected to the norms and policies of the organization.

Yes	No

4. The thinkers, doers, and streamers have equal space to express themselves in the organization.

Yes	No

5. The silent ones and the vocal ones are treated at par in assessing and nurturing individual strengths.

Yes	No

6. Identify all the attributes (from the 'A to Z of leading' given in this chapter) that best describe you during the entire day. Count the total number that best describes you.

Less than 5	5–15	Greater than 15

7. Write the one attribute pair in the 'A-Z of leading' that you want to cultivate and practice every day.

Leading with a Strategy

Being realistic is the most commonly travelled road to mediocrity.

Will Smith, actor

The concept of strategy as a central idea or the core of a plan had been part of the polity used by kings to conquer new territories, usurp a kingdom, or defend themselves against invaders and sabotage. Every successful side has a winning strategy, and the defeated side had a failed strategy. The ingredients of this strategy are the element of surprise in striking, the timing of striking, the special formations, the methods of use of force, the tactical withdrawals from the scene, the creation of confusion, the shift of attention, and several other tactics as per a well-guarded game plan known in its entirety only to the king and his top lieutenants. The fulcrum of a king's strategy was projecting a great *purpose* that was attractive to the masses.

The first book of Chronicles in the Bible describes this strategy in the life and conquests of David to build the house of God, which must be exceedingly magnificent, famous, and glorious throughout all countries, and all his wars were preparations for it (1 Chronicles 22:5, New King James Bible). David advises his son Solomon, 'Be strong and of good courage, do not fear nor be dismayed.' And thus gave him charge. The preparation for the great purpose involved conquests; plundering of the gold, silver, bronze, iron, timber; and bringing them to Jerusalem to build the house of God. The kings in ancient China and India also had great purposes communicated to their followers as reasons for their conquests.

The second element of strategy is the *resources*. David chose for himself five smooth stones from the brook and a sling. Even though David was given by Saul, the then king, a bronze helmet, heavy armor, a coat of mail, and a sword, he could not walk with these untested resources. He removed all untested resources and chose the tested sling and stones and killed the mighty heavily armed Goliath. Tested and befitting resources enable success when used at the correct time.

The third element of the strategy is having a *cause*. When David, a youth, decided to take on Goliath, who was a man of war from his youth, David's brothers dissuaded him as Goliath was tall and a champion. David countered, 'Is there not a cause?' (1 Samuel 7:29);

Insight Box 7.1

Fire-and-fear leadership strategy
Steve Jobs is known for a leadership strategy founded on fire (igniting a big fire inside every follower) with the fear of burning oneself.

the cause was salvaging the esteem of his kingdom. A cause arises from the deprivation, deficiency, or need that requires action to remediate. A cause provides justification and moral power for actions. Purpose gives direction for those actions.

The fourth element of leadership strategy is *confidence*. Leaders who are confident welcome challenges and set difficult goals (Luthans 2001), and a leader's confidence increases the follower's willingness to work toward the leader's vision (Luthens and Peterson 2002). Confidence involves a belief in one's capability to be successful and in self-perceptions of competence in knowledge, skills, and abilities (Hollenbeck and Hall 2004). It is a judgment of whether one is capable to do something. Self-confidence and self-efficacy (an estimate of one's capability to perform successfully) are one and the same (Yukl 2002; Hannah, Avolio, Luthens, and Harms 2008).

Insight Box 7.2

Origin of strategy
Strategy is a management team's way of selecting its place in its environment as well as the firm's way of interacting with the environment. Thus, strategy is manifested in both cognition and action. Strategy exists in the leader's mind and reified in a firms activities, rules, routines (Gavetti and Rivkin 2007; Hulf and Jenkins 2002; March et al. 2000).

Setting direction, gaining commitment, and overcoming obstacles are the behaviors associated with a confident leader (Palis and Green 2002). Internal locus of control, low neuroticism, high self-esteem, and general self-efficacy are the traits associated with confidence (Popper et al. 2004; Baline and Croder 1993). A sustainable leader will never become overconfident like narcissistic leaders (with inflated perception about themselves), hubristic

Jacob Thomas, PhD   142

leaders (unwilling or unable to see changes in the environment), or destructive leaders (exaggerating their positive achievements and pursuing their own self-interests) (Kroll et al. 2000; Campbell et al. 2004; Kaiser et al. 2008).

A hierarchy of leadership elements with confidence as the basic element (as shown in Fig. 7.1) defines a leadership strategy.

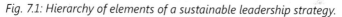

Fig. 7.1: Hierarchy of elements of a sustainable leadership strategy.

At the base of any leadership strategy, which is at the back of all influencing actions between the leader and his followers, is the confidence of the leader. A confident leader engages the followers and has the potential to excite and galvanize them to action in pursuit of an agreed vision. The confidence of the leader infects the followers, and together they can overcome obstacles in their march forward. Once confidence is there, the leader identifies a cause, a challenge, a need, a deprivation that requires attention.

A cause unites people and galvanizes them into action. If a cause is identified, resources are required. Resources can be tangible or intangible things that can be mobilized to address the cause effectively. Time is also considered a valuable resource. A confident leader who has mobilized the resources for a cause is required to clarify the purpose. The purpose may be vague in the beginning and gets clarified in due course as a cognitive activity of the leader. The purpose of using the resources differentiates a sustainable leadership strategy from other leadership strategies.

A sustainable leader imagines a roadmap based on the insights gained from investigating the context, potential followers, desirability of the purpose, elements of the vision and from introspecting about the self. The imagination with the intention to find the right path will unfold many directions or paths to take to achieve the purpose and thereby realize the vision.

Strategy is the choice of a purpose and the most fitting direction to follow (most fitting for the leader, for the followers, for the context, and for the time) with a game plan to advance that is different and difficult to imitate and a purpose that is beneficial to the present and future generations.

7.1 Leading game plan: Succeed with the least cost

Any initiative or effort has several costs. A sustainable leadership game plan is crafted in such a way that costs are minimum. The costs include personal costs of the leader, costs of resources required to put the leadership strategy into action, and any external costs on the environment.

The personal costs are basically three types: time costs, health costs, opportunity costs. A leader is devoted to a purpose to realize a vision. This devotion takes enormous time in investigation, introspection, imagination, implementation, and inspection of progress. Sustainable leadership involves hard work, which can create stress, leading to health effects, such as hypertension, heart diseases, headaches, stomach problems, excessive eating or drinking, etc. While devoting oneself to one purpose, the leader will not be able to devote to anything else, and thus opportunities for other pursuits are lost.

In addition to the costs of resources to meet the needs of followers, there are coordination costs and costs for communication. Even though costs can be planned neatly into long-term and short-term budgets and systematically accounted as expenses, the benefits of incurring all the costs are uncertain. Strategy bridges the certainty of all types of costs and the uncertainty of the benefits, as depicted in Fig. 7.2.

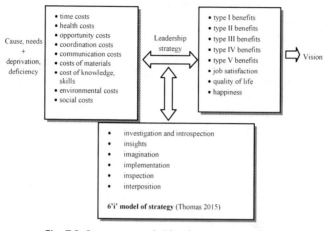

Fig. 7.2: Strategy as a bridge between certainty of costs and uncertainty of benefits.

The leader who invests and commits his and his follower's time, intelligence, and talents in a purpose expects benefits and need satisfaction commensurate with the costs incurred. Strategy is a best-fit line among the several uncertain benefits from each cost, cumulatively adding and leading to the vision through the common thread of purpose. Fig. 7.3 depicts the best-fit line of leadership strategy.

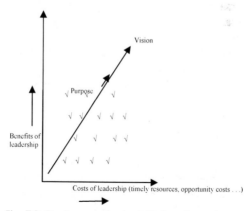

Fig. 7.3: Strategy as the best-fit line through several uncertain benefits from investments.

7.1.1 Strategy tenets of sustainable leadership

The strategy tenets of sustainable leadership are:

> ➤ Each person's insight about a situation and need is likely to be different.

> ➤ The insight and imagination of everyone in the organization need to be channelized.

> ➤ Differences in insights among the followers provide opportunities for cross-fertilization of insights, generating several fresh insights.

Insight Box: 7.3
Five *As* of leadership competence
Aspire — where to reach
Assess — capabilities
Architect — initiatives
Act — programs, action plans
Advance — cutting through
There are various frameworks on leadership competencies which are generally applicable to persons who were not born to inherit a kingdom or great fortune! Even in inherited leadership, sustainability depends on the incumbent's competence except in some monarchies.

> ➤ Environmental realities are complex yet local.
> ➤ Solutions to issues require multiple insights, collective intelligence, and knowledge.
> ➤ Three types of knowledge—traditional/tacit knowledge, modern scientific/empirical knowledge, and management knowledge—are required.
> ➤ There are several stakeholders of most public governance issues, with varying degrees of importance, interests and influence, that requires balancing. Multidimensional nature of socio-economic and environmental issues and changing natures of the external environmental conditions make continuous learning and adaptation an imperative.
> ➤ Leadership is the process of navigating from milestone to milestone linked through a strategic framework toward a vision.

7.1.2 Game plan for success

Success in a sustainable leadership endeavor starts with the beliefs of the leader. Final success depends on the effectiveness of the influence strategy adopted by the leader through a process, as depicted in Fig. 7.4.

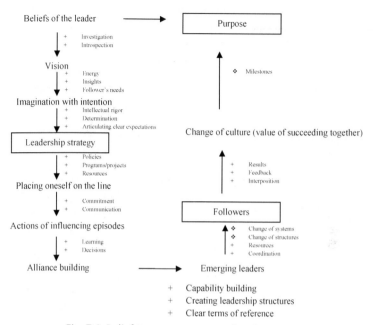

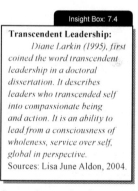

+ Capability building
+ Creating leadership structures
+ Clear terms of reference

Fig. 7.4: Belief-to-purpose game plan for success

The beliefs of the leader formed during socialization and early learning process combined with current observations and thoughts through *investigation and introspection* will lead to a vision about the leader's position and a purpose for his leadership. Vision combined with energy and *insights* about followers and their needs will advance the leader to *imagine with intention* to address the follower's needs. This imagination

> **Insight Box: 7.4**
>
> **Transcendent Leadership:**
> *Diane Larkin (1995), first coined the word transcendent leadership in a doctoral dissertation. It describes leaders who transcended self into compassionate being and action. It is an ability to lead from a consciousness of wholeness, service over self, global in perspective.*
> Sources: Lisa June Aldon, 2004.

process combined with intellectual rigor, determination, and articulation of expectations of the self and potential followers will give the design of the leadership strategy as the path to be taken to achieve the purpose of swaying the minds and influencing the thoughts of others. The leadership strategy has many initiatives as programs which require resources. With commitment and a communication plan, the leader places himself on the line, making him conspicuous. Placing oneself on the line is the act of *taking charge* of a situation, a cause, or a need of followers.

Episodes of influencing actions are the intermediary outputs of the leader once the leader has taken charge of the situation or started the journey toward the purpose with a leadership strategy. For each action episode, there will be impacts and responses from which a sustainable leader learns further about the inputs to leadership, unfelt needs of followers, unknown area of himself, and resource system, which leads to reframing decisions. The leader influences more people by building alliances, which is an act of creating more leaders through the process of empowerment.

> **Insight Box: 7.5**
>
> **Becoming conspicuous**
> *The best way to become conspicuous is to become a stranger. To become a stranger, one has to have strange thoughts, strange actions, strange personality, strange way of decision-making, and strange way of implementing those decisions. 'Strange' means not the way of the herd and not the way of the expected. By being consistent in strangeness, focusing on a purpose of significance, and creating new expectations, the herd will look up, notice, listen to, and probably follow the stranger! A sustainable leader creates expectations by being different from herd thoughts and actions.*

More leaders following the same path toward the same purpose are likely to emerge when appropriate leadership structures or climate is developed with clear terms of reference. With the power of the alliances of the emerging leader, more followers are likely to result if there are changes in systems and structures. The changes in structures in terms of roles, relationships, systems, communication, decision-making, resource mobilization, production, etc. will stabilize when a new culture is developed. Change of culture is a slow process with several milestones of results achieved along the path toward the ultimate purpose.

7.2 Follower analysis: The herding challenge and sustaining followership

> *The final test of a leader is that he leaves behind him in other men the convictions and the will to carry on.*
> *Walter Lippmann*

Followers of a sustainable leader are actors who generate the results based on the influences of the leader. Followers are not just the sum of individual followers but a system and a culture. They are parts of an interrelated whole working in harmony with the leadership strategy. Burns (1978) defines leadership as *the act of inducing followers to act for certain goals that represent the values and motivations, wants and needs, and aspirations and expectations of both the leaders and the followers*. Leaders cannot accomplish their vision without followers (Kelly 1992). Followers are also leaders in many other roles. People act as leaders and followers alternatively, and most people follow more than they lead in their lives.

A leader is like a conductor of an orchestra, where each player is an expert on his or her instruments, being a leader on their own right. They can enthrall an audience with their skills alone but submit to the authority and orchestration of the conductor while being in the team. The orchestra members contribute to the common purpose and are as passionate as the orchestra leader in pursuit of the common purpose.

Similarly, a chief surgeon conducting a heart operation acts like an orchestra conductor. The lifts, stretches, and the movement of the surgeon's hands are cues for actions by the followers. The head nurse, other surgeons, anesthesiologist, and other assistants in the operation theateract in unison for the common purpose of a successful operation to save or prolong the life of a person on the operation table.

The characteristics of followers are:

- recognize and acknowledge the authority of the leader
- make an active decision to contribute to a common purpose
- understand and own the common purpose and the leadership strategy
- stand up for the leader and his decisions
- work with other followers while holding on to one's values
- champion the vision and the need for change and stay with the leader till the vision is fully realized
- hold themselves accountable for the consequences of their actions
- stand up and voice the differences and views when a particular decision of the leader does not justify the service

Jacob Thomas, PhD

of the common purpose, thus acting as a sounding board for course corrections.

Hargreaves and Fink (2003) argue that *leadership is a culture of integrated qualities than merely an aggregate of common characteristics*, which is the essence of the holistic approach to sustainable leadership. The relationship between a sustainable leader and the follower is a long-term partnership.

There are four types of partnerships:

- transactional—a give-and-take relationship between the leader and the follower
- transformational—the leader providing a role model, articulating a vision, communicating high performance expectations, fostering the acceptance of common goals, providing intellectual stimulation, and providing individualized support to the follower; the followers experience social proximity with the leader (Podsako et al. 1996; Walter and Bruch 2010)

> **Insight Box 7.6**
>
> **Leader overcomes!**
> *Navigating a path which has hurdles, putting iron in the soul that keep the sturdiness and stability to advance is a mark of a sustainable leader with ambitions enclosed in the soul. By creating expectations step by step, deciding on bigger and longer steps, solving larger and complex problems, and unifying the followers rather than polarizing, the sustainable leader moves on.*

- transcendental—transformational plus service orientation (the manipulation aspect of transformational leadership is removed through the service orientation in this type of partnership)
- sustainable—transcendental plus vision of successive generations plus matters of significance for a meaningful and dignified life to all.

7.3 Leveraging resources Provider or appropriator

The purpose of leadership can be achieved only when there are required resources available in a resource system. The resources may be tangible or intangible, human or material, intellectual or social, current or historical, based on modern technology or traditional knowledge, natural or manmade, living or nonliving, temporal or spiritual, managerial or structural, and strategic or tactical that is necessary to satisfy the needs of the followers. What resources are needed, at what time, in what form, in which measure, and at what cost are the factors the leader should assess. A sustainable leader will use resources at such a rate that the outputs of the leadership pursuit do not harm the inputs and that the inputs can be replenished. A leader should be aware of the resource universe (the resources that are available), identify those that are useful, and develop methods to leverage those to fulfill the needs or achieve the vision.

This process of leadership starts when significant observations and insights are combined with the leader's beliefs, which are shaped by the culture in which the leader is rooted. The elements of the culture of both the leader and the follower and the role of the leader in enlightening the culture in ecological arena are depicted in Fig. 7.5. Similar cultural analysis need to be done for other action arenas of sustainable leadership which will show different cultural elements.

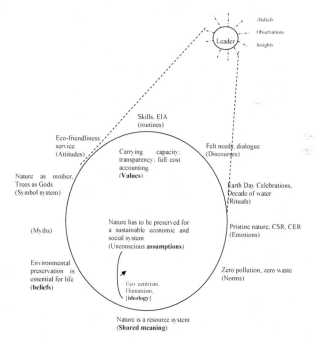

Fig. 7.5: Enlightening the follower culture as a resource

The leader is the sun that lights up the visible or invisible parts of the follower's culture. There are many elements of culture that are to be either influenced or leveraged by the leader–follower partnership. The cultural elements are not only intervening factors in the leadership process but are also a very valuable resource for implementing the leadership strategy. Personality attributes and experiences, ecological understanding, social sensitivity, and the leader's holistic view of interconnectedness are factors that affect each of the process steps once the leadership process starts, as depicted in Fig. 7.6.

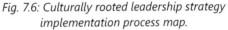

Intuition   Personality

Intention

Communication

Observations + belief ➤ inference from insights + sustainable strategy ➤ decision + influence methods ➤ sustainable leadership

Principles + concepts,
virtues, emotions

Leveraging resources.
Including cultural resources

Follower' needs,
expectations, culture

*Fig. 7.6: Culturally rooted leadership strategy
implementation process map.*

Soap has chemicals, whether synthetic or organic (has a natural origin), and it is used to cleanse the body either as solid soap, liquid soap, face wash, handwash, baby soap, or herbal soap. The observation is that soap has chemicals; the belief is that chemicals pollute water and that water is important for life. The inference from this observation plus belief is that soap is used with water, and thus it flows out as polluted water, requiring a removal process of the elements of soap. Such a soap-mixed bathwater or hand-washed water or face-washed water will reach a point of discharge. If this soap-mixed water is to be purified and recycled, it requires energy and equipment not affordable to many.

Considering the principle of waste management, reduction at the source is the ideal option among many options, if there is a way to do it. Thus, the need for a strategy comes in. Strategy formulation is an intuitive process of imagination with the clear intention of ameliorating the situation. At this point of strategy formulation, the resources available or those that can be mobilized are to be identified. A generic strategy that can be employed is resource leveraging.

While crafting the strategy, a sustainable leader assesses whether he or she acts as a provider of resource units to the resource system or as an appropriator. If he is not a provider, he undertakes an action at least to replenish in equal quantity and return in better quality that which is proposed to be used from the resource system. This point in the action series of leveraging the resources differentiates a sustainable leader from others. Thus, while imagining on these lines, several alternate options can come up.

Based on this sustainable strategy, a series of decisions needs to be taken by the leader with influence methods drawn from the innate strengths of the leader. The end result of the process is followers getting attracted and induced, implementing the strategy with the purpose of reducing soap use (reduction at the source was chosen as the ideal option). The strategy may be to use traditional materials for cleansing the body, which were in use before the industrial product of soap became ubiquitous. Another strategic option may be finding alternatives with technological advances where the quality of water that goes as input to bathing or washing comes out from the washroom in the same quality as that which goes in.

The leadership strategy needs to use influence methods that change the assumptions, beliefs, values, and attitudes of people to turn them into followers of the chosen strategy. There may be some people who believe that traditional materials for body cleaning are better than soap, and people with such beliefs can be partners in the influence strategy. This aspect of culture can thus be leveraged to influence others to reduce soap use.

7.4 Diversity inventory Converging challenges

A sustainable leader leads with the concept of ecosystem in mind for every aspect of leading. The ecosystem concept describes three types of diversity: genetic diversity, species diversity, and ecosystem diversity. Similarly, the leader experiences diversity of observations about causes, future scenarios, needs, beliefs, perspectives, concepts, principles, strategies, resources, communication methods, and finally, followers. Respecting and accepting such diversity in both the ecosystem level and among the people and followers and drawing the strength of such diversity is the hallmark of a sustainable leader.

Converging the challenges of diversity into strength as part of the leadership strategy will unite and synergize. Thus, the converged force of followers will become formidable, each one filling the deficiency of the other.

7.5 Expectation inventory Managing expectations

The diverse stakeholders and the diversity of followers of the strategy founded or crafted by the leader will have different expectations. Expectations are perceptions of a future event, action, or outcome that can change over the course of implementation of the strategy. Making an inventory of all such expectations, then finding out the central tendency (mean, median, and

Insight Box: 7.7
Seven cardinal characteristics of sustainable leadership:
• *authenticity*
• *reliability*
• *trustworthiness/success together*
• *stolidity/equanimity*
• *scholarship/strengths*
• *stoicism*
• *spiritual/transcendental orientation.*

mode) and dispersion (standard deviation, variance, frequency distribution) will enable the sustainable leader to manage the expectations well.

7.5.1 Leadership expectation matrix

Expectations are not a one-way process but are in multiple directions. Followers have their own expectations when they are aware of a leader in the beginning stage, when the influence process has not started. Subsequently, when the leader articulates his approach and communicates it, the followers' expectations about the leader shift. The approach that the leader articulates should be capable of influencing the expectations of the followers.

The central tendency of the expectations of all the current and potential followers will be the most likely realized vision of the leadership strategy. A sustainable leader also needs to manage the aspirations of those followers who are not near the central tendency. Fig. 7.7 shows four types of expectations in a leadership expectation matrix.

Leader to follower	Follower to follower
dyadic interactions between individual follower and the leader	individual followers' expectations from all other followers
leader's expectations from all other followers	mutually supporting relationships among followers, matching expectations among followers

Fig. 7.7: Leadership expectation matrix.

There are one-to-one dyadic relationships and mutual expectations between the leader and follower. This relationship is based on trust. There are also expectations between a group of followers and the leader. Some followers have individually more expectations from the other followers. Followers as a collective have expectations from all others as an organization in terms of organizational expectations.

Sustainable leaders approach the vision as a story told and enacted in a phased manner. The first phase of the story is the crafted leadership strategy to realize the vision. Realized-vision state is not the end of the story but only reaching the next phase, and from the first-vision state, a reframed leadership strategy appropriate for that context will take the story to the subsequent phases in an unending, rolling manner.

Insight Box 7.8

Prophetic leadership
It is an extreme visionary leadership style where the leader's vision extends to future generations in fifty or more years (Hall 1994).

A story has many twists, turns, subplots, and progresses through the actions of the lead characters (leaders, heroes) and supporting characters, with the script expanded from a plot or central concept. The reader of a story or an audience of a storyteller moves with the lead characters and expects a certain way of progressing of the story or next moves of the hero. The reader also may have an expectation about the fate of the heroes, their triumphs, and their tragedies. The reader/audience will be extremely happy if the ending of the story is as expected. However, there are many readers or audience who are more interested in the entertainment and information aspect of the story, and they will be extremely happy if their interest is sustained high till the end of the story; their expectations are about the thrills and suspense of the journey than the end.

A leader is thus a storyteller, and the follower is similar to the readers or the audience of the storyteller. The leader creates the expectations of the followers by the strengths of the central plot and the script that is yet to unfurl, which is the leadership strategy. The leadership strategy as a script with continuous evolution of the vision is depicted in Fig. 7.8.

There are two broad types of followers: those who look forward to the ending part (vision) and those who look forward to the thrills and the suspense to be experienced in the journey. Thus, there are likely to be two major central tendencies with a two-peak frequency distribution when all the expectations of the followers are plotted in a graph. The expectation inventory can be depicted as having three vertices, as shown in Fig. 7.8.

> **Insight Box 7.9**
>
> **Therapeutic leadership**
> *Some leaders define themselves (self-identity) as persons who provide solace to the physical and psychological ailments afflicting people. The classic example is the Sermon on the Mount by Jesus Christ, giving solace to all the deprived, disabled, downtrodden, disempowered, dispossessed, and distressed people. Such leaders provide:*
> - *hope and purpose in life*
> - *connectedness to the world*
> - *a healthy mind that cures many physical ailments.*
>
> *Honore de Balzac wrote* La Comedie Humaine, *which is rated as a therapeutic novel, and the School of Life was established in Bloomsbury in UK as a bibliotherapy service center, using the 'curative' powers of the novel.*

Expectations are created through the strategy by the leader toward the strategy implementation process. Through the process of dialogue, the process-orientated expectations and the vision are managed by the leader. The leader's role is to ensure that the *process* expectations do not derail the *vision* expectation and that both are balanced.

Fig. 7.8: Leadership strategy as a script influencing the process and vision expectations.

John F. Kennedy used a sustainable leadership strategy with his script told in 1961—landing people in the moon and returning them safely before the close of the decade. The vision was to enhance the self-esteem and pride of America, which was perceived as behind the USSR in space success at that time. The script was trusted by all and was implemented, giving euphoria to the whole world when Neil Armstrong landed on the moon on 21 July and returned safely in 1969 before the close of the decade.

> **Insight Box 7.10**
>
> **Copernicus created new expectations**
> *He has overturned the church doctrine on man's place in the universe through his book* On the Revolutions of the Heavenly Spheres *starting in 1514. He contradicted Aristotle and Ptolemy by stating that our planet Earth is not the centre about which all else turns. Even though Nicolaus Copernicus died on 24 May 1543 in Poland, he still lives and will live in coming generations as well for his courage to tell the world what he observed, the significance of what he told, the expectations raised by him, and the influence he wielded as his theories changed the perspective about the world and mankind.*

There were many subplots and elements of story from the articulation of the vision by the leader in 1961 till its realization in 1969, which gave to the world 'one small step for a man, one giant leap for mankind'. The announcement of the strategy and vision in 1961 created expectations about how it would be done and about the end state. The story did not stop with the landing; it went forward with further probes into other planets, the space

Jacob Thomas, PhD

shuttle program, space stations, and space probes going beyond the solar system.

7.5.2 Characteristics of the script

The script of the story carries the followers through the journey that the leadership strategy envisages. The characteristics of the best script are:

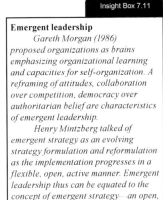

> ➢ It is based on the central tendency of the expectations of the potential followers
> ➢ It considers the marginal expectation categories through side stories to bring their expectations to the mainstream.
> ➢ The end of the story opens up possibilities to multiple story leads to the followers.
> ➢ There are significant roles for many in the story.
> ➢ The story should have enough material to keep up the interest of the follower.
> ➢ It should inform, enthuse, entertain, and enable the follower.

Insight Box 7.11

Emergent leadership
Gareth Morgan (1986) proposed organizations as brains emphasizing organizational learning and capacities for self-organization. A reframing of attitudes, collaboration over competition, democracy over authoritarian belief are characteristics of emergent leadership.
Henry Mintzberg talked of emergent strategy as an evolving strategy formulation and reformulation as the implementation progresses in a flexible, open, active manner. Emergent leadership thus can be equated to the concept of emergent strategy—an open, active, flexible, evolving, adaptive leadership strategy.

7.6 Sustainable leadership model

Sustainable leaders unite people in two ways: under one cause or under one vision. The leader crafts a leadership strategy with the cause or vision as the anchor to wield influence among a set of followers through a portfolio of means, such as:

Insight Box 7.12

Vision salience (Oswalled et al. 1994):
- clarity
- sharedness
- appropriateness.

> being aspirational about a dream, clarified and communicated as a purpose
> being inspirational to follow certain core values or virtues
> being ambitious in fulfilling a need
> being rehabilitating by going to the basics
> revitalizing a dissipated system
> championing a cause
> focusing on a differential strategy
> leveraging all resources while developing them.

By choosing one or a combination of the routes above to unite and excite the potential followers, a leader carves out a more impactful role for them. This leadership model can be graphically represented, as given in Fig. 7.9.

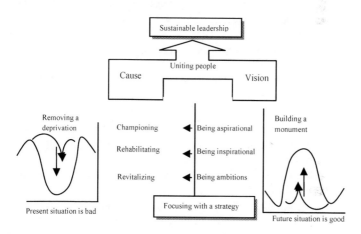

Fig. 7.9: Sustainable leadership model.

Every organization and institution can be categorized, based on the sustainable leadership model, into two: those that fulfill a need arising from a deprivation and those that fulfill a need arising from a vision. The driving force of the first is hope, and for the second, it's the ambition of the followers and the leader. The leader thus sells hope or ambition, as the case may be, among the followers.

7.6.1 Types of sustainable leadership models

A leadership strategy is essential either way, whether the hope route or ambition route. The strategy may revolve around the skill set of the leader, such as:

> ➢ oratorical/communication skills
> ➢ dialogue skills
> ➢ resource leveraging skills
> ➢ strategy crafting and implementing skills
> ➢ visioning skills along with action orientation.

Models enable an understanding about what makes leaders act and how they influence followers. It is similar to business models that conceptualize the product market scope and how profits can be generated by influencing customers to pay a good price for a product or service.

Every type of vision and every type of need requires a different model of sustainable leadership. Models also vary with contexts. These three variables—needs, vision, and context—make a multitude of leadership models in the following systems:

> ➢ leadership in economic systems: business firms, industries
> ➢ leadership in political or legal systems: local, national, global
> ➢ leadership in sociocultural systems: ethnic, local, multicultural
> ➢ technological leadership: traditional knowledge, modern scientific knowledge, and experience-based knowledge systems
> ➢ environmental leadership models: holistic, involving components of the environment, and based on opportunities, problems, and issues.

One of the earlier documented leadership models is the managerial grid by Robert Blake and Jane Mouton, with the concern for people and concern for results resulting in four types called the country club, impoverished, authoritarian, and team leader. Bolman and Deal (1991) proposed the four frameworks of structural, human relations, political, and symbolic leadership models. There are models of leadership where a leader's role is not exclusive to interpersonal domains but includes complex cognitive activities and social problem-solving skills (Conway 2000; Mumford et al. 2007; Yukl 2002; Qwinn 1988; Hunt and Phillips 1981).

7.6.2 Articulating an approach to sustainable leadership

Sustainable leadership does not happen automatically. It has to be modeled and undertaken by articulation of an approach so that doors to opportunities of influencing become visible for further progress. In order to articulate an approach, investigation and introspection are the first steps. Make a list of probing questions to clearly understand the context in terms of time, occurrences, events, space, people, resources, risks, and hurdles revolving around the need and/or vision. This process of making the list itself is likely to open up the different aspects of the need or the vision.

While thinking and getting insights on the answers to these questions, make the second list of actionable propositions as an output of the list of probing questions. Attempt to prepare the documentation work of the propositions as if you're about to act, which will enable the gathering of more details by way of imagination with intention.

Insight Box 7.13

Thought leadership

The power of an idea is well known. Ideas come from imagination. Ideas that constitute strategy come from imagination with intention. When the imagination process is channelized towards the vision elements with a view to get connections between the insights about the present situation and the vision (future situation), the script of a leadership strategy forms.

A fertile mind or imaginative mind produces a good crop of ideas. The ideas generated in one's mind have the potential to influence others if they are appropriately communicated. The medium of communication can be a blog, a book, a speech, an act, an art, a song, an entrepreneurial venture, an association or congregation, an NGO, a social business, or any initiative. The idea is encoded in such a way that the targeted followers or audience can understand it. Without the intended understanding, the action of followership is not likely to occur.

Thus, thought leadership is the art and design of packaging and encoding an idea and choosing the correct medium to reach the target or potential followers, with the purpose of the idea entering their minds and working like a virus, creating more follow-up action ideas.

---

161   Jacob Thomas, PhD

During the process of imagination, an attempt can be made to draw up a model of the direction to take by writing down the vision for clarity and the elements of the influence strategy that are likely to motivate the followers. This second step will lead to articulation of an approach which defines the boundaries of action and potential ways to move forward. The third step is assessing the risks, hurdles, resources required, and probability of success of each of the paths. The fourth step is the final choice for implementation of an action plan with the least-costly, sustainable, and sure-to-succeed actions.

7.7 Creating structures for engagement: Horses for the courses, cavalry to advance

The first idea that comes to mind when the term 'structure' is mentioned is the pattern of relationships between the leader and his followers. It is a relationship between the roles in the organization of followers. The classic unity of command and span of control principles define the relationship of roles in most of the organized endeavors. However, there are many developments that are movements toward the sustainable leadership structure. One illustration is given in Fig. 7.10.

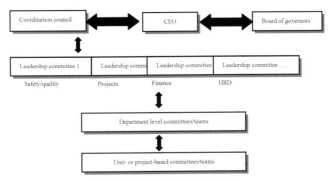

Fig. 7.10: Sustainable leadership structure.

As part of the structure, the leader needs to choose and place at appropriate places, in the formation of his followers, solitary horses for the courses and cavalry to advance. Solitary horses are in terms of devotion to the cause.

7.7.1 Characteristics of a sustainable leadership structure

There are four types of relationships that a sustainable leadership structure has.

- relationships with mutual expectations between the leader and followers
- relationships with mutual expectations between the followers themselves
- relationships of the leader–follower organization with other stakeholders
- relationships of both the leader and followers with nature or the universe, the connectedness and the transcendental aspect.

The structure is expected to provide the following:

- autonomy to the followers to express their full potential, talents, and true interests
- meaning to all their actions as per the articulated approach
- connectedness to their souls with the universe and other followers
- feelings in followers of being independent leaders pursuing the vision or addressing the defined need.

7.7.2 Structure for motivating followers

The motivation to lead and motivation to follow a leader are psychological processes inherent in any leadership process. A person who has a wish to lead (Popper and Mayseless 2007) creates a formal or informal structure made up of followers or joins an existing organizational structure at leadership positions. Such persons who have a wish to lead cultivate orientations toward mastery, curiosity, persistence, task endogeny, and engagement in challenging, difficult, and novel

Insight Box 7.14

Sustainable leaders rest after victory

Jesse Owens, at the age of twenty-one, in one hour's time in the afternoon of 25 May 1935, set five world records and equaled a sixth in six different athletic events. Thus, he became a legend, influencing athletes in successive generations.

Jacob Thomas, PhD

tasks (Goufried et al. 2011). The academic intrinsic motivation theory (Chan and Drasgow 2001) suggests that a person engages in leadership activities for the pleasure inherent in the leadership process rather than for external rewards. They chart new directions, effect change, organize members, and persist in the face of challenging, difficult, and novel situations and tasks. They have affective identity (enjoyment of leading), noncalculative motivation (leading for its own sake, not for rewards), and social normative aspect entailing leading to serve one's duty.

Just as leaders have a motivation to lead, followers have a motivation to follow, and this follower motivation also has three aspects: affective identity (enjoyment of following), noncalculative motivation (following a leader not for rewards), and social normative aspect of being guided by the call of duty. Even though motivation to follow may be intrinsic among many followers, such a motivation is nurtured by a structure created by the leader as part of the leadership strategy. Motivation strategies emphasizing task endogeny is shown to be more motivating than task-extrinsic practices, such as rewards. Task endogeny as a motivation strategy can be provided to followers by designing appropriate roles and role relationships among followers, involving exploration, intellectual stimulation, enjoyment of the process of doing the activities, tasks of optimal match to the follower's abilities, and tasks that provide autonomy and stimulate challenge and roles that provide variety of stimulation.

7.8 Not a resource to waste

The types of resources that a sustainable leader leverages include rare, unique, valuable, and nonsubstitutable resources or assets. The value and rarity comes from the fact that every resource unit used from the resource system needs to be at best replenished in equal measure if not returned with augmentation. However, a highly effective sustainable leader enhances the resource units by becoming a provider than an appropriator. Thus, the efficient use of resources without any wastage is an imperative.

A network resource, particular location, climate, unique history, ethnic cuisine, local medical knowledge, deep knowledge of a subject, etc. are very valuable, unique, and nonsubstitutable resources that unless used to their advantage, will remain a waste. Even the energy and spare time of potential followers is a unique and valuable resource. Underutilized skills, tools and knowledge of persons which have use in addressing a need or cause are also valuable for the implementation of the strategy.

The most important resource a leader has is his followers. The followers are individuals with needs, motives, drives, intelligence, time and energy. If the energy and intelligence of the followers are channelized, they become a formidable resource. Getting this formidable force by uniting followers for a cause or for realizing a vision is the process of leadership. The lever that a leader uses to tap this resource is ideology, as in the case of the revolutionary model's motivational tactics. Other levers often used are enlightening, dialogue; providing mastery, meaning, and mission; and raising the expectations. Followers have physical strengths, knowledge, attitudes, skills, and relationships, and each of these five aspects are assets.

7.9 Strategy script: How well is the sustainable leadership strategy crafted?

1. Do you have an enduring purpose for your most important activity that benefits future generations as well?

Yes	No

2. Do you engage yourself in a cause, addressing the benefits that are likely to flow to many people by engaging in the cause?

Yes	No

3. If you are in a leadership situation, do you craft a vision and think of various approaches to realize the vision?

Yes	No

4. Do you leverage the existing resources at your command or incur more costs to mobilize more resources?

Yes	No

5. Do you always articulate an approach to solve a problem or to address an issue?

Yes	No

6. Are the roles that the followers perform sufficiently stimulating to themselves, and do they enjoy doing their jobs?

Yes	No

7. Do you consider yourself a good storyteller to your followers, and do followers enjoy the script of your story?

Yes	No

8. Does your leadership strategy include every follower in the story, or is anyone left out without a stimulating role?

Yes	No

9. Does your leadership strategy make it clear among your followers that the benefits of following you are far greater than not following you?

Yes	No

10. Does it cost much to the follower to be a follower to your vision?

Yes	No

11. How you searched and identified all types of resources and assets among the current and potential followers that have value in implementing the strategy

Yes	No

Leading with Decisions

8

Everyone makes thousands of decisions on aspects occuring in their lives, studies, careers, jobs, people, relationships, nature, hobbies, investments, and beliefs. There are several small-impact decisions and big-impact decisions. There are stand-alone decisions and decision series. Each decision, big or small, affects yourself, other people, and your surroundings.

8.1 Decisiveness: Taking the reins and not shrinking to management decisions

An indecisive person is a confused and stressed person. A decision offers clarity and removes the stress in situations that require a decision.

Taking charge of situations, events, and people gives enormous responsibility to a leader. After taking the reins, the leader should not be restricted to management decisions, which are execution decisions; leaders are expected to expand their decision arenas with performance-enhancing decisions and those that have long-term consequences.

8.1.1 From decisions to judgments

Judgments are more than decisions even though there is an element of decision-making in all judgments. Judgments are made when there are multiple options, with the pros and cons of each alternative being weighed, and are based on evidence and certain norms or values. Insights about decisions in one kind of circumstances are of no use in making judgments as situations, people involved, issues, impacts, and decision importance vary. In judgments, the issues are framed first, followed by collecting evidence for and against each of the issues framed in the nature of collecting all available positive and negative information. With more information, the issues get more light, and all knowable information gives clarity to the issues.

8.1.2 Rationality of the decision process

Decisions that are logical in pursuing the goals toward the vision are said to be rational decisions. In economics, rationality equates to utility maximization. Individuals are assumed to seek the maximization of their expected utility. Leaders in organizations, however, are rational within the limits of their own capabilities, and the decision-making process is limited by cognitive, social, and political realities, which is the concept of bounded rationality (Eisenhardt 1997; Snyman and Orew 2003; Dean and Sharfman 1993). Boundedness of decision rationality is largely a function of limitations of information relevant to the decision (Dean and Sharfman 1996).

> **Insight Box 8.1**
>
> **Core skills and orientations for good judgments:**
> * *courage and risk-taking*
> * *honesty*
> * *passion*
> * *innovation*
> * *curiosity*
> * *selflessness and sharing*
> * *communication and knowledge flow*
> * *impact anticipation*
> * *triangulation*
> * *uncertainty reduction*
> * *cognitive diversity*
> * *autonomy*
> * *speed: cycle time of decision-making*
> * *forecasting inflection points*
> * *butterfly effect of decisions.*

Decision guides	
Purpose:	the last why of pursuing a vision with a mission which is nonnegotiable and lasting
Mission:	the basic purpose and the scope of operations, the method by which the vision will be achieved
Vision:	where one is going, wants to be, and what he can become in the future
Goal:	different compartments of the vision

Objectives:	defining tasks to achieve the vision
Targets:	specific measurable components of objectives
KPI:	performance indicators that will tell whether the objectives have been achieved
Strategy:	choice of calculated and well-informed sequence of steps leading to the vision and avoiding missteps
Values:	the attributes of a person that forms the basis for his thoughts, words, deeds, and decisions

8.1.3 Decision-making models

Several models of decision-making exists, which can be grouped into categories.

- rational decision-making model
- incremental model or trial-and-error model
- coalition model
- garbage can model
- virtue ethics decision-making model (Jordan and Meura 1995)
- integrative decision-making model
- participatory decision-making model

The rational decision-making model has the following six steps, as described by Schwartz (2004).

Figure out the goals or issues or problems.

Evaluate the importance of each goal or issue.

Identify the options to reach the goal or resolve the issue.

Evaluate the probability of each option meeting the goal.

Select the winning option which may be the best fit or a trade-off.

Use the consequences of the choice to generate future possibilities.

Six steps in the rational decision making model

The steps in most of the models are similar, but the methods at each step vary, depending on situations. The trial-and-error model is employed when the parties agree on goals but do not agree on methods about how to achieve the goal. When uncertainty is high, a succession of small decisions that can fit together is taken, which over time solves the issues.

Coalition models are used when parties do not agree on the goal but agree on methods. When there is conflict of interest or goals and competition over resources, there will be high ambiguity, and coalitions are formed, representing each interest groups to gain what each group wants. The decisions arrived at are a trade-off, accommodating alternate or multiple interests.

In the garbage can model, there is disagreement on both the goals and the methods, and the decision-makers face both uncertainty and ambiguity. Random solutions attach themselves to some problems, proposed by random individuals at a random point in time. Some problems get solved by chance, and often solutions may be proposed where no problem exists.

No model can be said to be superior as even in the rational model, final selection of the option can be influenced by personal biases, established relationships, and environmental influences.

8.2 Decision dilemmas Choices all along

The values that a leader uses as an anchor to label his thoughts and emotions and base a decision on can be grouped into several boxes. Normal leaders usually have six boxes, invariably having a self-growth orientation as one among them. However, as the leader graduates into a sustainable leader, the number of boxes to which all the values in a value universe that he is aware of can be grouped expands, as depicted in Table 8.1.

Table 8.1 Value–variable matrix of decision-making

Growth	Growth		
	Self	**Organization**	**Others/ followers**
Performing Energizing Empowering Partnering	Self-growth; Achievement; Wealth; Mastery; Nonconformity; Creativity; Adventure.	Organizational growth; Purpose; Risk; Service; Openness; Passion for the mission.	Contribution; Challenge; Change; Autonomy; Helpfulness; Health.
Harmonizing Balancing Controlling	Self-knowledge; Accuracy; Stability; Tradition; Power; Moderation; Leisure.	Honesty; Authority; Responsibility; Duty; Order; Humor.	Humility; Safety; Tolerance; Justice; Friendship; Popularity; Fun.

Individual followers			
		Growth	**Energizing**
Organization of followers	Growth	Self-knowledge; Creativity; Responsibility; Achievement; Change; Growth; Mastery; Openness; Power.	Generosity; Autonomy; Challenge; Contribution; Passion; Purpose; Risk; Service.
	Harmony	Accuracy; Humility; Moderation; Safety; Order; Stability; Honesty; Authority; Tradition; Dependability; Duty. Justice; Rationality; Realizing.	Courtesy; Forgiveness; Tolerance; Generosity; Helpfulness; Adventure; Friendship; Health; Fun; Humor; Leisure. Popularity;

Jacob Thomas, PhD

Each leader has a pattern of thoughts, emotions, and decisions which sets in as one grows in age and experience. Often they get feedback, criticism, responses, and reactions for their emotional expressions and actions based on intents, which may bring about change and/or frustration and stress. A sustainable leader allows the patterns of decisions of each follower with the harmonizing role of hybridizing all those patterns to get hybrid vigor in the organization.

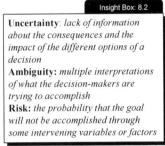

Insight Box: 8.2

Uncertainty: *lack of information about the consequences and the impact of the different options of a decision*
Ambiguity: *multiple interpretations of what the decision-makers are trying to accomplish*
Risk: *the probability that the goal will not be accomplished through some intervening variables or factors*

The concept of workability, whether your response with a decision in a context is good for the organization or good for individual followers, are evaluated with the underlying values that guide those decisions or responses. Whenever a decision dilemma occurs, if the situation is put to a quick test using the matrix given in Table 8.1 for identifying a value that should guide that decision, stress can be avoided, and there will be more control in decision-making.

8.2.1 Influencing factors of decision-making

The factors that influence the decision-making process of a leader are:

- leader's individual characteristics, values, and virtues
- followers' diversity of expectations
- nature of the decision (decision-specific characteristics), whether strategic or managerial, and nature of the problem
- organizational culture, vision, size, and performance orientation
- environmental characteristics, such as turbulence, uncertainty, and munificence
- national cultural characteristics
- influence and importance of different stakeholders.
- Compliance in letter and intent of local, national and international laws, codes and covenants.

All these factors assume more importance in stable environments even though they influence the process of decision-making and the decision-specific characteristics, such as importance of the decision, decision uncertainty, and decision motive. However, in very turbulent environments, decisions are mostly externally influenced where a participatory decision-making model, one that uses both empirical knowledge and tacit knowledge in evaluating the choices, is proposed to have less risks.

8.2.2 Decision uncertainties

The future is already arrived; it is just not evenly distributed yet.

William Gibson, novelist

Knowledge uncertainties and residual uncertainties are two types of uncertainties faced by a leader while making strategic decisions.

A decision is needed when there are alternatives or options, and each alternative have different consequences. The uncertainties faced by a leader are numerous.

- uncertainty about the salience of the needs of the followers that are addressed
- uncertainty about the galvanizing power of the cause
- uncertainty about the number of followers to the vision state
- uncertainty about other needs that overshadow the current needs but identified as important due to changes in the environment.

> **Insight Box: 8.3**
>
> **Could these events, which led to crises, have been predicted?**
> - *Enron fraud*
> - *dot-com bubble*
> - *September 11 WTC terrorist attack*
> - *Kuwait war*
> - *Iraq war*
> - *rise of emerging markets*
> - *concerns on global warming*
> - *Eurozone crisis (Greece)*
> - *coal allocation scandal in India*
> - *2G spectrum scandal in India*
> - *2008 US mortgage crisis.*
>
> *Are there turbulence triggers and levers?*

Courtrey et al. (2014) identified four levels of uncertainties surrounding strategic decisions.

- level 1—There is a clear-enough future where the residual uncertainty is not very relevant.
- level 2—The future can be one of a few outcomes, and the probabilities of each outcome can be estimated through decision analysis, game theory, and option valuation models.
- level 3—There are no natural discrete scenarios, but a range of potential future state can be identified. Scenario planning and technology forecasting are useful tools in such situations.
- level 4—There is true ambiguity, where the range of potential outcomes cannot be identified as multiple dimensions of uncertainty interact. Analogies and pattern recognition and nonlinear dynamic modes are analytic tools useful in truly ambiguous decision situations.

8.3 Dimensions of decision-making

Decisions have two major dimensions: performance and control.
How much or to what degree the decision is going to impact the performance of the organization and how much control the decision maker has on the outcome of each decision are depicted in Fig. 8.1

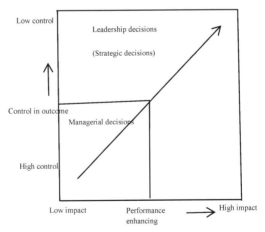

Fig. 8.1: Direction in which a decision is moving in a sustainable leadership.

The extent of rationality in decision-making, incrementalism (fragmentation), and intuition are other three dimensions of the decision-making process. The decision process may not always be characterized by analysis but short cut decision-making heuristics, such as simplification, reference to past cases, imitation, risk-aversion, and satisficing are adopted to simplify the decision process (Krabuanrat and Phelps 1988; Quinn 1980; Starbuck and Milliken 1988).

8.3 Machine learning Algorithms to use data for better predictions

'Anything that does not fit into the current knowledge or frameworks is termed as mad idea, mad method, mad action and mad strategy, yet that madness may be a pointer to the future.'

Any decision has some amount of risk. Any nondecision also has some amount of risk. The risk analysis of any decision versus nondecision can be done by using frameworks and tools in order to predict better the cost of the decision or nondecision. Along with this, another dimension is the several options or choices available in each decision situation, like a fork, any one of which are potential candidates for selection.

Each decision option has separate consequences or impact which needs analysis. A third aspect is the reactions to each decision apart from the consequences and impact. Sometimes the reactions to a decision may worsen a situation than improve it. Everyone takes decisions by expecting the benefits but often forgetting to analyze the risks, costs, impact, and reactions.

Jacob Thomas, PhD

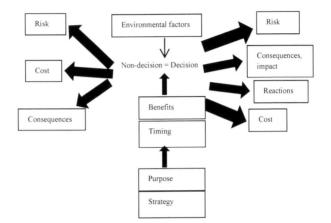

Fig. 8.2: Two options in a decision situation.

Both decision and nondecision have consequences, risks, and costs, as depicted in Fig. 8.2. The cost of not deciding may be the loss of an opportunity, or preventing a situation from worsening and recovering with a later decision is likely to have higher costs. To make or not to make the decision at a particular time is mediated by the environmental factors. The decisions or nondecisions at a time depends on environmental factors, such as uncertainty about a law, success of new technologies, tax rates, interest rates, political turmoil in a country, terrorist attacks, serious frauds, etc.

A good organizational leader engages the followers in such uncertain situations, discussing about the situation, analyzing options, gathering information, performing maintenance and cleanup tasks, focusing on CSR projects, and engaging customers and suppliers to build relationships. Till such times that the uncertainty gives way to clarity, these engagement decisions rather than strategic decisions keep the costs low. This way, the consequences of nondecisions are made positive, and risks are minimized.

The decision or nondecision is also a decision which is made based on the strategy and purpose, while all decisions are taken anticipating the benefits emanating from the decision. Nonlinear dynamic models, latent-demand research, decision analysis, option valuation modes, game theory, pattern recognition, etc. are some of the tools used for better prediction.

8.4 Leading without controls: No one likes to be controlled

Everyone likes freedom, and no one likes to be controlled. A leader who makes fewer rules and norms for the followers is likely to get more followers. However, rules and controls that discipline followers, whereby everyone gets equal opportunities and freedom to pursue their goals and everyone's efforts are guided in the direction of vision is a mark of good leadership. Absence of control is chaos,

> **Insight Box: 8.4**
>
> **Traits of a strategic decision-maker:**
> * *confidence in capabilities*
> * *credibility to gain trust*
> * *courage to take risks*
> * *integrity to be objective*
> * *imagination to consider all scenarios*
> * *making inferences*
> * *listening to and entertaining other views*
> * *humility for best judgment*

which is not conducive for followers to pursue actions as uncertainty looms large. Morten T. Hansen (2011) defines discipline as the consistency of action—consistency with values, long-term goals, performance standards; consistency of methods; and consistency over time. Sustainable leaders show consistency between their thoughts (strategy), words (goals and plans), and behaviors (execution methods and matrix to measure performance).

Defining too narrowly a role of the followers with very detailed job descriptions and micromanaging will be felt by the follower as very constraining. Such a follower is not likely to exhibit creativity in his actions and may resort to work-to-rule, making just enough performance to escape from punishments.

8.5 Leadership risks: Risks in decision-making, risks of success

Risks are uncertainties and unpredictable consequences of the decisions, investments, commitments, and actions that we intend or propose to take or make. Risks come from unexamined and unwarranted assumptions and information about the present context and future scenario. Leadership risks are of the following three types:

* path-dependent risks: pursuing a wrong path which involves waste of time and efforts of both the leader and the follower will diminish the influencing ability of the

leader as his credibility is eroded; this results from the influence strategy that is wrongly formulated.

- trust-eroding risks: these are relationship risks resulting from the actions of a leader that erode trust and faith in the leader by the followers and vice versa.
- decision risks: these are low-impact risks arising from each decision of a leader.

The initiatives that the leader–follower system decides to execute have the following four types of execution risks (Loren Gary 2005). These are risks that an organizational leader faces often.

- financial resource risk: a cash flow shortage
- human resource risk: some key followers leaving the organization
- supply risk: a problem in one of the suppliers' end may delay a component
- quality risk: the standards are not reached in a service.

A systematic audit of all the things that can go wrong by collecting opinions from stakeholders and estimating the negative impact of each risk and ranking the risks for taking action to avoid or minimize risks is essential for success. For risks that cannot be avoided, developing a contingency plan should the anticipated risk strike saves time and prevents possible derailment of the leadership strategy.

8.5.1 Decision paralysis

Risk-averse leaders leading in highly turbulent environments sometimes may not take strategic decisions based on their gut instincts, which is called decision paralysis. Being aware of the correct tools for each uncertainty or decision dilemma, collecting as much information as possible, and then basing decisions on interactions is the best bet for leadership success than making no decisions.

8.5.2 Biases in decision-making

There are several biases that creep in while making decisions, which are risks in decision-making. A few are listed below:

- sunk-cost error
- overconfidence bias
- anchoring effect
- hindsight bias
- immediate-gratification bias
- selective-perception bias
- confirmation bias
- framing bias
- availability bias
- representation bias
- randomness bias
- self-serving bias.

An awareness about the potential biases in each decision situation helps in making less biased decisions.

8.6 Integrative decisions

Decisions made by considering all factors, including when to make the announcement or publish a decision, is by a process, as depicted in Fig. 8.3. When faced with a decision situation, there exists a need to make a decision. The urgency and importance of the decision is first assessed, which is the first step.

Fig. 8.3: The process map of integrative decisions.

The integrative decision-making model involves the basic steps of the rational decision model but integrates with it the factors that cause biases in decision-making, situational variables, and involvement of stakeholders. An overarching purpose will permeate all the steps in the integrative decision process, and the final choice of options is a judgment based on justice and ethics and devoid of biases from a ranking of all options. The ranking itself is done through exploration and knowing all consequences of each option if enacted based on both information and tacit knowledge. The timing of announcing the decision and implementing it are also a matter of choice for the execution success.

8.7 Social justice in decisions

All decisions have impacts. The impacts are either on the people in a society (individually or collectively) or on the resource system in the environment. A sustainable leader's decision aims at creating more leaders among the followers and has equal opportunities for all followers to participate and contribute in the endeavor with equity as a motive. Justice in decisions ensures judiciousness by following a fair process and fair ends for the process of decision-making.

Justice perspective in decisions is usually not applied to strategic decisions in organizations which are aimed at performance. However, a sustainable leader looks toward the performance of his followers in a holistic manner, which includes the conditions for the performance of future-generation followers also.

8.8 Ethics in decisions

All decisions have an element of ethicality in it, which is a manifestation of the ethical orientation of the decision-maker. This orientation enables weighing alternatives in a balance of right or wrong, and the decision manifests what the leader stands for.

8.9 Rewarding decisions

Strategic decision-making in a business organization involves decisions on a strategy context, such as portfolio management, diversification, acquisitions, mergers, selling businesses, and the alignment of the strategy with environmental characteristics. All these are intended to reward the stakeholders, primarily the shareholder followers, of a business firm. Decisions that lead to superior performance with sustainable competitive advantages for the firm reward the shareholders with higher and sustained dividends and share price, employees with higher bonuses, society with higher taxes, suppliers with assured purchases, and consumers with higher satisfaction. All strategic decisions are aimed at benefitting one or more stakeholder categories. A sustainable leader takes decisions with a view to maximize value not only to shareholders (owners) and agents (employees) but also to the community, present and future.

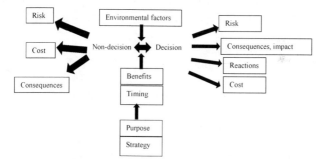

Fig. 8.4: Leader's decision balance model.

Benefits to stakeholder categories—such as suppliers, government, consumers—are benefits to the present community directly and indirectly. Even employees, if they are from a local community, it is a benefit to the present community. An organization which takes decisions on CSR and CER initiatives—such as education of children, reducing pollution, conserving natural resources, and practicing a green strategy—will benefit the future community.

8.10 Monitoring decisions

Any development typically follows the shape of an S curve, where the change starts slowly and incrementally based on a strategic decision to change and then gathers momentum and expands or explodes, eventually tapering off, reaching a plateau of stability, and dropping down. In an S curve, there are four major inflection points, as depicted in Fig. 8.7.

Jacob Thomas, PhD

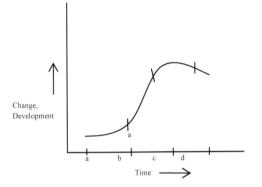

Fig. 8.5: The four major inflection points in an S curve.

The inflection points are the dramatic moments or drastic shifts or moments of truth in case of opportunity seeking in any development, change, or evolution. Each inflection point has precursors that can be estimated or forecast like the ripening of a fruit. The growth or development of a fruit is a change in size, quality (sweetness), texture and structure (chemical composition), and appearance (color change). Both the growth of the fruit from pollination and the fruit setting to final senescence—or the change from raw fruit to ripe fruit—follow an S curve.

The inflection points of the growth of a fruit can be correctly forecast from its precursor events. For the event of fruit set, they are opening of the flower and pollinators visiting the flower. The precursor events for the inflection point of rapid growth in size of the fruit are the potassium and other nutrients in the rhizosphere of the plant, greenness and robustness of the plant, and absence of pests and diseases. The inflection point of the start of ripening can be judged from the TSS (total soluble solids), fructose content, and change of color. The dropping down of the growth as an inflection point can be predicted from the change of color, texture, structure, and abscisic acid concentration in the fruit peduncle.

Similarly, a knowledgeable person of an organizational process and systems can forecast inflection points of developments in the organization accurately from the precursors of each inflection point. Identifying such precursors and taking decisions before the reach of each inflection point are the monitoring decisions which ensure that the steps planned are progressing as per the strategy toward the goals set.

Making decisions after reaching the inflection point precludes the freedom and flexibility in taking course-correcting decisions. For example, if the fruit set is judged as much higher than the carrying capacity or fruit-bearing capability of a plant, the planter needs to take a decision about thinning the fruits for optimum growth of the remaining fruits. If the ripened fruits are to be transported to a distant market, the planter needs to decide on the correct harvesting date to harvest before the ripening process advances. If the fruit is to be consumed locally or at home, the climacteric point of ripening is to be identified for maximum sweetness and thus high quality of the table fruit. Thus, monitoring decisions vary with the purpose of the initiative or course of action planned.

Another aspect of monitoring decisions apart from inflection points, timing, and purpose is deciding on the appropriate indicators, metrics, time frame, responsibilities, and use of the monitoring data.

8.11 Sustainable leadership's decision-making process

Sustainable leadership decisions have two dimensions: uncertainty and complexity. Uncertainty has three levels, as identified by Coutesy et al. (2014), and complexity has also three levels, as identified by Sargut and McCoratte (2014). Interaction of these two dimensions makes nine possible scenarios, as given in Table 8.3.

Complexity (interactions of elements of a system are continually changing)		Uncertainty (future is uncertain)		
		Known	Knowable	Residual uncertainty
	Multiplicity of elements	Current followers' expectations	Stakeholder categories of a strategic decision	Unfelt needs of followers
	Interdependence of elements	Ecosystem components	Impacts on the resource system from the decision	Present and future generation's interdependence
	Diversity (degree of heterogeneity)	Diversity of interests of stakeholders	Hopes and ambitions of followers	Interest of future generations

Jacob Thomas, PhD

A sustainable leader's uncertainty is high as he anticipates the needs of future generations and, at the same time, intends to fulfill the diverse expectations of the community. Thus, the residual uncertainty exists beyond the knowable arena after collecting all information. The technology that will be available 100 years from now, the food habits of people, and the interests of people are truly ambiguous. He also deals with the nonvocal ecosystem, which has multiple interacting and diverse elements. A sustainable leader minimizes the risk of each of his decision by identifying the multiple elements, understanding the interdependencies and the degree of heterogeneity of the elements, and developing contingency plans for the residual uncertainty. Adaptation, absorption, agility, and participation are employed by the sustainable leader to manage complexity and uncertainty.

8.11.1 Participatory decision-making

Participation of the diverse stakeholders in a decision reduces the risk when dealing with complex systems. The diverse perspectives and information that different participants bring to the decision process enables the decision to absorb the shocks and quickly adapt. Participation of both young and old in a decision reduces the residual uncertainty by bringing the generation gaps in perspectives to a great extent. Participation allows triangulation and use of diversity of thoughts, which mitigate the risks inherent in decisions influencing a diverse follower base.

8.11.2 Adaptive decision process

Adaptability is a competitive advantage (Reeves and Deimler 2014). Quick to get, understand, and act on signals from the external and internal environments will give adaptive advantage. In a highly uncertain environment, developing hypothesis of the likely consequences of the decisions and then enacting the decisions as experiments are suggested. Even though experiments are local and done mostly on a sample or as a pilot, the results and discussion about it has global value. The leadership strategy will be adaptive in a limited way to the inputs from such results of hypothesis testing. A leader who disperses the decision rights among the followers and leaders and who communicates freely among themselves increases the adaptive decision process. Every risk or uncertainty should be converted into a strategic initiative, which will enable learning more about it, thereby the information for good decision-making can be obtained.

8.12 Decision script: How adept I am at making leadership decisions?

1. I normally take decisions after weighing all options, and impacts of each option on the community and other stakeholders.

Yes	No

2. I check for the possibilities of decision biases before finalizing each decision

Yes	No

3. The guides that I use to make decisions are the mission, vision and values, than the opinion of others or information gathered.

Yes	No

4. I follow a participatory and integrative decision making model

Yes	No

5. When I take decisions, always look for the growth of others and the organization, resulting from the decision.

Yes	No

6. I foresee the risks, especially trust eroding risks, while taking strategic decisions

Yes	No

7. I do not take decisions which are clearly in the domain of others to take, but only remind them with adequate information to take their own decisions.

Yes	No

Jacob Thomas, PhD

8. I always try to take decisions much before the critical juncture when a decision is done.

Yes	No

9. I enjoy taking decisions in ambiguous and uncertain situations.

Yes	No

10. I believe that making a decision is better than not taking a decision.

Yes	No

Leading for Impact

Are leaders doing it for themselves?

Sustainable leaders are not there in the arena of leadership for self-flagellation but for making a difference in themselves and in other's lives, generating improvements, and making followers strive toward excellence.

9.1 Types of leadership impacts

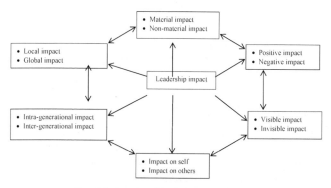

Fig. 9.1: Leadership impact polygon.

A highly ambitious and sustainability-oriented leader strives for several impacts, as depicted in Fig. 9.1. The first step is to establish an emotional connection with the followers. Emotional connection can be established if the leader demonstrates determination, trustworthiness, and faith in the desirability of the destination, as depicted in Fig. 4.1. Followers have their own psychological and emotional needs which are expected to be satisfied by following the leader. If the leader satisfies these emotional and psychological needs of followers, emotional impact is higher, which paves the way to achieve physical impacts in the form of organizational outcomes.

The hierarchy of sustainable leadership's impacts is depicted in Fig. 9.2. Physical impacts are the measurable results or objectively verifiable indicators of performance or milestones in a PERT chart. Since long-term success is a succession of small achievements and improvements, celebrating a few small achievements is likely to lead to a culture change of organizational routines and how things are done.

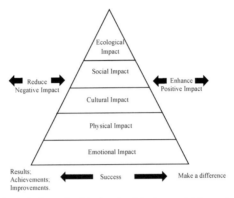

Fig. 9.2: Sustainable leadership impact hierarchy.

When the organizational culture is impacted, a stable pattern toward excellence sets in if the balance of impacts is positive, which in turn potentially develops a community of practice. Sustainable leadership gives significant benefits to the community marked by high levels of trust and faith in the intentions of the leader. When society is considered as a primary stakeholder, the ecological impact upon major commons that are shared by the community, such as air, water, forests, landscape, biodiversity, good climate, etc. becomes important for the leader.

For every leadership decision and action, there are both positive and negative impacts for some vocal or nonvocal stakeholders. To make a positive difference and have sustainable results, the leader should not only proactively anticipate the impacts through an impact assessment of each of the decision but also choose those actions that enhance positive impacts and minimize negative impacts. The success of sustainable leadership in terms of impact is getting the expected results, thereby making a difference in the lives of the followers and the wider community of today and those yet to be born.

9.2 Leadership impact fit

The leadership impact is assessed in terms of its significance on the growth of the leader and the followers. There are two types of followers: those who are directly involved under the sphere of influence of the leader and those who are outside the direct sphere of influence but within a sphere of impact. The impacts that positively affect the quality of life come from three levers: structure, environment, and value. The structure is defined as the intrapersonal and interpersonal relationships between the leader and the follower and among the followers themselves. The impact fit is conceptually depicted in Fig. 9.3.

	Self (shaping)	Sphere of influence	Sphere of impact
Structure (intrapersonal, interpersonal)	• trust • commitment • faith • interdependence	Organization structures	External networks, self-help groups, social media groups
Environment (social, economic, ecological)	• personality traits • leadership styles	Prosocial, eco-friendly inclusive orientation and values	• consistency of impact • monitoring, mitigation measures • internalization of all externalities • minimization of negative impacts
Value (economic, ecological, social value)	• cognitive competence • affective competence • technical competence	• cooperate • perform roles	• providing feedback • participate in programs

Fig. 9.3: Sustainable leadership's impact fit map.

Intrapersonal relationship is the relation one has with oneself, which is the domain of the mind and different levels of consciousness. There is a structure to one's intrapersonal relations, which are the domains of thought, imagination, dream, self-concepts, self-confidence, aspirations, ambitions, passions. These are all shaped by interpersonal processes, mostly in interaction with the environment and all of which add value to the self and others. Interpersonal relations in the case of a leader is a relational aspect with the people in the circle of influence. The self is thus social and contextual (Tice and Baumeister 2001). A relational self of the leader is developed when the self becomes defined, at least in part, in terms of interpersonal relationships (Arraiga and Agnus 2001; Anderson and Chan 2002).

Social identity theory (Tajfel and Turner 1986), interdependence theory (Rusbult et al. 2001), attachment theory (Simpson and Rholes 1998; Fraley 2002), and self-discrepancy theory (Shah 2003) postulate how highly interdependent people, as in a leader–follower ecosystem, develop sets of knowledge about each other as well as cognitive, affective, and behavioral structures unique to their relationships.

A sustainable leader crafts a befitting organization structure for the performance of the roles of the followers in the circle of influence, who are employees or staff or alliance partners mostly. The structure enables the expression of leadership in order to create an impact in the circle of impact. Henry Mintzberg (1989) suggested entrepreneurial, machine, diversified, professional, innovative, missionary, and political organization structures. The people in the circle of impact are often the receivers of the consequences of leadership decisions with less voice and choices to influence the leader directly except through campaigns, protests, boycotts, and noncooperation measures. Social media has opened technical opportunities to develop structures for the people in the circle of impact as extended networks or social media group.

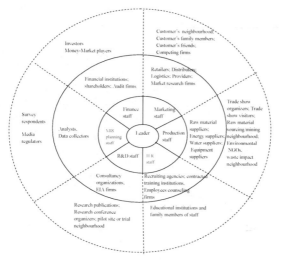

Fig. 9.4: Sustainable leadership impact sphere

The impacts in the environmental domain also needs alignment of the leader's self and his circle of influence and impact with the particular socioeconomic ecosystems in which the leadership is enacted. If the leader's personality traits and leadership styles are not a good fit for a particular social or economic system, there will be suboptimal impact. The sphere of influence of a leader within appropriate organizational structures performing with collective orientation and values are prosocial, eco-friendly, and economically inclusive. People in the sphere of impact are the constituencies, customer segments, etc. (as depicted in Fig. 9.4).

The leader of a business firm has as his primary circle of influence the staff or employees who constitute the organization and as his secondary circle of influences those who are outside the traditional boundary structure but who facilitate the performance of the activities of the staff in the primary circle of influence. The sphere of impact has a variety of parties who are impacted by the decisions and actions of the leader through the organizational members in the circle of influence.

The sphere of impact has both the current generation and future generation at the local, regional, and global levels who expect more of positive impacts from the actions of a sustainable leader by internalizing the externalities and regular impact monitoring.

Jacob Thomas, PhD

9.3 Define results that make impact on profit, people, planet, and person (self)

The results of leadership make impacts on profit, people, planet, and the person of the leader himself. Results are value creation for the self of the leader, circle of influence, and the sphere of impact through a set of best-fit actions, as depicted in the last row of Fig. 9.2. The intention forms the backdrop for defining the results as usually there is a gap between the intention and impact, as depicted in Fig. 9.5.

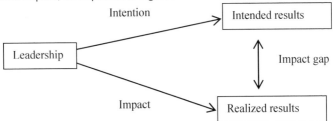

Fig. 9.5: Leadership intention-impact gap analysis

The results are defined by a sustainable leader to reduce the impact gap in the following action framework:

- defining the intention in the minds of all followers as a vision to reach or a mission to follow
- transforming their worldview and expanding the capacity of followers to internalize the mission or larger purpose
- creating structures for the circle of influence and sphere of impact to engage everyone with the mission
- generating challenge and excitement by defining the milestones (targets) and large signposts (strategic objectives) till the destination.
- preparing the hurdle map and resolving the blockers
- practicing flexible leadership styles at different phases of the path and for different groups of followers
- monitoring the degree of negative impacts and responding rapidly to restore faith
- measuring the well-being and experience of the followers periodically

- showing the differences from the baseline situation to create positive emotions and to sustain trust in the leader.

In a business organizational setting, individual-, organizational-, and societal-level outcomes are defined a priori by organizational leaders.

9.4 Expedient way to results

The expedient way is the easy way to achieve results without losing time and other resources and without diluting the faith and belief of the followers in the leadership. The second chapter of Lotus Sutra of Buddhism's Tiantai (538–597) is titled 'Expedient Means' and describes three types of expedient means:

- The teachings of the leader are adapted in accordance with people's capacities.
- Leader's mission and vision is the gateway that can lead one.
- The secret to the well-being of each is present inside everyone, which is a wonderful jewel sewn in the body, but most people are unaware of it.

Adapting the expedient means to organizational leadership— this teaching can be compared to the strategy in accordance with the capacity of the followers. The leader in the second type of means creates opportunities through foresight and insight. The third means can be sharpening the capabilities of people by leveraging the unique strengths that are already present in each person for excellence by integrating the strengths of all in strategic partnerships.

9.5 Define methodology

Having a method even in madness generates results than having madness in methods. There is 'one best way' to reach the results, which is to be identified considering the sustainable leadership impact hierarchy given in Fig. 9.2. 'One best way' to lead and manage had been the teachings of the founding fathers of scientific management, such as Taylor, Fayol, and Likert. Later, it was realized that there is no one best way of leadership for results fitting all situations and times.

Methodology means a specific sequence of actions, leadership traits, and skills that produce the intended results (Tongy 1996). The sequence of goal-achieving actions is defined by a sustainable leader, considering the perspectives of internal causation, abundance, order out of chaos, wholeness, probability, and continuous process in the place of the industrial-era mindset of external causation, scarcity, order into chaos, separate parts, predictability, and discrete events.

9.6 Hurdle mapping

The destination of the leadership journey that was chosen through the leadership destination tripod in Fig. 4.1 is neither a straight course nor hurdle-free. Just as there are milestones to identify and mark progress in the path toward the destination, in

Insight Box 9.1

Outcome indicators:
- *individual outcome*
- *organizational outcome*
- *community outcome*
- *project/program outcome*
- *systematic outcome*
- *policy outcome*
- *learning outcome.*

a milestone chart or PERT chart or CPM chart, the hurdles and obstacles on the course are identified and marked in a leadership hurdle map. Unlike the hurdles in a 100-meter hurdle race, the hurdles are neither of uniform height nor at a uniform distance. Worse still, the hurdles may not be visible and can be felt only on touching them. This characteristic makes the leadership journey different from a steeple chase, where the obstacles (such as fences, fires hedges, and ditches) are known to exist en route. This is not to say that all hurdles are invisible and unknowable; some hurdles, which are normally called risks, are knowable and hence anticipated and addressed.

A leadership hurdle map (Fig. 9.5) follows in part the principle of a PERT chart in time and space but has the additional features of an alternative plan, vigilance intelligence, stakeholder interest map, and emergency toolkit.

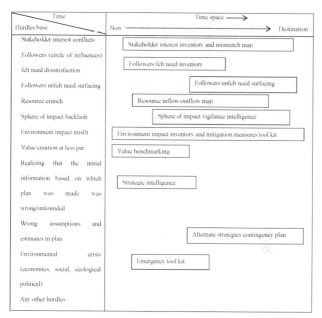

Fig. 9.6: Leadership hurdle map

9.7 Time frames: Short-, medium-, long-term results

The impacts of sustainable leadership are not only in the short term by satisfying the needs of the current followers, but the long term needs of the community are of equal importance. Creating short-term impacts is necessary to satisfy the current followers' needs lest the leader will not be trusted. A sustainable leader therefore identifies opportunities to make short-term impacts with more emphasis on individual-level, project-level, and policy-level outcomes for which expedient means to results are resorted to.

9.7.1 Leadership impact index (LII)

The potential for impact from leadership can be predicted by LII (Fig. 9.7), which considers the hurdles in the implementation of a proposed leadership strategy and the opportunities for action estimated for their impacts at individual, collective, and community levels.

High hurdles	Leadership action focus								
	Individual level (self + circle of influence)			Organization/ group level (team + larger organization)			Community level (social + economic + ecological)		
	Self	Primary circle	Secondary circle	Upper	Middle	Lower	Social	Economic	Ecological
	3	2	3	2	3	4	2	4	4
High opportunities (space for action)	2	4	3	3	2	1	3	3	5

Fig. 9.7: Leadership impact index(LII)

Give a number from 1 to 5 based on self-assessment, with 1 as less possible and 5 as the most probable, and rate where you place the leadership action in influencing the outcome intended despite the hurdles.

The leadership hurdle map will give some insight about the bases of hurdles and the appropriate time when they can strike. Only high hurdles are considered for their potential to block the leader in the march ahead while tapping the high opportunities as spaces for action. There are spaces for action at the self (shaping self) and others at individual level. Out of 90 points, if a leader gets more than 50 LII units, the leadership impact will be substantial.

9.7.2 Strategies for higher and earlier impact

The impact of leadership can be high or low and easy or difficult depends on the availability of spaces and arena for leadership action, along with the competence of the leader in addressing the hurdles in the journey toward the vision. Mapping of the extent of opportunities for leadership action and the degree of hurdles gives a four action framework as depicted in Fig 9.8. This framework will be helpful in attuning the leadership strategy for the desired impact.

| | Hurdles identified blocking leadership action | |
	Low	High
Low Opportunities identified for leadership action	Expedient means to sustain the circle of influence	Postpone action or reframe issues
High	Harvest short-term results by tapping the opportunities	Plan for long-term impact by removing the hurdles

Fig. 9.8: Four action leadership strategy framework

When the leader finds that, even though the opportunities for action are very high the hurdles are likely to hamper the achievement of results, he should re-design his leadership strategy imagining on a methodology to remove the hurdles.

9.8 Measuring results, the indicators of progress

The shifts or changes that are likely to occur as a result of the implementation of the sustainable leadership strategy are measured through objectively verifiable indicators that are causatively linked to the strategy. There may be many shifts occurring that are not caused by the leadership and points to the need of reliability, validity, and accuracy in the measures selected. Some measures of sustainable leadership impacts are:

- shifts in collective identity and action while creating space and safety for people to operate outside their current thinking habits
- shifts in engagement among followers
- shifts in the performance metrics used
- shifts in institutions and policies, resulting from changed rules

Jacob Thomas, PhD

- shifts in framing the issues, resulting from shifts in beliefs, norms, and practices. More of thematic and strategic framing of issues than episodic and issue framing.
- shifts in natural capital as a result of the leadership strategy
- shifts in social capital and human capital.
- shifts in ecological intelligence among followers.

Embedding assessment tools in all leadership objectives, in all the elements of the leadership objectives, in all the elements of the leadership impact polygon, and in the elements of the leadership impact hierarchy similar to a radio tracer in a physiological system or a dashboard or tachograph in a motor vehicle enables measurements of progress objectively by the actors themselves.

The genuine progress indicator (GPI) given in Table 9.1 is a single framework of twenty-six indicators of critical economic, environmental, and social factors, giving a balanced picture of progress and enabling everyone to understand the true impacts of the actions toward the destination of a sustainable economy. GPI is an alternative to GDP, evolved from the Index of sustainable Economic Welfare (ISEW) proposed by Daly and Cobb (1989).

Table 9.1 GPI being used by GRI

Economic indicators	Environmental indicators	Social indicators
Personal consumption expansion	Cost of water pollution	Value of housework, parenting
Income inequality	Cost of air pollution	Cost of family changes
Adjusted personal consumption	Cost of voice pollution	Cost of crimes
Cost of consumer durables	Loss of wetlands	Cost of household pollution
Value of consumer durables	Loss of farmland	Value of volunteer work
Cost of underemployment	Loss of primary forests	Loss of leisure time
Net capital investment	CO_2 emission damage	Value of higher education
	Cost of ozone depletion	Value of highways and streets
	Depletion of nonrenewable resources	Cost of commuting
		Cost of automobile accidents

9.9 Implementation with improvement

Impact is a result of the implementation of change or development or improvement programs and projects. If nothing is implemented, there is still impact of not implementing a program which could have been implemented. Some leadership actions are aimed at not implementing a project, such as the Narmada Sarovar project objected to by Medha Patkar and her followers. However, human tendency is to implement projects rather than to not implement as any implementation has economic and social benefits in terms of at least consumption and employment. Should a program be implemented if there is going to be substantial improvements in the economic and social sectors but substantial degradation in the environmental aspects? The concept of implementation with improvement addresses this decision dilemma by quantifying the net improvements through indicators similar to a measure such as GPI.

9.9.1 System improvements required for leadership impact

There are system improvements required for leadership impact. They include the following:

- For transparent and data-based decision-making, data systems that collect, collate, tabulate, analyze reliable and valid data is to be developed.
- The 'next steps' are planning systems in a bottom–up method, which incorporates the needs and capabilities of people at all levels.
- Feedback and suggestion collection systems at all levels, groups, and milestones should be part of the communication protocol.
- An impact assessment system in a proactive manner for each decision should be part of the decision support systems.
- There should be a process innovation system to change policies in an adaptive manner and to achieve multiple fit, as depicted in Fig. 9.2.

Jacob Thomas, PhD

9.9.2 Positive-to-negative ratio (PNR)

Psychologist John Gottman has predicted with 94 percent accuracy that married people whose positive-to-negative interaction ratios are above 5:1 in a fifteen-minute interaction session are likely to stay together. A PNR of 3:1 is identified as optimum for better performance in an organizational setting from a study by Barbara Fredrickson and Marcial Losada with an upper limit of 13:1, beyond which the productivity worsens.

Sustainable leaders can create positive emotions among their followers in each episode of interaction, which are likely to have a ripple effect. When the leader genuinely praises good work, shows care, and empathetically deals with each person, there is a chance of improving the PNR, thereby energizing the teams and the whole organization of followers as energy moves fast through the follower networks. While high PNR improves the morale or esprit de corps within the followers, it improves the engagement of each one with the leadership vision. Sustainable leaders thus invest in such interaction opportunities, which improve impact.

9.10 Leadership impact script

1. Number of leadership hurdles identified:

4	8	12

2. Number of opportunities for leadership action identified:

4	8	12

3. Number of emotional impact levers identified

2	4	6

4. The extent to which you are shaped by others in a scale of 1 to 5:

1	2	3	4	5

5. The extent to which you are shaping yourself for more impacts on the indicators of progress:

1	2	3	4	5

6. The extent of value you are creating in other individuals' lives:

1	2	3	4	5

7. The number of persons you are energizing on an average day:

Less than five	five to ten	More than ten

Jacob Thomas, PhD

Leadership Audit

Saviors are remembered and revered eternally, but heroes are not.

Leadership is explained as one of the most important intangible resources (Schein 1985) that bring lasting positive changes in the lives of people in organizations or outside. Leadership is also capable of bringing negative changes as can be seen in examples of many political leaders who pollute the minds of people and business leaders who pollute and overexploit natural resource systems to satisfy their greed, self-interest, and ego. Leadership audit is a mechanism to differentiate these important aspects that impact us.

There are various types of audits—such as financial audit, performance audit, environmental audit, social audit, etc.—with different objectives and procedures. Leadership audit is a systematic, objective assessment of the leadership process to check whether the expectations of the followers are going to be realized by the leadership factor. Conventionally, leadership effectiveness audit is carried out to measure the strength and impact of leaders in different contexts but primarily to measure how effectively the leadership drives performance. The ingredients of sustainable leadership's effectiveness are given in Fig. 10.1.

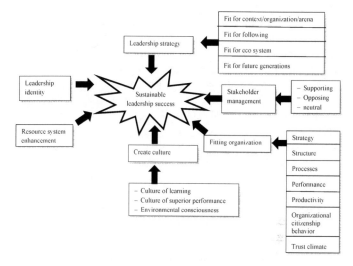

Fig. 10.1: Ingredients for sustainable leadership's effectiveness.

Leadership is viewed as a social process of exerting influence that involves two or more people (Yukl and Van Fleet 1990). In this process, there are different elements (as depicted in Fig. 10.1), and a leadership audit examines these ingredients. Some of these are predictors, some are outcomes, and a few are mediators of sustainable leadership. Every leader has followers, those who get influenced by the leader, and as the number increases, there forms an organization. The organization may be formal or informal, hierarchical or networked, real world or virtual world. There are many virtual organizations of followers transcending space, cultures, and political boundaries where the leadership strategy is more indirect yet close.

Whatever the organization type and the context of leadership, audit inspects the effectiveness of six primary parameters, such as the leadership strategy fit, leadership identity, resource system enhancement, culture creation, fitting organization and stakeholder management. The fitting organization of followers that the leader develops itself has an organization strategy, structure, process, performance, productivity orientation, trust climate, and organizational citizenship behavior.

In organizations, leaders rarely act in isolation; they work together with other leaders. Thus, the followers are exposed to the influence of not a single leader, but they observe and interact with other leaders at various levels throughout the organization. When all such leaders to whom the followers are exposed behave in a similar fashion, the leadership strategy can be assessed to be effective.

10.1 Inspecting leader effectiveness providing what is needed, managing expectations

Never lead queens if you are not a king.

House, Javidan, Hanges, and Dorfman (2002) define leadership as the 'ability of an individual to influence, motivate, and enable others to contribute toward the effectiveness and success of an organization of which they are members'. This definition has the following ingredients of leadership:

- an *ability* of an individual (leader)
- a process of *influencing*
- a process of *motivating* (inspiring)
- a process of *enabling* (developing)
- *involvement* of others as members (followers)
- *contribution* from others as a collective effort
- *effectiveness* measured against a purpose
- *success* defined by the expectations of the followers
- *organization* of followers with a befitting structure.

This definition does not include other necessary ingredients of leadership success, such as strategy formulation and implementation, a befitting culture, organizational structure, processes, sharing of benefits, and celebrating. The effectiveness of leadership is when the success defined by the followers and the leader are achieved. Thus, a clear articulation of what constitutes success is a precondition to measure or assess whether the leadership is effective.

To be effective, a fitting culture among the followers is also a necessary condition. Even though building a new culture or changing a culture within an organization is not an easy task, a sustainable leader needs to build a culture for the desired impact of sustainable leadership to be realized. The elements of culture and the change required for making the organization environment-friendly is given in Fig. 7.6, enlightening the follower culture model.

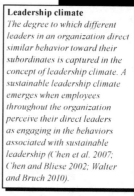

Insight Box: 10.2

Leadership climate
The degree to which different leaders in an organization direct similar behavior toward their subordinates is captured in the concept of leadership climate. A sustainable leadership climate emerges when employees throughout the organization perceive their direct leaders as engaging in the behaviors associated with sustainable leadership (Chen et al. 2007; Chen and Bliese 2002; Walter and Bruch 2010).

Leadership effectiveness can be understood as the satisfaction of the needs of the followers and realization of the vision, with the leadership strategy employed within the time frame estimated. The purpose for which the influence was applied on the followers is to be achieved for the leader to be effective; if not, the whole effort is a waste, and the leadership is a failure.

Insight Box: 10.3

Test of sustainable leadership
Most leaders' efforts and initiatives are like drawing a line on water; the moment the finger is removed, the line disappears. Often in organizations, when one leader is replaced by another leader, the previous leader's initiatives fade unless the previous leader developed leaders within and carried them to some distance towards the purpose. A sustainable leader does the following:
- *creates changes that are lasting*
- *creates changes that matters to people and to the planet*
- *creates changes that enhance the well-being of people*
- *creates changes that enhance the resource system*
- *leaves a feeling among others as a savior*
- *creates multiple leaders to carry forward the initiative*
- *articulate clearly a purpose that is significant, enduring, and beneficial to future generations.*

As the leader takes the decision to be in charge, takes the reins on the march toward the vision or a cause, others develop expectations from the leader. The sum of expectations of the followers is one of the driving or distracting forces for a leader in addition to the power of the vision or strength of the cause. If the sum of expectations of followers is fully aligned with the leadership strategy, the riding of leadership will be effective, and if the expectations are distracting, the likelihood of effectiveness is lower. Thus, a

205 Jacob Thomas, PhD

sustainable leader is the one who is able to identify the distracting expectations of the followers and realign them toward the vision or cause without any wavering. The effectiveness audit will thus be a process of leadership impact assessment in realigning followers toward the vision or the cause.

10.2 Leader efficiency: Less generating more

> *If your actions inspire others to dream more, learn more, do more and become more, you are a leader.*
> John Quincy Adams

A leader who realizes the purpose with fewer resources and shorter time and/or makes a larger impact with the same resources is considered efficient. A sustainable leader's actions can be grouped into the following seven categories:

- founding: the path, vision, mission, purpose, strategy
- influencing: for acceptance of the concept, vision, strategy
- encouraging: for adoption, change of behavior, action
- developing followers/collaborators/partners to excel, use their individual strengths
- motivating to sustain the enthusiasm, energy levels, and the activities
- inspiring to transform the methods, ways, purpose
- celebrating successes, achievements, and self-actualization.

This seven-action sustainable leadership framework (Fig. 10.2) is best represented as a cycle as the celebration of one achievement or the success of a leadership episode leads to the founding of a new level of vision or a new level of the need to pursue, and the process goes on.

Insight Box: 10.4

Dignity of life
Jean-Paul Sartre was awarded the Nobel Prize for literature in 1964, which he refused to accept. The Roads to Freedom, The Flies, Being and Nothingness, Existentialism Is a Humanism, No exit *are his major contributions to philosophy and literature.*

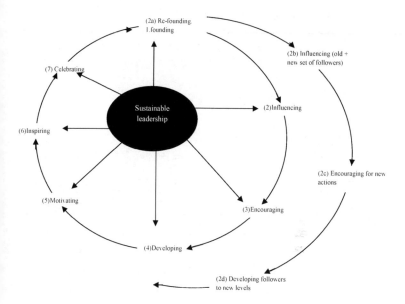

Fig. 10.2: Seven-action sustainable leadership framework.

Thus, the audit examines whether the initial less influence, less encouragement, less development, and less motivation are generating more cycles, gathering momentum in a never-ending quest for excellence and celebration of success.

10.3 Stakeholder management Vocal and non-vocal

There are three levels of stakeholders for any leadership action—primary, secondary, and tertiary stakeholders. Which one among them is the primary stakeholder depends on the perspective that guides a leader. There are ten perspectives that guide a leader, starting from profit maxim, as listed below:

- profit maxim orientation—business leaders
- people orientation—social, political leaders
- aesthetic orientation—fashion, art leaders
- spiritual orientation- religious, spiritual leaders;

Jacob Thomas, PhD

- leisure, entertainment orientation—sports, entertainment, media, cinema leaders
- profit plus people maximization—social business leader
- profit plus people plus planet maximization—sustainable business leader
- planet maximization—environmental leader
- knowledge maximization—academic leader
- people plus planet plus aesthetics—sustainable leader.

The leadership strategy can be depicted as a combination or stand-alone of any of the perspectives (as depicted in Fig. 10.3).

Effect or aspects	Enhance, maximize	No effect—degrade or ignore
Profit	√	
People	√	
Planet	√	
Knowledge		
Aesthetics		

Fig. 10.3: Ten possible perspectives that guide a leader.

A leader who considers people, planet, and aesthetics will inherently see the beauty and wonder of life in its totality. People orientation includes their well-being and quality of life not only in one generation but inclusive of children, youth, old men and women and the differently abled as each one is a life with expressed or unexpressed beauty.

> **Insight Box 10.5**
>
> **Leadership circle**
>
> Gardiner, J. J. developed the concept of leadership circle as a frame evolving from the leadership team, emphasizing cooperation and focusing on abundance and possibility. He proposes that circles remind interconnectedness promoting life, discipline, and sacrifice for a common goal. The circle enable shared governance. (Gardiner 2001, 1995).

For a business leader with a profit maximization perspective, the primary stakeholders are shareholders. The leader is bothered to anticipate the expectations of the shareholders and to meet them even at the cost of all other stakeholders' expectations.

Expectations are deeper and broader than requirements. They embody the perception of a future state of their situation when their current needs are fulfilled by the actions of the leaders. There are three components to managing expectations, which starts at the first contact.

- forming expectations
- influencing expectations both ways
- monitoring fulfillment of expectations.

The expectation ecosystem of the stakeholders of a sustainable leader has the following characteristics:

- context specificity—The present needs of the stakeholder category projects as more forceful expectations in the form of the requirements.
- dynamic stability—Expectations change, yet they're stable in an evolutionary manner.
- homeostasis
- resilience—There will be resistance to change the expectations from outside the leader–follower ecosystem.
- integrity—Expectations are rooted in some ethical values and universal virtues.
- complexity—There are multiple stakeholders for any leadership initiative with a web of expectations.
- diversity—The needs and requirements of all stakeholder categories are not likely to be similar. Even among a simple stakeholder category, the expectations of different persons are likely to be not uniform.

> **Insight Box 10.6**
>
> **Narcissistic leadership**
> *Such individuals have an unwavering desire for glory and to exhibit their competence. They possess in abundance all attributes expected from a leader: overconfidence, extraversion, dominance, high self-esteem, and superficial charm. Narcissism, however, is accompanied by a sense of entitlement and egoism, which may lead to unethical, exploitative behavior (Rosenthel and Piltinsky 2006; Maccoby 2000; Wallace and Baumeister 2002). Grandiosity, exaggerated sense of self-importance, exploitation of others, lack of empathy, sense of entitlement, self-centeredness, feeling of superiority, and vanity are characteristics of narcissistic leaders, who constantly seek social stages to show off their superiority. They crave admiration and need constant validation from the external world. They amplify their positive personality characteristics before an audience of admiring followers. Non-narcissistic sustainable leaders do not show any of the above characteristics.*

Jacob Thomas, PhD

For a sustainable leader also, the stakeholders are in three levels. The stakeholders in the unorganized and nonvocal categories (as given in section 5.8) are the primary stakeholders for the sustainable leader. The three levels of stakeholders of a sustainable leader are as given in Fig. 10.4.

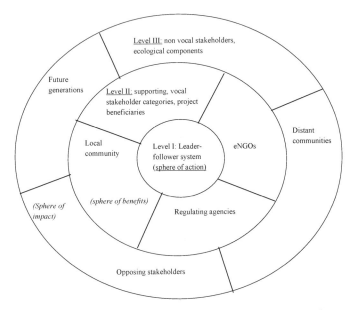

Fig. 10.4: Three levels of stakeholders for a sustainable leader.

Normal leaders see as far as the level II sphere of stakeholders, whereas sustainable leaders not only see the level III sphere but craft the leadership strategy, considering the level III as the primary stakeholder group. They see not only the individual categories of stakeholders but identify the interconnections between the stakeholder categories within each level and between level II and level III.

He or she crafts the leadership strategy to create positive impacts among the stakeholders in the sphere of impact by inspiring and interconnecting the stakeholders in the other two spheres toward a compelling vision.

10.4 Leadership identity: Stages and strengths

> *Leadership can be thought of as a capacity to define*
> *oneself to others in a way that clarifies and expands*
> *a vision of the future.*
> Edwin N. Friedman

Leadership identity is how the leader is defined by the followers relative to other leaders. A leader also has a self-identity of how he or she defines himself or herself relative to other people and other leaders (Lord and Brown 2004; Uhl Bien 2006; Hogg 2001). The way people view a leader, a leader's connections to followers and other people, and the value the leader places on other people's goals and welfare depends on identity (Brewer and Gardner 1996). Identity is a stable element in the case of a sustainable leader, and it will not shift in response to situational cues.

Identity comes from uniqueness of motives and vision that guide attention and behavior during social interactions. Leader differentiates herself as part of the leadership strategy and how well that differentiation is felt in social interactions which define the leader's identity. Sustainable leadership strategy differentiates the leader by virtue of the seven big personality traits, leadership process uniqueness, strength of the vision that is appealing to both the present and future generations, and the leadership strategy to maximize the personal uniqueness and difference from other leaders.

Who are the leaders who sustain their leadership in terms of their influence even after their bodies are no more in this world? They influence generations without any dilution in their influencing potential. Some of the winners in different walks of life

> **Insight Box 10.7**
>
> **Charismatic leadership**
> *Charisma is a leader's dimension usually associated with articulating a vision that relates followers' self-concepts to their roles, and followers internalize the values associated with the vision. Fluid speaking styles, symbolic behavior, storytelling about bold decisions, expressing confidence in followers, demonstrating boldness and competence are important behaviors exhibited by charismatic leaders. However, there is no conclusive evidence that the charisma of a leader and effectiveness are linked (Galvin, Balkundi, and Waldman 2010; Pentland 2010; Lowe et al. 1996; House 1997; Paulsen et al. 2009).*

Jacob Thomas, PhD

who made life and living more meaningful, wholesome, beautiful, and enabling are:

- ❖ Abraham Lincoln
- ❖ Alfred Nobel
- ❖ Albert Einstein
- ❖ Al Gore
- ❖ Aristotle
- ❖ Asoka
- ❖ Beethoven
- ❖ Bernard Shaw
- ❖ Bertrand Russell
- ❖ Bill Gates
- ❖ Graham Bell
- ❖ Madam Curie
- ❖ Rachael Carson
- ❖ Karl Marx
- ❖ Charles Darwin
- ❖ Dalai Lama
- ❖ Gautama Buddha
- ❖ Gregor Mendel
- ❖ Helen Keller
- ❖ Jean Paul Sartre
- ❖ Jesus Christ
- ❖ Leonardo da Vinci
- ❖ Leo Tolstoy
- ❖ Mother Teresa
- ❖ Martin Luther King Jr
- ❖ Mohandas K. Gandhi
- ❖ Confucius
- ❖ Prophet Mohammad
- ❖ Greger Mendel
- ❖ Adam Smith
- ❖ Max Weber
- ❖ Voltaire
- ❖ William Shakespeare
- ❖ René Descartes
- ❖ Salim Ali
- ❖ Sergei Bubka
- ❖ Socrates
- ❖ Vangai Mathai
- ❖ Nelson Mandela

The list is not exclusive. There are many at the global and the regional level that passed on strong messages through their way of living to succeeding generations. What are common to them? They all lived by example or gave lasting concepts or frameworks that enhances life and living. Each of them influences positively millions through their concepts, inventions, lives, brilliance, products, or principles globally and cross-culturally.

10.5 Strategy fit audit: fit for context, fit for people, fit for nature, fit for the future

A sustainable leader takes people to a pristine nature with the vision of harmonious coexistence of people, respecting the interdependencies among people and the resource system. A four-way leadership strategy fit assures the effectiveness of sustainable leadership. The leadership strategy should be aligned (Fig. 10.4) with the context (chapter 5), people, nature (ecological environment), and future. The leadership strategy should also lead to flourishing development or enhancement of the context (growth of the organization), people development, natural resource enhancement, and a flourishing future generation who should be thankful to the leaders who preserved or nurtured a good world for them. The leadership strategy should not leave any negative effect or impact in the organization, people, nature, and future generations. If in any of the twelve boxes in Fig. 10.5 is a no, then the sustainable leadership strategy needs a relook.

	Aligned	Flourishing	No negative effect No negative impact
Context	√	√	√
People	√	√	√
Nature	√	√	√
Future	√	√	√

Fig. 10.5: Four-way leadership strategy matrix.

The strategy fit of the leadership is audited for the congruence of the following sub-elements of the four factors with the leader's competence, aspirations, ambitions, values, and the organization/sector in which he or she is involved.

Context: vision and mission (of the organization or the region or community)
organizational strategy
communication systems
growth stage of the organization

People: stage of empowerment of people
emotional and social intelligence of people
management systems
relational and collective similarity in motives, values, and goals

Nature: ecological footprint of the organization
ecological footprint of the country
nature of materials used in the products
nature of waste generated from the products during use and at the end of life

Jacob Thomas, PhD

Future: the nature of the need, the firm satisfies in society;
degree of valence of the need;
scope for substitution of the organization and/or its
products, services

The four-way leadership fit is pictorially represented in Fig.
10.6.

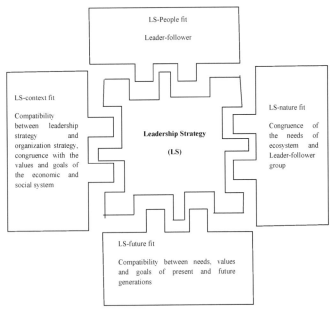

Fig. 10.6: Four-way sustainable leadership strategy fit.

Person–person fit or misfit and personal work–environment
fit (P–E fit) improves leader–follower relationship quality, cohesive
interactions, compatible motivations, and shared outlooks (Kristof
1996; Kristof-Brown, Zimmerman, and Johnson 2005; Chang and
Johnson 2010). The four-way fit of sustainable leadership strategy
(as depicted in Fig. 10.6) fulfills the expectations of all relevant
stakeholders, including future generations and ecosystems, in the
vision and actions of the leader–follower group. An investigation
of a sustainable leadership strategy's effectiveness views this fit
in four directions as an essential feature of sustainable leadership.

10.6 Are there leadership skills?

The enlightened leader is equipped to create a world that existed in beautiful dreams.

Leadership in business organizations exist at many levels in many forms and in many styles. There is leadership at team level, unit level, functional level, and enterprise level. There are leadership in cross-functional teams, inter-organizational level (post-merger), and business ecosystem level (industry association). Every leader at every level oversees a group of people of diverse nature.

- Are such leaders at different levels differentiated by their skills?
- Are the leadership skills required at different levels, transferable?
- Does a person leading at the unit level fully acquire the skills at the enterprise level?
- Is there a leadership profession with a body of knowledge?

The skills required for a potential sustainable leader compared with other levels and types of leadership are given in Table 10.1.

Table 10.1 The essential skills of a sustainable leader

From leader	To sustainable leader	How does the sustainable leader act?
Managing/ governing	Institution building	Identifying all stakeholders and their interests and get cooperation
Focusing on details	Whole conceiving	Harmonizing with the external environment
Deciding	Judging	Every decision arena having multiple aspects for fair judgment
Performing	Entrepreneurial skills	Creative, novel ways
Being professional	Perspectives	Larger view on events and interests of different people
Analyzing	Synthesizing	Sum of different parts in synergistic array

Jacob Thomas, PhD

Directing	Commanding	Carrying the entire function in one direction, knowing the strengths of every unit
Observing	Imagining	Reflecting on phenomena and insights
Action planning	Strategizing	Setting the direction and trends for lasting positive results
Negotiating	Mediating	Trading off from contra-interests of stakeholders
Goal setting	Visioning	Focusing on a future state and impact on future generations
Being a process owner	Having designer skills	Understanding interconnections between all subsystems and larger systems
Coordinating	Enabling	Enabling the followers to perform by creating the organizational leadership climate
Delegating	Partnering	Developing followers as partners and co-leaders
Communicating	Storytelling	Making the leader vulnerable and open, placing himself in a context, that has a history, hope, with full awareness of the sunk cost, and other biases, displaying emotions appropriately

Whether leaders are born or made is an age old question. Leaders are born, and every person has a seed of leadership in him or her in some specific domain or arena. Many potential leaders are at a wrong arena forever or come to the right arena very late without getting the required time to flourish and blossom. The identification of the right arena for the leadership seed to germinate and flourish early on enables any person to blossom. Unless the leadership seed is fully grown to blossom, a leader won't be visible.

Leadership audit is self-reflection combined with an external counsel to identify the variety or type of leadership seed inherently existing and then identifying the nourishments needed for enablement in the right arena.

10.7 Resource enhancement, not resource depletion or degradation

As per the model of sustainable leadership given in Fig. 1.3, the leader draws on the resource units from the resource system to meet the needs of the followers in such a way that the resource system is not depleted or degraded in any way. The resource systems valuable to sustain human life and well-being are:

> **Insight Box: 10.8**
>
> **Leader–member exchange (LMX) theory**
>
> *LMX theory states that leaders form relationships of differing quality with their followers (Graen et al. 1982). The exchange relationships can occur between leaders and followers within a dyad or within multiple dyads in organizations. LMX is a social exchange of psychological benefits between leaders and followers, which are characterized as being low or high quality based on the extent of mutual trust, respect, liking, and obligation between the two parties (Graen and Uhl-Bien 1995). The quality of these exchanges determines leadership outcomes among followers (Ilies, Nahrgang, and Morgeson 2007; Gerstner and Day 1997). Follower competence and personality also affect LMX quality apart from the traits of leaders.*

- space with unpolluted air
- ecosystem services
- human resources: health, skills, community feeling, pride
- biodiversity: use and nonuse values
- metallic and nonmetallic minerals
- climate: communities are adapted to specific climate parameters
- landscape
- water resources versus polluted water
- fertile soil versus eroded soil
- traditional knowledge and cultural resources.
- Literature and history
- Myths and ideologies.

A sustainable leader is, first of all, aware of the different resource systems and the value of them in relation to quality of life. For example, polluted air and water diminishes the health of people and eroded soil diminishes the capability to produce food for the people, thereby reducing the carrying capacity.

Jacob Thomas, PhD

10.7.1 Carrying capacity

Every resource system has an optimum carrying capacity of people, projects, and quality of life. A leadership strategy also has an optimum carrying capacity of followers. A best-fit leadership strategy is when the carrying capacity of the leadership strategy is in consonance with the carrying capacity of the resource system from which the resource units are intended to be drawn for the actions.

10.7.2 Biodiversity values

The life aspects of earth distributed in different life forms at micro to macro levels are interlinked and interdependent in complex ways. The total life energy in earth is the sum total of this life, and hence, each life has a value, whether a visible life form or an invisible life form. For example, a small bacterium that lives in the mouth of an animal or leaf of a plant or rhizosphere in the earth has some specific role or job to do in the larger scheme of life.

10.7.3 Ecosystem services

Each ecosystem performs several vital functions that sustain life directly or indirectly. For example, pollination by wind, water, insects, birds, and rains is an essential service for food production. Filtering of storm water as a sponge by wetlands to aid drainage and purification of the water is a service that gives fresh water. Interferences by human actions on the ecosystem disrupt or block some of these essential services on earth, the effects of which will become apparent only after years.

10.8 Leadership degradation versus upgrade

> *What you get by achieving your goals is not as important as what you become by achieving your goals.*
> *Thoreau*

'Once a leader, always a leader' is not valid in all situations except in hereditary positions in clans and primitive monarchies.

The leadership degrades when the external environment changes and when the leader is unable to anticipate the early signals of change and all the interconnections of the change happening. The changes may overwhelm the leader.

Leadership upgrade occurs when the leader–follower need congruence is shifted with the changing external environmental conditions and/or changing internal psychological conditions without shifting the purpose. The social, political, legal, economic, and technological external environmental changes are likely to make yesterday's insights irrelevant and invalid. The resulting alteration in the situation calls for a redefinition of the why, what, how, when, where and the leader–follower congruence on these. The leadership upgrade may involve a change of who, change of how, change of what, and change of where at both ends of the leader–follower continuum. Sustainable leadership includes a leadership succession wherein the who leads may change toward better-fitting who or a better follower base by attracting new followers to achieve the purpose. Drawing on the LMX theory, leadership can be upgraded by improving the exchange quality through more agreeableness, compassion, honesty, and humility.

Thus, there may be a continuum of leaders in a sustainable leadership with a few shining stars close by and many distant stars to light up the way forward, some of whom may be in future generations. The shining stars may be at any point in the continuum. This is the relevance and importance of developing followers through dialogue and partnership process. Fig. 10.7 illustrates the progression of leaders.

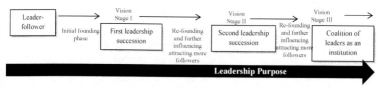

Fig. 10.7: Upgrading leadership process map.

Martin Luther King Jr is not the first leader who rallied blacks toward freedom, fraternity, and equity, but he shone more than the others in the constellation of many leaders with the same purpose.

10.9 Interposition to recharge

> *Climb to the shoulder of giants to see farther than*
> *others.*
> *adapted from Isaac Newton*

The result of leadership actions can have two types of consequences.

- intended consequences—results as expected
- unintended consequence—results not expected

The new observations give new insights to reframe the influence strategy to get more of intended consequences. With the constant flux in the external environment, new inputs come to the knowledge of both the follower and the leader, which are interpositioned in the leadership strategy. Every instability in the instability–adaptation–stability (IAS) cycle provides widows of opportunities when inspected closely. If such opportunities are interpositioned in the leadership strategy, both the leader and the followers get recharged through the renewed hope that the reframed strategy provides.

Both the leader and her followers need frequent recharging so that the leadership is sustained. The purpose for which the people who are influenced are following a leader cannot be achieved without the leadership sustaining it. Recharging is done in several ways by the leader.

1. actively seeking feedback; positive feedback energizes
2. identifying small wins from closer inspections
3. taking time off for reflection as a pause in the journey forward, which will give new perspectives
4. getting new followers with new skills and knowledge
5. celebrations at milestones.

The followers get recharged from the energy emanating from the leader.

10.10 Best-leader script: Am I considered the best leader?

1. Are my intentions authentic and contestable?

Yes	No

2. Am I able to accept responsibility for all the actions of my followers?

Yes	No

3. Do I anticipate opposition from any stakeholder group for my actions, and does the strategy have an inbuilt mechanism to make opposing stakeholders be included?

Yes	No

4. Are my hopes, aspirations, and desires congruent with those of my followers?

Yes	No

5. Do I share the worries, concerns, and fears of my followers?

Yes	No

6. Does my leadership strategy change the followers' thoughts, attitudes, knowledge, expectations, and actions?

Yes	No

7. Is my strategy capable of overcoming the barriers foreseen to bring about the change in (f)?

Yes	No

8. Am I aware of the aspects that I don't know but should know?

Yes	No

Jacob Thomas, PhD

9. Does my leadership strategy have the potential to earn the attention, loyalty, trust, and confidence of future generations?

Yes	No

10. Am I focusing on what matters most to my followers, and will my followers' well-being be enhanced together with enhancing the resource system?

Yes	No

Leading with Wonder

11

Universe has an algorithm, which God only knows.

Each follower or potential follower evokes wonder with respect to his natural qualities, relationships with others, and the perspectives he carries in the head. Such diversity is both a challenge and a source of possibilities in drawing strengths in the march toward the destination. An analysis of the different perspectives a follower can carry in one among the aspects of today's way of living is the views on man–nature relationships. For example, the ecological evolutionary states of man–nature relationships in the history of mankind (Thomas 2014) is a source of diverse views on development, resources, end state of a vision, manner of living, etc., such as the following:

- pristine nature
- mysterious nature
- transparent nature
- romantic nature
- resourceful nature
- sustainable nature
- transcendental nature.

Before the Industrial Revolution, nature was pristine in most parts of the world. The Industrial Revolution started the exploitation of nature, which became a worse situation in today's competitive economy, leading to the current views about sustainable nature. Just as nature is mysterious, romantic, resourceful at the macro level, a follower, being a part of the same nature at the micro level, embodies the same man-to-man or man-to-woman or woman-to-woman relationship. The concept of leading with wonder emanates from these premises.

11.1 Leadership as an expedition

> *Management is efficiency in climbing the ladder of*
> *success. Leadership determines whether the ladder*
> *is leaning against the right wall.*
> Stephen Covey

A leader who embraces a cause or a dream or a vision takes determined steps toward the vision. Each step gives him new learning, new meaning, new followers as new people to interact and share with, and new issues of these new followers to care about, and his next step is again a new step. It is like an expedition where each step gives new sights and new experiences. A sustainable leader sees the plants, birds, flowers, pollinators, and the interconnection between them and his own connection with them. This leadership is a process of realization of the self as a part of the world around, and he guides the followers to the same effects.

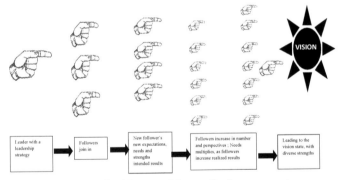

Fig. 11.1: Leadership expedition gathering momentum.

The new expectations, perspectives, and interests that the new followers bring before the leader at each step provides new experiences and insights to the leader, and the influence strategy needs to be adapted to accommodate all perspectives and most of the new expectations. Thus, the entire process is like a journey through unknown territory fraught with unanticipated challenges. Thus, to move forward, the leader needs the ability to wonder at each step and welcome things as it, is with curiosity.

Since leadership is a process of discovery, the person who leads sets the followers up a path. A leader who leads with wonder does not put any boundaries or restraints on the followers. The leader frees up the psychological, relational, and physical resources of the multitude of persons in a less uncertain and less risky setting.

Furv and Dyer (2014) propose three kinds of value from conducting business experiments, which are explorations into the unknown.

- insight value: insights into the unknown
- option value: the option to use some learning in some way
- strategic value: value which is of use on the long term and at a higher relational level.

11.2 Leadership emotions (joy of leading, anxiety of the led, anger) and emotional health

When leadership is taken as an expedition, every step offers causes of joy, the joy that a child gets in his first steps and in every new experience. Since the environment around is complex and each step offers diverse experiences, the followers feel anxious about the utility or futility of the next steps unless the leader is able to carry every follower and explains fully and clearly the next step. However, the next steps are generally not very clear even to the leader in terms of the challenges in store, which gives rise to anxiety of the led, and sometimes anxiety turns to anger. A sustainable leader who carries the followers through a difficult process thus has to look after the emotional health of the followers.

There are primary emotions and derived secondary and tertiary emotions. Primary emotions are joy, anger, love, surprise, sadness, and fear (according to Shaver et al. 2001). Jack et al. (2014) came up with four basic emotions: anger, fear, happiness, and sadness. Identifying the emotional state of the followers while leading them is important to get the desired results as emotions have their own functional value for each person. The most simple categorization of emotions as pain and pleasure are given by Mowrer (1960).

11.3 Ecosystem wonder: Interconnectedness

> *Deciphering the algorithm of nature unravels wonders.*

A correct, full understanding of any natural ecosystem and its functioning creates awe in any thinking individual. The millions of life forms interacting in multiple ways and the interconnectedness of nature's various living and nonliving components, many of which are unknown and may even be unknowable, evokes wonder. Man's superiority leads him into these ecosystems as intruders, encroachers, appropriators, and often as destroyers that bring about changes in an otherwise resilient system. A sustainable leader undertakes the job of interfacing the interconnectedness of man to his ecosystem and to be cautious in not interfering with something which is wonderful in its original state.

> **Insight Box: 11.1**
>
> **Emotional competency of leaders:**
> *Ellie Filler and Dave Ulrich (2014) describes emotional competency as the way leaders deal with such things as ambiguity, pressure, and risk-taking. They identified six aspects of emotional competency of leaders.*
> - *ambiguity tolerance*
> - *composure*
> - *empathy*
> - *energy*
> - *humility*
> - *confidence.*
>
> *Leading with wonder involves a lot of ambiguity about every decision and situation.*

11.4 Wonder of multitudes: The abundance in everything (water, energy, materials)

The world's life units are beyond counting. The human beings are more or less counted, which is also subject to change every minute by deletions and additions. The number of plants is not counted; the number of animals is not counted even though estimates are available for a few species. The numbers of fish, bacteria, fungi, butterflies, birds, insects, etc. are in multitudes, the number unknown. When the number itself is not known, the interactions among them is beyond comprehension. The purpose of each life form is another matter of wonder. Similar to the abundance of life in diverse forms and roles in nature, the forces and resources are also in multitudes and abundance. There is plenty of energy in diverse forms, water in different forms, and minerals in abundance, which seldom get destroyed even though place and form change.

11.5 Wonder of diversity of perspectives, skills, orientation, personalities, and interests

In biology, there is a phenomenon called heterosis or hybrid vigor produced by crossbreeding of two different species, and the resulting offspring is likely to be more vigorous than either of the parents. If the same species interbreed among themselves, after a few generations, the offspring are likely to be unhealthy and unadapted, which is called inbreeding depression. The same principle applies to an organizational setting also where cross-fertilization of different perspectives, orientations, skills, and personalities is likely to produce more-adaptable and robust decisions and performance. If all the followers of a leader are yes-men and only the leader's perspective and orientation are considered while making strategic decisions, in due course, adaptability to the external environment will diminish, and the performance slacks.

The diversity of perspectives and skills available within an organization of followers is enormous if an effort is made to identify and tap them. A perspective which may be assessed as dumb when viewed against a dominant perspective also has value as every perspective is evolved for some useful purpose based on tacit knowledge rooted in a sociocultural milieu or as a solution to a specific need. Diversity of interests demonstrates the hopes and aspirations of different segments of the followers; satisfying them will enhance the quality of life of those segments. A sustainable leader understands the value of those diversities in perspectives and interests and includes them in the leadership strategy to their advantage.

11.6 Beauty of nature: How nature leads its designs

Designers craft things of beauty for appreciation by others even from ordinary things by reshaping, reconfiguring, recombining, refining, or reconstituting. Just as a dexterous sculptor brings out the beauty inherent in an irregular rock by shaping and refining it, a leader brings out the beauty inherent in each follower and his surroundings through his dexterous handling. The followers, when they join the leader in a mission, are raw, but the leader's constant chiseling makes them shapely enough to advance in the course, thereby becoming very valuable. Since beauty lies in the eyes of the beholder, a particular leader's shaping of the personalities of his followers to suit the cause or vision that he is pursuing may not look beautiful to other interest groups. The process of mentoring and induction training are precisely doing this sculpting work to bring out the skills and perspectives inherent in each person, aligning them to the particular organization's mission and values.

Nature leads its design not in uniformity and independence but in diversity and interdependence. Diversity is nature's insurance against perishing of life by one cause as the multitudes of diverse forms of life cannot be destroyed by a few causes or forces. Similarly, interdependence is nature's way of assuring cooperation and mutualism, while the food chain predation ensures that populations are maintained as per the carrying capacity of the resource system. The balance of cooperation, competition, and predation sustains the resource systems for successive generations.

The social system in which organizations are transacting also mimics nature's design to a larger extent. However, the technological advancements during the last 200 years have interfered with the beauty of nature and its design. This interference is responded with reactions from nature in the form of extreme weather events, climate change, illness, and poverty, which generated concerns for the beauty of nature, and in the ultimate analysis, nature is likely to succeed in its design at a new equilibrium. A sustainable leader understands how nature leads its designs and goes along with it rather than against it to maintain the beauty and wonder of nature to which human beings are a part whether in business organizations or other forms of social organizations.

11.7 Aesthetic leadership: Infusing beauty into leadership actions

Algorithm of leadership is a process of artistry.

Leadership is a beautiful and a wonderful experience for the leader and his followers if the leader goes along with the flow and rhythm of nature, respecting diversity, considering the process as an expedition, and nurturing interdependence among followers.

There are leaders who specifically dwell in aesthetics, such as fashion designers, artists, writers, architects, and photographers. They derive joy from transacting in aesthetics by providing feelings and experiences of thrill, beauty, awe, wonder, admiration, design, magnificence, exhilaration, and excitement. An aesthetic leader also provides the same feelings and experiences to his followers by his leadership strategy, which should be enthusing, exhilarating, exciting, and enabling to the follower.

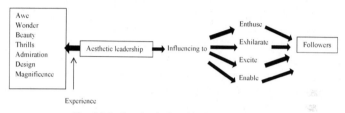

Fig. 11.2: Aesthetic leadership flow chart.

The leader excites the followers with the cause chosen and the vision crafted, which are communicated to followers as a beautiful experience of being there. The steps designed by the leader as actions to be taken will exhilarate the followers. The leader also enables by shaping each follower through individualized attention and by example in taking action or the steps planned to reach the vision state. The influence strategy by its sheer beauty and balance will enthuse the followers to follow the leader.

11.8 Ecological debit and credit

Since leading with wonder is an exploration, physical resources will be used along the way, and all physical resources come from nature. Since the perspectives of each person in the entourage are likely to be different, resource use, misuse, conservation, and wastage are at differential rates. What a person draws from nature directly or indirectly for his sustenance and for meeting all other needs are the ecological debit. Every individual takes in clean air and gives out air with more CO_2. This CO_2 is taken in by green leaves to produce food, which comes back to the human beings directly or indirectly. Everyone takes in good water and gives out urine and perspiration to the environment which is enriching for some plants. Thus, the drawing for sustenance (meeting basic physiological needs) simultaneously creates ecological debit and credit more or less in a balanced manner.

When iron ore is mined from one place, transported to a steel plant at another place, and converted as a machine part and sold in another region, the area which lost the iron ore and the people who should have been its stewards will become debtors. There is a need for recouping into the resource system. There will be an area at some future date where the iron is dumped when the machine's useful life is over unless it is recycled for further use. The waste dumps or polluted regions by the running of the machine also become debit areas as the productive capacity of the area gets diminished from waste and pollution.

The future generations, which also have an equal claim to the nature's resources, are deprived of the resource system if the current generation overdraws away resource or diminishes the quality of any resource. Thus, such an overdrawing or polluting person or group of persons will become an ecological creditor.

From a simultaneous ecological debit–credit balance in the subsistence economy to a region-to-region imbalance in ecological debit and credit in the market economy is the result of leadership consisting of appropriators and exploiters. The overexploitation of natural resources and degradation of the environment that occurred in the last 100 years due to the competitive economy has created an imbalance in the intergenerational ecological debit and credit, which points to the imperative of sustainable leadership (as depicted in Fig. 11.3).

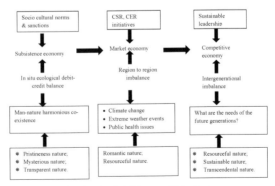

Fig. 11.3: Ecological debit–credit imbalance map.

In the subsistence economy that was prevalent in most parts of the world till the Industrial Revolution and the sociocultural norms and sanctions imposed by community or religion had been sufficient to maintain the ecological debit–credit balance. Such a state of affairs with harmonious man–nature relations left the nature pristine and relatively transparent even though mysterious. However, with the advent of market economy and horizontal diversification of economic activities considering nature as a resource system led to the present situation of region-to-region imbalance.

The buzzword 'corporate social responsibility' has come into corporate discourse as a reaction to the campaign that industrialization and capitalism are the root causes of the climate change. Thus, leadership came on both sides of the ongoing debate: a leader that uses and misuses nature for his or her benefit (anthropocentric view holders) and a leader that considers people and their vision within nature's design (ecocentric view holders).

Sustainable leadership is most likely to emerge from the anthropocentric view holders who had hitherto been using or misusing nature for its instrumental value. The compelling reasons for this shift in perspective and practice are the nature of competitive economy, where resource conservation becomes an imperative for the future of the anthropocentric organizations also. Those among such persons who immerse themselves in leadership actions that transcend the boundaries of material existence and present needs are not only leading sustainably but themselves become sustainable leaders. Sustainable leaders identify and apply the debit-credit concept on other aspects of human existence, living and inter-relationships.

11.9 Nature script: Are you experiencing the wonder and beauty of nature?

1. Have you seen a shooting star in the sky more than six times in an year?

Yes	No

2. Have you breathed in along with a breeze?

Yes	No

Jacob Thomas, PhD

3. Have you spotted at least five different types of butterflies during the past one month?

4. Could you see the magnificence and radiance of a sunrise during the last one week?

5. Have you taken a bath in the rain or river during the past six months (not sea or swimming pool or shower in a bathroom)?

6. Do you know the exact number and types of bacteria normally staying in your mouth?

7. Are you sure you have identified all the different perspectives, skills, and interests of your employees in your organization?

8. Are you an ecological creditor, and if yes, how much and when?

Yes	No

9. Which is the most frequent emotion that you experience when you are among the employees or in the workplace?

Joy	Anger	Fear	Happiness	Sadness

10. Have you walked through any pristine nature (unpolluted, unaltered) during the last one month?

Yes	No

Leadership Succession

"Succession assures success of the vision"

Leadership succession is understood normally as the development, education, election, and successful transition of each leader role in accordance with a leadership succession plan as part of the overall strategy of an organization. Sustainable leadership succession is conceived as the process of the leadership strategy evolving and becoming an ongoing process of an influence chain, transmuting the leadership vision in an ever-rolling manner toward higher levels of life connect, soul connect, and nature connect.

12.1 Influence chain: Making and distributing leadership

Just as the concept of value chain enhances the value of a product or service through a business process from its factory in-gate till it reaches the final consumer, a sustainable leader creates an influence chain as the core of his leadership strategy. This chain results in making and distributing leadership among his followers near and far so the leadership journey started never ends, continuing the influence over centuries. Fig. 12.1 gives a general framework of this influence chain.

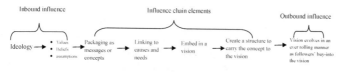

Fig. 12.1: Leadership influence chain.

The leadership influence chain has its foundation in the ideologies, beliefs, and values that shape the leader's vision and purpose. From the insights gained from the investigation and introspection processes, the leader packages the messages to his followers. The followers in turn link the messages from the leader to their own needs and causes that are dear to them. The next stage is enabling the followers to embed their self-interests in the leader's vision, which creates a powerful collective energy toward the purpose. The structure is a matrix of relationships between the leader and the followers and among the followers themselves. The structure is designed in such a way that many leaders emerge at different nodes in the network who roll the vision forward with their inventiveness and imagination in line with the ideologies and values of the founding leader.

> **Insight Box 12.1**
>
> **Rolling-ball structure**
>
> *A team of six is inducted into an organization with superior qualifications in expertise domains to implement an initiative that is linked to most of the activities of a normal organization. Should this team be given a separate identity or be integrated seamlessly with the normal organization structure? Integrating is the normal way of a hierarchical or matrix structure. Then the team's full potential will be dissipated at various locations and subsystems of the organization. If it is positioned as a separate entity, their output will be less as cooperation from the normal structure may be minimal.*
>
> *Alternatively, the team acts as a rolling ball in the larger arena of the organizational field, with units at different locations and fields acting as players. The team should be strong in expertise, resilient, flexible, and agile to absorb the shocks from different players.*

12.2 Leadership fatigue: Too much of the same thing

Unsustainable leaders create dependencies that curtail the enthusiasm of followers and do not address several cultural barriers to openness. Such leaders develop norms to restrict freedom of choice and fragment the followers to manage uncertainty and complexity. This is the legacy of the PLOC (planning, leading, organizing, and controlling) premise of the management that Henri Fayol (1842–1925) proposed through his book Administration Industrielle, which was presented in 1900, and the scientific management proposed by Frederick Winslow Taylor (1856–1915). From these foundations of management as an art and science, in which leadership science is an integral part, grew the frankness of Henry Mintzberg (1973), stating that management work is characterized by brevity, variety, and fragmentation. John

Kotter (1986) says managerial work is a kind of intuitive planning which is mostly reactive response to problems.

Conventional management theories and scientific, rational methods of leading create structures, processes, and leadership styles that restrict both the followers and the leader rather than liberate. Such self-created restrictions lead to fatigue and frustrations. The conventional strategic management process also can tell the leader where he needs to go as a continuation of where he has been going in the past. Exceptions are disruptive inventions. When leaders work in systems that are created to be leader centric, there will be too much of the same management theories applied month after month, year after year, resulting in fatigue, loss of energy, and loss of vitality.

Sustainable leadership is not based on management systems that are created as leader centric but created as nature centered, respecting the planet and its biodiversity, including the larger human needs. It is based on creativity, originality, inventiveness, intention, and imagination, which are liberating, defragmenting, synthesizing, and connecting rather than constraining. When a leader functions through imagination and inventiveness without any barriers of a structure or rules, there will be enthusiasm and energy. One leader alone cannot handle all the complexities of the nature's need—nature's needs expressed among the followers and their relationships not only with each other but also with the larger world. A true participatory leadership structure, which assures the enthusiasm of each follower to carry forward the agenda, is leadership succession wherein ownership of the strategy rests on all the followers. In such a situation, the strategy for moving forward is not viewed as a yoke having weight but as a yoke that unites all followers. Such a yoke that is viewed as a

---

Insight Box 12.2

Sir Alex Fergusson, after him!

Manchester United was nurtured well by Sir Alex Ferguson from 1986 till his retirement on 8 May 2013, with a thirteenfold increase in twenty years. It was listed at $2.3 billion at NY Stock Exchange, winning thirty-eight domestic and international titles in addition to thirteen Premier League wins. He built the club to victory.

After Alex's retirement, the new manager, David Moyes, saw the same club struggling at number 12 on the league charts, eight points behind leader Arsenal, with a series of stunning losses. It even had a 4–1 thrashing by rival Manchester City—all this within four months of retirement of Sir Alex Ferguson! Was his leadership sustainable! Why did the organization crumble immediately after his departure?

Jacob Thomas, PhD

uniting force is not felt as a burden by the follower, which results in fatigue by carrying.

Leadership fatigue, if not addressed, will lead to decisions of overstaying by doing the same thing or decision to leave the purpose. In such situations, a sustainable leader steps back to go outside of everything and view the influence chain and the leadership strategy afresh as an outsider. Leadership fatigue sets in if the influence chain has completed one cycle and effective reframing of next issues and next needs are not done to enthuse the followers sufficiently.

12.3 Leader's legacy: Continuity of initiatives, sustainability

Leadership is a process of evolving, dissolving, becoming, and leaving a legacy in time scale. Becoming a sustainable leader is an evolutionary process of adding and removing, increasing and decreasing, dividing and multiplying various attributes of the personality traits of both the leader and the followers and aspects of the leadership strategy. A sustainable leader necessarily leaves a legacy for the followers to multiply or scale up in an ongoing process, as depicted in Fig. 12.2.

People strategy	Psychological, relational, transcendental aspects of people		
	Increasing(↑)	Adding(+)	Multiplying (×)
Decreasing(↓)	?	?	?
Removing (−)	?	?	?
Dividing (÷)	?	?	?

Fig. 12.2: People strategy synergy matrix.

There are many characteristics, traits, attitudes, and perspectives that the leaders and the followers need to assay periodically which are not aligned to the sustainable leadership strategy. In order to make a perfect fit, certain elements of the psychological, relational, and transcendental aspects of the people domain are to be increased, added, or multiplied. Instead of attempting to remove or decrease any psychological or relational element, which are far more difficult to realize, overwhelming what are to be removed or decreased with positive aspects by increasing or adding or multiplying them will leave a legacy. Many leaders waste their time in removing certain negative traits of followers, which is nearly impossible to do in a sustainable way. As long as the perseverance or pressure is there, the trait will not surface, but it never goes away completely and can be overwhelmed by positive aspects through the leadership strategy.

The leadership strategy also is a process of evolving, dissolving, and becoming by decreasing, removing, or dividing some of its elements and aspects as the leader–follower characteristics evolve and when the number of followers multiplies. Certain aspects which were important in the beginning of a course are to be shed at the next stage to retain the focus on an aspect significant to that stage.

Insight Box 12.3

Ten incarnations of the leader

The ten incarnations of Lord Vishnu—Fish, Kurma, Varaha, lionman, Vamana, Parashuram, Ram, Krishna, Buddha (Balarama), and Kalki—are interpreted in different ways.

- *As the ten states of mind evolving and dissolving*
- *As the ten stages in the journey of the soul from conception to enlightenment*
- *As the ten phases in the life of a person from birth till liberation*
- *As the ten phases of the evolution of life*
- *As the ten states of nature or the cosmos*
- *As the ten styles of leadership*
- *As the ten ways life can be lived*
- *As the ten virtues of the world*
- *As a guide to find out the meaning of life in chaos*
- *As the ten measures of time as a ladder to eternity.*

The context in which each of these ten incarnations of the same leader occurs, each type of incarnation's characteristics as the likely ten steps of the same leader to become a sustainable influence, etc provide inferences of leadership succession.

12.4 Making monuments: Institute heaven on earth

Omnicom Group compiles the Best Global Brands report since the year 2011. In the year 2013, Apple replaced the thirteen-year reign of Coca-Cola as number 1, and Coca-Cola was relegated to number 3 after Google at number 2. Apple was number 2 in 2012 and number 8 in 2011. Google was number 4 in 2012. Samsung reached position number 8 on account of their adoption of a new brand strategy called

Brand Ideal focusing on social purposes. This shift in focus was based on the observation of Samsung leadership that consumers will prefer brands that are associated with improving people's lives. A company changes the lives of people living in the present and in the future not only with its products but with its ethos. The ascent of brands to top positions was based on how much and how far its products and ethos have changed the lives of people in the ultimate analysis.

The lives of people are touched, thrilled, or chilled by the leadership ideologies and ethics of a company. The categories of people whose lives a company impacts are the internal staff consumers of its products or services, its suppliers, its distributers, the community where it operates, the larger society where its messages are aired, and the other organizations in its business ecosystem. By touching the lives of many people toward greater happiness not only in the present but the future generations as well through its sustainability policies and values, the company/organization's leadership creates a monument, a lasting evidence of greatness.

Every person who wants to matter gets an opportunity to speak, create, organize, and get fulfillment by doing what he wants to do, create, and feel when he tries to connect with the lives of people with the focus on making their lives happier, easier, or more comfortable.

12.5 Taking care of leaders: Leadership sharing

Leadership is a relational process in as much as a strategic process requiring inventiveness and imagination. New forms of relating to followers are to be invented in accordance with the follower characteristics, the vision, and the context. Sustainable leadership is a complex, difficult process of knowing what to do and getting others to do the way the leader wants them to act so that the vision is realized without harming the resource systems. The process progresses based on several hypotheses, and the unfurling of the leadership strategy is the testing of these hypotheses. Since leadership is a voluntary action process, those who agree with the leadership strategy will get in as followers, and those who don't will get out of the followership. Management by decree or persuasions can lead to one-time success, but the forces against the decree get reinforced when the second-time leadership persuasion cycle arrives. Compulsions and persuasion will wilt the enthusiasm of the followers as it dries up the sources of motivation. Enthusiasm is gained and enhanced among the followers by sharing, caring, pairing, and daring leadership processes, which are essentially the principles of participation. The dwindling of enthusiasm among the followers is the primary reason why many robust strategies of growth or institution building wither away after some time.

Participation is a process of sharing of information, knowledge, skills, perspectives, activities, vision, and leadership. There are different levels of participation, as given in Table 12.1

Table 12.1 Levels of participation in the leadership strategy

Levels of participation	Extent of sharing, caring, pairing, and daring by the leader
Information sharing	Information about the vision, methods, and aspects of activities are shared. The leader is not daring enough to pair with the followers.
Participation by consultation	The leader listens to the views of followers and appears to be caring and willing to share his or her views
Functional participation	Structures such as teams or groups as tools of participation are formed.
Interactive participation	Decisions are jointly taken through joint analysis.
Leadership sharing (self-mobilization)	The leader's enthusiasm and vision are shared fully, and the followers become leaders on their own volition with full self-awareness.

12.6 Predicting succession success

The success of sustainable leadership is leadership succession in perpetuity with unbridled, undiminished enthusiasm. Succession is for the leader–follower ecosystem to evolve in perceptivity with resilience and dynamic stability. Like the Macedonian army's

Jacob Thomas, PhD

formation of a section with a big sphere, the followers should maintain their formidability and focus. The two most important predictors for succession success are:

- how early the succession as an essential aspect of leadership is conceived and the succession strategy imagined
- how early the succession strategy is rolled out to the arena.

Succession is not about individuals but about the systems, processes, and institutionalized mechanisms. It is also about resources and long-term performance in the case of organizations. Thus, success of succession is also predicted on the rate of use of resources and institutionalization. Fig. 12.3 shows these factors in graphical form.

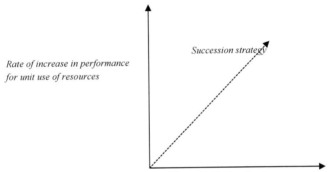

Fig. 12.3: Succession success indicators.

Examples of succession success are the Hemis Monastery in Ladakh and leadership of the Roman Catholic Church, both of which are performing well even after 1,500 years, and some of the oldest universities in Europe and the US, which are maintaining high performance in the world's university ranking. Compare these organizations against those organizations that started during the last fifty years: Grameen Bank led by the Nobel laureate Dr Muhammad Yunus, Reliance Industries Pvt Ltd led by Mukesh Ambani, and Microsoft Corporation led by Bill Gates. These three are great organizations in the present. But will they be great organizations 500 years from now?

12.7 Success script: How well and how far will you be succeeded?

1. What is the extent of buy-in into the vision of the leader among the followers, measured in terms of sustained enthusiasm?

Less than 50 percent	50 to 80 percent	Great than 90 percent

2. How many of the followers have become leaders already?

Less than 50 percent	50 to 80 percent	Greater than 90 percent

3. How many of the current leader followers are expected to multiply further leaders among their own influence chain through leadership sharing?

Less than 50 percent	50 to 80 percent	Greater than 90 percent

4. What is the extent of inventiveness and imagination with intention among the leader followers in terms of the number of touchpoints with the lives of followers that are initiated?

Less than 50 percent	50 to 80 percent	Greater than 90 percent

5. What is the probability of the leadership's vision evolving in an ever-rolling manner and in an expansive manner rather than losing its luster?

Low	Medium	High

6. What is the level of participation strategy as an element of the leadership strategy that the leadership process has achieved so far?

Information sharing level	Interactive level	Mobilization level

Jacob Thomas, PhD

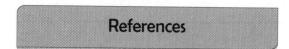

References

Aldon, L. J. (2004), *Transcendent Leadership and the Evolution of Consciousness* (London: Lightning Source UK Ltd).

Armenakis, A. A., and A. G. Bedeain (1999), 'Organizational Change: A Review of Theory and Research in the 1990s', *Journal of Management*, 25: 293–315.

Barnard, C. (1938), *The Functions of the Executive* (Cambridge, MA: Harvard University Press).

Bass, B. M. (1985), *Leadership and Performance Beyond Expectations* (New York: Free Press).

Bass, B. M., and P. C. Burger (1979), *Assessment of Mangers: An International Comparison* (Free Press).

Bass, B. M. (1990), *Bass & Stogdill's Handbook of Leadership: Theory, Research, and Managerial Applications* (3rd edn, New York: The Free Press).

Bass, B. M. (1990), 'From Transactional to Transformational Leadership: Learning to Share the Vision', *Organizational Dynamics*, 18/3: 19–31.

Bass, B. M. (1997), 'Does the Transactional to Transformational Leadership Paradigm Transcend Organizational and National Borders?', *American Psychologist*, 52/2: 130–139.

Blake, R. R., and J. S. Mouton (1982), 'Comparative Analysis of Situationalism and the 9, 9 Approach of Management by Principle', *Organizational Dynamics* (Spring).

Blanchard, K., and P. Hersey (1969), 'Life Cycle Theory of Leadership in Training and Development', 23/5.

Block, P. (1993), *Stewardship: Choosing Service over Self-Interest* (San Francisco: Berret-Koehler Publishers).

Brass, D. J., and M. E. Burkhart (1993), 'Potential Power and Power Use: An Investigation of Structure and Behavior', *Academy of Management Journal*, 36: 441–470.

Burns, J. M. (1978), *Leadership* (New York: Harper & Row).

Burns, G. J. (1978), *Leadership* (New York: Harper Touch Books).

Cardona, P. (2000), 'Transcendental Leadership', *The Leadership and Organization Development Journal*, 21: n. 4.

Cameron, K., J. Dutton, and R. Quinn, ed. (2003), *Positive Organizational Scholarship. Foundations of a New Discipline* (San Francisco: Berret-Koehler Publishers).

Carter, J. (1997), *Boards That Make a Difference* (San Fransisco: Jossey-Bass Publishers).

Chaleff, I. (2002), *The Courageous Follower: Standing Up to and for Our Leaders* (2nd edn, San Fransisco: Berrett-Koehler Publishers Inc.).

Chalmers, D. J. (1996), *The Conscious Mind: In Search of a Fundamental Theory* (New York: Oxford University Press).

Chopra, D. (2001), *How to Know God: The Soul's Journey into the Mystery of Mysteries* (New York, NY: Running Press Book Publishers).

Cohen, M. D. et al. (1972), 'A Garbage Can Model of Organizational Change', *Administrative Science Quarterly*, 17: 1–25.

Cotton, J. L. et al. (1988), 'Employee Participation: Diverse Forms and Different Outcomes', *Academy of Management Review*, 13: 8–22.

Cremo, M. A., and M. Goswami (1995), *Divine Nature: A Spiritual Perspective on the Environmental Crisis* (Sydney: Bhaktivedam Book Trust International).

Dahl, R. A. (1957), 'The Concept of Power', *Behavioral Science*, 2: 201–218.

Dean, J. W., and M. P. Sharfman (1996). 'Does Decision Process Matter? A Study of Strategic Decision-Making Effectiveness', *Academy of Management Journal*, 39: 368–396.

De Boer, H. (2002), 'Trust the Essence of Governance?', in A. Amaral, G. A. Jones, and B. Karseth, eds., *Governing Higher Education: National Perspectives on Institutional Governance* (New York: Springer).

Dirk, K. T. et al. (1996), 'Psychological Ownership in Organizations: Conditions Under Which Individuals Promote and Resist Change', in R. W. Woodman and W. A. Pasmore, eds., *Research in Organizational Change and Development*, vol. 9 (Stamford CT: JAI Press).

Dutton, J. E. et al. (2001), 'Moves That Matter: Issue Selling and Organizational Change', *Academy of Management Journal*, 44: 716–736.

Elder, N. et al. (1988), *The Consensual Democracies* (New York: Blackwell).

Ellsworth, Richard (2002), *Leading with Purpose: The New Corporate Realities* (California: Stanford Business Books, Stanford University Press).

Emery, F. E., and E. Thorsrud (1976), *Democracy at Work* (Leiden: Martinus Nijhoff).

Ercetin,S.S., and M.C.Kameet (2008), 'Quantum Leadership Paradigm', World Applied Science Journal, 3/6

Farmer, S. M. et al. (1997), 'Putting Upward Influence Strategies in Context', *Journal of Organizational Behavior*, 18: 17–42.

Fieldler, F. E. (1974), *A Contingency Model of Leadership Effectiveness*.

Filler E., and D. Ulrich (2014), 'Talent: Why Chief Human Resources Officers Make Great CEOs', *Harvard Business Review* (December), 20–22.

Folger, R. (1977), 'Distributive and Procedural Justice: Combined Impact of 'Voice' and Improvement on Experienced Equality', *Journal of Personality and Social Psychology*, 35: 108–119.

Furr, Nathan, and Jeffrey H. Dyer (2014), 'Leading Your Team into Unknowing', *Harvard Business Review* (December), 76–82.

French, J. R. P., and B. H. Raven (1959), 'The Bases of Social Power', in D. Cartwright, ed., *Studies of Social Power* (Ann Arbour, MI: Institute for Social Research).

French, J. R. P., and B. H. Raven (1959), 'The Bases of Social Power', in D. Cartwright, ed., *Studies of Social Power* (Ann Arbour, MI: Institute for Social Research), 150–157.

Gandhi, A. (2003), 'Leadership and Nonviolence', in C. Cherry, J. J. Gardiner, and N. Huber, eds., *Building Leadership Bridges 2003* (College Park, Maryland: International Leadership Association and Center for Creative Leadership), 1–11.

Gardiner, J. J. (1998), 'Quiet Presence: The Holy Ground of Leadership', in L. C. Spears, ed., *Insights on Leadership* (New York: John Wiley & Sons), 116–125.

Gardiner, J. J. (2005), 'Building Leadership Teams: A Comprehensive Study of American's College and University Presidents, 1988–2003'. Paper presented at the annual meeting of the International Leadership Association, Amsterdam, Netherlands, 6 November 2005.

Gardiner, J. J. (2001), 'Growing Leadership Circles for Rotary's Emergent Future'. Paper presented at the annual meeting of the International Leadership Association, Miami, Florida, 3 November 2001.

Jacob Thomas, PhD

Gardner, H. (1995), *Leading Minds: An Anatomy of Leadership* (New York: Basic Books).

Gardner, J. W. (1990), *On Leadership* (New York: The Free Press).

Gioia, D. A., and K. Chittipeddi (1991), 'Sense Making and Sense Giving in Strategic Change Initiation', *Strategic Management Journal*, 12: 433–448.

Gioia, D. A., and J. B. Thomas (1996), 'Identity, Image, and Issue Interpretation: Sense Making During Strategic Change in Academia', *Administrative Science Quarterly*, 41: 370–403.

Glew, D. J. et al. (1995), 'Participation in Organizations: A Preview of Issues and Proposed Framework for Future Analysis', *Journal of Management*, 26/1: 63–83.

Grayer, P. H. et al. (1990), 'The Sharp Benders: Achieving a Sustained Improvement versus Middle Management Self-Interest', *Strategic Management Journal*, 7: 263–279.

Greenleaf, R. K. (1977), *Servant Leadership* (New York: Paulist Press).

Hackman, R. (2002), *Leading Teams: Setting the Stage for Great Performances* (Cambridge: Harvard Business School Publishing).

Hall, B. P. (1994), *Values Shift: A Guide to Personal and Organizational Transformation* (Rockport, MA: Twin Lights Publishers).

Hambrick, D. C., and P. Mason (1984), 'Upper Echelons: The Organization as a Reflection of Its Top Managers', *Academy of Management Review*, 9: 193–206.

Hameroff, S. (2007), The Brain Is Both Neuro Computer and Quantum Computer', *Cognitive Science*, 31: 1035–1045.

Hameroff, S. R., and R. Penrose (1996), 'Conscious Events as Orchestrated Space Time Selections', *Journal of Consciousness Studies*, 3/1: 36–53.

Hannan, M. T., and J. Freeman (1984), 'Structural Inertia and Organizational Change', *American Sociological Review*, 49: 149–164.

Hardy, C. (1995), 'Managing Strategic Change: Power, Paralysis, and Perspective', in P. Srivastava and R. Lamb, eds., *Advances in Strategic Management*, vol. 6 (Greenwich, CT: JAI Press).

Hargreaves, Andy, and Dean Fink (2003), 'Sustainable Leadership', *Phi Delta Kappan*, 84/9 (May 2003).

Hargreaves, Andy, and Dean Fink (2003), 'The Seven Principles of Sustainable Leadership.

Havelock, R. G., and M. C. Havelock (1973), *Training for Change Agents* (Center for Research of Utilization of Scientific Knowledge, Institute for Social Research, University of Michigan).

Hawking, S., and L. Mlodinow (2010), *Grand Design* (New York: Bantam).

Hebb, D. O. (1949), *Organization of Behavior: A Neuropsychological Theory* (New York: Wiley).

Heracleous, L., and M. Barrett (2001), 'Organizational Change as Discourse: Communicative Actions and Deep Structures in the Context of Information Technology Development', *Academy of Management Journal*, 44: 755–778.

Hersey, P., K. H. Blanchard, and D. E. Johnson (1996), *Management of Organizational Behavior* (7th edn, Englewood Cliffs, NJ: Prentice Hall).

Hickson, D. J. et al. (1986), *Top Decisions: Strategic Decision-Making in Organizations* (San Francisco: Jossey Bass).

Hinkin, T. R., and C. M. Schriesheim (1989), 'Development and Application of New Scales to Measure the French and Raven (1959) Bases of Social Power', *Journal of Applied Psychology*, 74/4: 561–567.

Hinkin, T. R., and C. M. Schriesheim (1990), 'Relationship between Perceptions of Supervisor Influence Tactics and Attributed Bases of Supervisor Power', *Human Relations*, 43: 221–237.

House, R. J. (1988), 'Power and Personality in Complex Organizations', in L. L. Cummings and B. M. Staw, *Research in Organizational Behavior*, 10: 305–357.

House R. J., N. S. Wright, and R. N. Aditya (1997), 'Cross-Cultural Research on Organizational Leadership'.

> *http://www.truepoint.com/who-we-are/our-people/nathaniel-foote/*
> *http://www.britannica.com/biography/Johann-Wolfgang-von-Goethe*
> *http://iae-pedia.org/Abraham_Maslow*
> *http://www.rand.org/topics/delphi-method.html*
> *http://www.thehindubusinessline.com/news/juhi-chawla-ups-the-ante-against-mobile-radiation/article5082835.ece*
> *http://www.biography.com/people/ernest-shackleton-9480091*

Jacob Thomas, PhD

- *http://www.oxforddictionaries.com/definition/american_english/marx-karl?q=Karl+Marx*
- *http://www.biography.com/people/nicolaus-copernicus-9256984*
- *http://www.nasa.gov/mission_pages/apollo/apollo11.html*
- *http://www.nobelprize.org/nobel_prizes/literature/laureates/1964/sartre-bio.html*
- *http://www.amazon.com/Existentialism-Is-Humanism-Jean-Paul-Sartre/dp/0300115466*
- *http://www.cliffsnotes.com/literature/f/the-flies/about-the-flies*
- *http://www.biography.com/people/alex-ferguson-9293262*
- *https://books.google.com.ph/books?id=G6ZYTUHVKlQC&pg=PA66&lpg=PA66&dq=Henri+Fayol+1842-1925&source=bl&ots=UFYPG3Zlm9&sig=f-f09TtFn2gfN73M7IUW3tbKX4Y&hl=en&sa=X&ved=0ahUKEwi-qMD0x6XJAhVLFJQKHbnjBZUQ6AEIITAB#v=onepage&q=Henri%20Fayol%201842-1925&f=false*
- *http://interbrand.com/newsroom/interbrand-releases-2015-best-global-brands-report/*
- *http://www.coca-cola.com/global/glp.html*
- *http://www.lonelyplanet.com/india/jammu-and-kashmir/ladakh*
- *http://www.grameen-info.org/*

Jack, R. E., O. G. B. Garrod, and P. G. Schyne (2014), 'Dynamic Facial Expressions of Emotion Transport on Evolutionary Hierarch of Signals over Time', *Current Biology*, 24/2: 99–112.

Jacob Thomas (2006), 'Study of Relationship between Empowering Forces and the Empowering Process among Women in Managerial Positions in Business Organization', doctoral dissertation, XLRI.

Jaworski, J. (1996), *Synchronicity: The Inner Path of Leadership* (San Francisco: Berrett-Koehler Publishers).

Kabanoff, B. et al. (1995), 'Espoused Values and Organizational Change Themes', *Academy of Management Journal*, 38/4: 1075–1104.

Kabilsigh, C. (1987), 'An Ethical Approach to Environmental Education', in S. Davis, ed., *Tree of Life* (Geneva: Buddhist Perception of Nature).

Kabilsigh, C., J. Chankaew, and P. Kabilsigh (1991), *Buddhism for Preservation of Nature* (Bangkok: Thammasart University Press) (in Thai).

Kelley, R. E. (1992), *The Power of Followership: How to Create Leaders People Want to Follow and Followers Who Lead Themselves* (New York: Currency Doubleday).

Kipnis, D., and S. M. Schmidt (1988), 'Upward Influence Styles: Relationship with Performance, Evaluation, Salary and Stress', *Administrative Science Quarterly*, 33: 528–542.

Koch, C. (2004), *The Quest for Consciousness: A Neurobiological Approach* (Englewood: Roberts and Company).

Korsgaard, A. et al. (1995), 'Building Commitment, Attachment, and Trust in Strategic Decision-Making Teams', *Academy of Management Journal*, 38: 60–84.

Kotter, J. P. (1995), *Leading Change* (New York: The Free Press).

Kush, Brian D. (2009). *Auditing Leadership: The Professional and Leadership Skills You Need.* ISBN 928-0470450017.

Larkin, D. (1995), 'Beyond Self to Compassionate Healer: Transcendent Leadership', doctoral dissertation, Seattle University.

Lee, C. et al. (2000), 'Power-Distance, Gender and Organizational Justice', *Journal of Management*, 26/4: 685–704.

Lipman-Blumen, J. (1996), *The Connective Edge: Leading in an Inner-Dependent World* (San Francisco: Jossey-Bass Publishers).

Makiphere, Kristine, and George Yip (2008), 'Sustainable Leadership', *Business Strategy Review* (Spring).

Martin, C. L. et al. (1995), 'The Influence of Employee Involvement Program Membership during Downsizing: Attitudes toward the Employer and the Union', *Journal of Management*, 21/5: 879–890.

McFarlin, D. B., and P. D. Sweeney (1992), 'Distributive and Procedural Justice as Predictors of Satisfaction with Personal and Organizational Outcomes', *Academy of Management Journal*, 35/3: 626–637.

Miller, K. L., and P. R. Monge (1988), 'Participation, Satisfaction, and Productivity: A Meta-Analytic Review', *Academy of Management Journal*, 29: 727–753.

Jacob Thomas, PhD

Mintzberg, H. et al. (1976), 'The Structure of Unstructured Decision Processes', *Administrative Science Quarterly*, 21: 246–275.

Mintzberg, H. (1983), *Power in and around Organizations* (Englewood Cliffs, NJ: Prentice Hall).

Molm, L. D. et al. (1990), 'Structure, Action, and Outcomes: The Dynamics of Power in Social Exchange', *American Sociological Review*, 55: 427–447.

Morgan, G. (1986), *Images of Organization* (Beverly Hills, CA: SAGE Publications).

Mowrer, O. H. (1960), *Learning Theory and Behaviour* (New York: Wiley).

Pasmore, W. A., and M. R. Fagans (1992), 'Participation, Individual Development, and Organizational Change: A Review and Synthesis', *Journal of Management*, 18: 375–397.

Penrose, R., and S. R. Hameroff (1995), 'Gaps, What gaps? Reply to Grush and Churchland', *Journal of Consciousness Studies*, 2/2: 99–112.

Peterson, C., and M. Seligman (2004), *Character Strengths and Virtues: A Handbook and Classification* (APA and Oxford University Press).

Pettigrew, A. M. (1985), *The Awakening Giant: Continuity and Change in ICI* (Oxford: Blackwell).

Pfeffer, J. (1981), *Power in Organizations* (Marshfield, MA: Pittman).

Pfeffer, J., and G. Salancik (1978), *The External Control of Organizations: A Resource Dependence Perspective* (New York: Harper & Row).

Plante, Patricia R. (1990), 'Leadership and the Making of New Words', *Liberal Education*, 76/1: 31.

Rost, J. C. (1991), *Leadership for the Twenty-First Century* (New York: Praeger).

Simon, H. A. (1964), 'On the Concept of Organizational Goal', *Administrative Science Quarterly*, 9: 1–22.

Skamp, K. (1991), 'Spirituality and Environmental Education', *Australian Journal of Environmental Education*, 7: 79–86.

Smart, N. (1999), *World Philosophies* (Routledge).

Seligman, M., and M. Csikzentmihalyi (2000), 'Positive Psychology: An Introduction', *American Psychology*, 55: 5–14.

Shaver, P., J. Schwartz, D. Kirson, and C. O'Conner (2001), 'Emotional Knowledge: Further Exploration of a Prologue Approach', in G.

Parrot, eds., *Emotions in Social Psychology: Essential Readings* (Philadelphia, CA: Psychological Press), 26–56.

Synder, C. R., and S. J. Lopez (2002), *Handbook of Positive Psychology* (New York: University Press).

Thurman, R. (1992), 'Buddhist Views on the Environmental Crisis', in F. B. Miracle, ed., *Conference Proceedings on Human Values and the Environment* (Wisconsin: Wisconsin Academy of Sciences, Arts and Letters), 23–31.

Valentine, Scott Victor (2009), 'The Green Onion: A Corporate Environmental Strategy Framework', *Corporate Social Responsibility and Environmental Management* (John Wiley & Sons), DOI: 10, 1002/csr.217.

Wagner, J. A., III (1994). 'Participation's Effects on Performance and Satisfaction: A Reconsideration of Research Evidence', *Academy of Management Review*, 19: 312–330.

Walsh, J. P. (1988), 'Selectivity and Selective Perception: An Investigation of Managers' Belief Structures and Information Processing', *Academy of Management Journal*, 31: 873–896.

Wegner, D. M. (2002), *The Illusion of Conscious Will* (Cambridge: MIT Press).

Wooldridge, B., and S. W. Floyd (1990), 'The Strategy Process, Middle Management Involvement, and Organizational Performance', *Strategic Management Journal*, 11: 231–241.

Yukl, G. (1994), *Leadership in Organizations* (3rd edn, Englewood Cliffs, NJ: Prentice Hall).

Yukl, G., and J. B. Tracy (1992), 'Consequences of Influence Tactics Used with Subordinates, Peers, and the Boss', *Journal of Applied Psychology*, 77: 525–535.

Yukl, G. (1998). *Leadership in Organizations* (4th edn, Upper Saddle River, New Jersey: Prentice Hall).

Zizzi, P. A. (2004), 'Emergent Consciousness: From the Early Universe to Our Mind' <http://arxiv.org/abs/gr-qc/0007006>.

Jacob Thomas, PhD

Index

255   Jacob Thomas, PhD

Jacob Thomas, PhD

Printed in the United States
By Bookmasters